HOW TO SURVIVE
IN YOUR
LIBERAL SCHOOL

HOW TO SURVIVE IN YOUR LIBERAL SCHOOL

JAMES K. FITZPATRICK

ARLINGTON HOUSE·PUBLISHERS
NEW ROCHELLE, NEW YORK

101796

To the Parents of South Boston
and Kanawha, West Virginia.

Copyright © 1975 by Arlington House Publishers, New Rochelle, N.Y.

Library of Congress Catalog Card Number

Manufactured in the United States of America

Library of Congress Cataloging in Publication Data

Fitzpatrick, James K
    How to survive in your liberal school.

    Includes indes.
    1. High school students' socio-economic status--
United States. 2. United States--Social conditions--
1960-   3. Catholic high schools--United States--
Administration. I. Title.
LC205.F57   373.1'8'1   75-8796
ISBN 0-87000-323-2

Contents

Introduction

More and more of America's young people are becoming aware of a truly strange and confusing tension in their lives. Perhaps you are one of them. They hear their parents complaining—frequently and angrily in many cases—about "what is going on" in the schools. Often their teachers come across in these complaints as some kind of menacing group of aliens, out to "corrupt" the minds of their students, as teachers of a "new morality," of "anti-American" ideas, of "slovenly ways." In school on the other hand, in teacher-directed "rap sessions," students learn of the dangers implicit in their parents' "narrow," "Archie Bunker-like," "anti-intellectual" "ethnocentric" rigidities. The teachers, the men and women hired to properly educate our future citizens, to preserve, protect, and extend our way of life, seem to be doing something closer to the opposite from where the parents sit.

But that is not what makes the situation most strange and most confusing. The parents not only complain that they do not like the kind of job being done by the schools. They complain, perhaps even more frequently, that they are being forced to pay excessively high taxes to subsidize the effort—more and more taxes for more and more of what they do not want.

It really is a unique situation. There just is not anything quite comparable in American life. Where else in our economy do you find a situation where people cannot control either the quality of the product they purchase, or the price they pay for it, or even whether they want to make a purchase at all? Even during the gasoline shortage, as bad as that was, and as smelling of monopolistic practices as many social studies teachers told us it was, you at least could refuse to buy the gas, even if only at the price of great hardship to yourself. There is no way, short of leaving the country, or joining a hobo colony, that you can manage to escape the local school taxes.

This is, however, exactly the kind of situation which has developed in the American's relationship to his public schools. No one in touch with reality would argue the point. Defenders of the public schools, in fact, most especially teacher unions, speak proudly and openly of how this situation has been promoted through years of struggle in the courts and arduous contract negotiations. "Academic freedom" clauses in teacher contracts clearly protect the teachers' rights to define for themselves what is an acceptable topic for their students. Parental pressures are most often treated in these contracts, and in supportive court decisions, as narrow and threatening sectarian forces which would menace the "free pursuit of truth" if they were allowed a presence in the classroom atmosphere. The teachers, in the truest sense, are given control over the ultimate directive thrust of the educational process, the kind of power which our Founding Fathers struggled so determinedly to never allow in government through their delicately constructed system of checks and balances.

The only corrective pressure deemed legitimate by teacher groups, and educational interest groups in general, is the so-called "collegial" pressure a misguided teacher would supposedly receive from his fellow teachers and school administrators. Even this pressure, however, is made near to non-existent after "tenure" status is reached by a teacher—which usually comes about three years or so after a teacher is hired. Tenure protects a teacher's job, and makes it virtually impossible to fire him except for the grossest, and most unlikely, forms of misbehavior in the classroom.

But even if tenure were abolished it would do little to solve the problem. Since administrators of the public schools—department heads, principals, superintendents, etc.—almost always rise to their jobs by moving up through the system, and by taking the same graduate education courses at the same graduate schools of education as the teachers, they tend to share most of the teacher notions about academic freedom. In fact, they often exceed them since these administrators tend to be "upward bound" and concerned with adhering to the standards of "professional educators" set by the schools of education around the country so that they will have the proper credentials for future promotions. The pressure they apply on teachers usually centers around administrative and procedural inadequacies—i.e., excessive absences, lateness, lack of classroom discipline, poor record keeping. American school administrators, to be direct, would seldom feel as if they were acting appropriately—as "professional educators" —if they pressured a teacher for making Marxism look a little too attractive to his students, or sexual promiscuity an acceptable American lifestyle. And you can sympathize with them in many ways. Can you imagine the way the *N.Y. Times, Newsweek,* CBS, to say nothing of the leading educational journals and teacher union publications, in our day and age, would cover the story of a principal who fired a teacher for pushing anti-Christian or pro-Marxist ideas in his classes? The poor soul would come across as part Archie Bunker, part Benito Mussolini, and part Beetle Bailey.

State laws on collective bargaining make it impossible, as well, for the community to show its indignation by withholding any pay increases until teachers "toe the line," so to speak, on educational philosophy. Citizens can vote down school budgets in many communities. In many city areas they cannot even do that. But even if the budget is defeated resoundingly, and if schoolboards are forced to cut back to the bare bones on books, lab equipment, extra-curricular activities, maintenance, buses, heating oil and office rubber bands, the teacher salary scales stay put. They cannot be voted down. There have been cases of school districts which have had to close down completely for months at a time—no classes whatsoever—because of a lack of funds, but the teachers' salaries went on as usual, as negotiated. Of course, there is nothing wrong with a group of workers insisting on this kind of job security. But it is surprising that anyone could demand it, and receive it, for a job performance that is not to the buyers' liking.

The ultimate protest, then, for the average citizen is an angry phone call or a letter of complaint to a school administrator, who will expeditiously summon the teacher to his office for some "old pro" advice on how a teacher can protect himself from giving the wrong impression to the community.

So the schools go on with professional educators devising a curriculum that they think is "best for the community" (which really means as close as possible to whatever is the going educational rage at various "leading" schools of teacher training around the country), and the taxes go up to finance it. And the average parent has to sit back and either stew in powerlessness, or learn to love it, to see the light, to learn to think like a correct-thinking secular liberal.

Of course, you might argue that prices go up all the time, not just school taxes. But, remember, you might pay more to have a garage built this year than last, but you get the design, the color, and the quality you specify—not what the carpenter wants.

And it is true that doctors and lawyers and other professionals do not really consult you about how they are going to remove your kidney stones, or file your last will and testament. But you can select these professionals according to their reputation, and price. You can fire them at will—at whim, in fact. You can refuse their advice.

Or what about other public officials—elected leaders, for example? Don't they keep raising the taxes for their salaries and programs for the public? No one in America ever votes for that and it happens anyway. True, but they at least can be removed from office every two, or four, or six years. They do not have tenure.

There is no need to beat the issue to death. There is a wide range of freedom of choice in the purchase of cars, clothing, toothpaste, phonograph records. But there is none in the schools, unless a parent is willing to pay high tuition for private schools, in addition to the high taxes for the operation of the public system. The taxes go up. The parents continue to complain about the "quality of education." The same Americans who can select their socks and their beer and their deodorant to suit their needs and their pocketbooks cannot control what happens, from nine to three, ten months a year, to their own flesh and blood, the young people for whose upbringing most Americans feel they will one day be answerable to God. It boggles the mind when you think about it. And you should think about it.

You should think about it not to find justification for any kind of external show of rebelliousness in the classroom. That would solve few, and create many additional, problems. It is near to impossible to imagine students having a solution to this tension. Their very role as student, as learner, implies that they do not have at their disposal an outline for the directive norms for running a school. Genuine reform can only come from an aroused adult America. But today's student is tomorrow's adult.

If you come to develop some inner resistance, therefore, some understanding of the nature of the conflict between what you hear from your parents and what you hear in school, you will not only promote your own moral development in the short run, but prepare yourself to battle intelligently for this educational reform as an adult.

It is possible, in short, to go through your school years without being "educated out" of your acceptance of your parents' ideals and standards of behavior. Being educated simply does not mean learning why Mom and Dad and the pastor of your local Church are all wet.

But, for charity's, and decency's, sake, try to remember that being determined to stay loyal to the ideals of your parents, and the ways of your people, does not require any hostility to your teachers as individuals. Although you probably know that by intuition. It must puzzle you to find that your parents can get so distressed by what kind and gentle Mr. Smith says to you in class, or what cute, and with-it, Ms. Jones said in her interview in the school newspaper. In many ways it is not your teachers' fault. Not fully anyway. The teacher does not have to be a "sinister" sort of character to get your parents riled up a bit. Remember, too, that teachers more often than not are parents too. And as parents they just might sound like your own. Maybe they even send their children to private schools. It is only when they act as teachers, what they call "professional educators," that they mount the attack against so many community standards.

American teachers are not as much to blame as the ideology which provided the overall direction to their own education. That ideology goes by the name of liberalism, and it has had such a grip over the process by which teachers are trained, and educational objectives defined in this country, that it would be surprising if the schools acted in any manner other than the one we are familiar with today. Liberalism is the disease.

1

Liberalism: A Disease of the Heart

There is neither space, nor is it necessary, here to attempt to dig down to the tap root of what has come to be called "liberalism." What we are concerned with is more the way the liberal attitude shows itself in modern American education than in the exact convergence of historical forces "way back when" which caused the birth of the liberal way of looking at man and the world. Books such as James Burnham's *Suicide of the West,* Thomas Molnar's *Utopia: The Perennial Heresy,* Russell Kirk's *The Conservative Mind,* and Willmoore Kendall's *The Conservative Affirmation,* are just a few of the classic studies of liberalism's malignant presence in the history of Europe and America, the "West," and the way defenders of our civilization have attempted to innoculate society in defense down through the ages. What is said within the pages of this book will serve an important service if it does nothing other than persuade the reader to tackle any one of them somewhere along the line.

Just to get our bearings, however, to establish a historical perspec-

13

tive, it is necessary to look at some of the theories advanced by conservatives, and other thoughtful historians, to explain liberalism's historical origins—even if only in the most surface manner.

A case could be made—and quite well at that—that liberalism, like everything else, started with Eve. For part and parcel of the modern liberal attitude is a rebelliousness toward current authority and the orderly patterns of behavior prescribed by that authority. The words "self-rule," "independence," "individualism," and "liberation,"—which must have been pretty much the way that Eve framed her pitch to Adam on that fatal picnic lunch—slide easily into the modern liberal vocabulary.

But let us leave that theme and move into the periods of written history where the demanded analysis becomes more workable and more easily documented.

In current historical theory there seem to be two periods which vie for the lead as the most-mentioned birthplace of the liberal: the Renaissance, and the Eighteenth Century Enlightenment. Those historians and philosophers who push their analysis most rigorously find it difficult to accept both periods as equally and partially responsible. Those who want to "blame" the Enlightenment often insist that the Renaissance was, by and large, a healthy and praiseworthy period of human historical development. Those whose analysis takes them back to the Renaissance insist that to blame only the Enlightenment is to miss the point, and that attacking the Enlightenment alone is to strike out at the symptom while ignoring its cause—very much like lopping off a branch that hangs menacingly over your garage only to find out that what you really have done is to prune the tree and promote six new shoots of growth where there used to be just one.

This is not just a trivial academic difference of opinion. There is substance to the arguments. More importantly, the kind of remedies that you will propose for what the liberals have done to life in our country will vary according to which analysis you accept. We will have more to say about this later, but just to make the point: Those who see the Renaissance as the villain tend to insist that the only hope for our society is in some kind of revival of the underlying religious spirit of medieval Christendom; those who blame the Enlightenment rely less on revealed religious truths as such, and insist more on good government and a healthy respect for our past based on an appreciation of the value of our tradition, and a respect for the need for a strong sense of national unity.

14

THE RENAISSANCE

It used to be fairly easy to make the assumption that anyone who had reached junior or senior year in high school was familiar with the term "Renaissance." Students used to spend a large portion of their time in high school history courses taking a course called "World History" or "World Civilization" in which the Renaissance was a major topic of concern. There are courses in most schools today that still carry those titles, but there is more than a slight chance that a modern student might have taken that course with a teacher in search of "relevance" instead of dusty old "antiquarian topics." The result just could be that the student knows all about Angela Davis, Charles Reich, Yogi Gupta, the Black Panthers, Timothy Leary, hippy commune pottery, Andy Warhol, how to raise marijuana from seed, transvestitism, and Yoko Ono's poetry, and never have heard of Machiavelli, Galileo, or Leonardo da Vinci. So, just a brief historical sketch is in order.

The Renaissance, or rebirth, was a social, economic, political and religious outlook which both resulted from, and helped cause, the downfall of the medieval Church-dominated social order in the late fourteenth and fifteenth centuries. The growth in trade which came about with the discovery that the products of the Middle East, which Europeans first learned about while fighting their "Crusades" to recapture the Holy Land from Mohammedan invaders, could be sold for high profit in Europe was the primary impetus for the change. New ways of making a living (trade and connected services) and new places to live (the trade centers, the cities of Europe) made the medieval feudal manor no longer necessary. Commercial wealth grew, and with it a taste for the luxuries of life—including, of course, the fine arts. Artists, sculptors, poets, metalsmiths, for example, found in wealthy *patrons d'arts* a new market for their works. Churches were no longer the only buyers around. But not only the style of art was affected. The interests of commerce redesigned society as a whole.

New worldly interests challenged the old church concern about this world as only a place to prepare men for their eternal reward after death. Man's creative energies were directed toward the new values, the earthly concerns of profit, pleasure, and efficiency. Scientists, for example, became more concerned with gears, compasses, and the use of the convex and concave lens than in theology and metaphysics—the number of angels that could dance on the head of a pin for

15

one thing. A person or thing was evaluated by the extent to which he or it served these purposes.

This was the rebirth. Men began to think consciously and deliberately of living their lives by the earthly—"humanist"—standards of the glory years of ancient Greece and Rome. They chose to look on the medieval world they were rejecting as the "Dark Ages," an age whose religious focus blinded men to their full potential as men, as creators of newer and better ways of living their lives.

It was an age of tremendous energy. In the arts and the sciences, men like Galileo, Leonardo da Vinci, and Michelangelo strode impressively, making everlasting impressions on history. Machiavelli, in his brilliant little book, *The Prince*, rejected the medieval notion of the pious, Christian ruler, and substituted a new, worldly standard of success for rulers. He rejected the idea that a ruler should be bound by the Church-defined codes of behavior, and substituted the standard of worldly success—"The end justifies the means."

Men not only attempted to escape and rise above the confines of their Church-dominated culture, they even tried to escape its geographical setting. It was the Age of Discovery, of Exploration—the age of Columbus, Cabot, Hudson, Magellan, Balboa, and Drake. It was an age of boundless confidence, optimism, and faith. Not the Christian faith of the medieval man, but a faith in man as man, and in his power to refashion and improve his world.

Well? And what is so bad about that, you might ask. In many ways nothing. Nothing at all. Clearly, the progress we have experienced since then can be attributed to the Renaissance shift in emphasis towards improving life on earth, rather than tolerating it as a penance. And by progress we do not just mean flashy cars and stretch pants. It is unlikely that the progress in the field of medicine, just to take the obvious example, would have come about without the Renaissance outlook on life.

There are, however, other attitudes, and prejudices if you will, related to what we now call liberalism, which have their roots in this period as well. Perhaps we could call it an "intellectual arrogance"—not held by the Renaissance greats as much as by their fourth-rate imitators in the modern world. Whatever Leonardo da Vinci was, he was not a "liberal."

The liberal confidence in man's ability to solve all of man's problems without reference to the teachings of the Christian revelation; the liberal view of religious belief as a hindrance, an obsolete superstition which stands as an obstacle to man's fulfillment; the search for the new experience, the new pleasure, even when these pleasures are violations of the accepted moral codes—it could be said they all grew, perhaps in a perverted way, from the Renaissance world-view.

A contempt for old ways as backward ways develops. A prejudice that the "new" is the "better" takes hold. A desire to escape the past, rather than to build upon it in conservative fashion, becomes the ideal of those who get caught up in this drift. The logic develops, for example, that a school is a place to attack the "outdated," the traditional "prejudices," the "accepted ways," a place to teach "progressive thoughts," to "expand the child's horizons," to give the child "new experiences," to "liberate the child's mind." It is the logic which allows every version of Marxism and atheism under the sun to be reflected in course content, but outlaws prayers and religious instruction, as if religion were some kind of sinister presence which hinders the scholarly search for truth.

THE ENLIGHTENMENT

In most high school history textbooks you come across, there is a section called "The Age of Reason," or the "Age of Revolution," or the "Enlightenment," or all three. The point that the authors try to make by this grouping is that the same spirit of inquiry which led an Isaac Newton to question "why" the apple plunked him on the head, led a Thomas Paine and a Jean Jacques Rousseau to question the logic behind the governmental structures of their time, and, like Isaac Newton, to reject the explanation that they "just always" operated like that.

It was an age which specifically rejected any answer other than those which could be demonstrated logically, scientifically, *empirically*, the way that you would conduct a laboratory experiment. It was the age of the scientific method, of Harvey, Bacon, Jenner, Lavoisier, as well as Newton.

Without this kind of measurable explanation, no relationship between any cause and effect would be acceptable. Superstition, witches, toad's urine, and other mysterious explanations for earthly phenomena were rejected out of hand. But, by and large, so were religious faith and hallowed national traditions. It was not enough to say that a thing should be done in this way or that way because the Bible said so, or because our forefathers did it that way. Before a government, or a religion, or a polite and gentle way of behavior, could be judged acceptable by these men of enlightenment, it had to meet

17

this test of "reason." And, of course, the governments and religions of the eighteenth century came up lacking. Which is why it was also called the "Age of Revolution." It was also, you see, the age of Voltaire, and Locke, and Rousseau, and Robespierre.

The bright young men of this age, the *philosophes* as they were called in France, through scholarly tracts, lectures, pamphlets and novels, began their openly, and admittedly, seditious work—to establish a new order, a new regime which would be reasonable and enlightened in its structure. Once the "primitive" pretensions of kings and nobles, lords and ladies, were exposed as fraudulent, and destroyed; and once the people were able to construct a new government based on "rational" premises, a new age of equality, prosperity, and freedom would rise from the ashes. Rational man viewing his world without the constricting hobgoblins of the old regime would be able to construct governmental structures which would maximize the opportunities for human freedom, and thus allow other rational men the opportunity to improve and improve and improve the world. If there was a limit to human potential for these eighteenth-century men it was so far beyond the level of human development of the time that it was hardly worth thinking about. For them, man's greatest need was for liberation—from their kings, their governments, their religions, their folkways, their pieties.

This "liberation" of course, was the key. For if "rational" man was not building a better and better world with each succeeding year, it must have been because of the faulty social structures of the time.

Democracy, then, of one sort or another, (and there were as many versions as there were *philosophes*) became the system of government which would provide the answer. It would free rational men, give them the freedom of speech, press, religion, etc. which they needed to unleash their constructive energies, to build a world of peace and human brotherhood based on rational, not mystical, needs.

This, too, must sound attractive to many—especially to Americans. After all, we are a democracy. We believe in freedom. Right?

Well, yes and no. Our Founding Fathers did not set up quite the kind of thing envisioned by the more extreme of the *philosophes*. True, the Declaration of Independence might easily be used as a summary of many of the Enlightenment attitudes toward man, his revolutionary rights, and his autonomy as an individual in society. But remember, America's revolutionary history did not end with the Declaration of Independence.

The Declaration of Independence was a statement of revolutionary

18

intent, of the destruction of the political bonds between one people, one government, and another. Statements like that tend to be *hortatory* rather than analytic, designed for dramatic effect, to inspire revolutionary emotions, rather than a careful statement of political philosophy. This is not meant to be a criticism. You do not start a drive to raise money for the school band, much less a revolution, with a legal brief or a philosophical dissertation.

It was later at the Constitutional Convention in 1789, and in a brilliant collection of articles known as the Federalist papers, that America got down to the business of defining how it would operate as a government.

Perhaps the best way to make this point is to use the criticism of our Constitution which is made by the liberals. If you can get your opponents to make your argument for you, you have a sure sign that you have won the debate.

Quite frequently in recent years American liberals have been critical of what they call the "anti-democratic" features in operation in the early days of the American republic—property qualifications for voting, election of Senators by state legislators instead of by the people directly, the electoral college, seniority systems, the toleration of the filibuster, etc. Some of these criticisms just might be valid. Many conservatives oppose certain of them. But that is not the point. What is important here, is the clear indication that our Founding Fathers were not as confident as the *philosophes* in the results of political "freedom" in the unqualified sense of the term. Freedom, by the Founding Fathers' definition, was not an early version of "do your own thing." They were more interested in the orderly process of government, social stability, and a defense against impetuous and radical change. They were eager to make change come slowly so that no temporary democratic majority—which is after all only 50% plus one of the people—could act irresponsibly, and do permanent damage to the nation. Their view of government, as the liberals and radicals remind us in criticism, was a conservative one, designed to maintain much of the legal and social structure of the former thirteen colonies.

A better example of what the *philosophes* had in mind came in France in 1789 when a revolution toppled the French monarch, Louis XVI, and in a few short years had him and his family and his court, thousands of priests and tens of thousands of suspected monarchist sympathizers executed in order to protect the reasonable spirit of brotherhood and equality which was being built by the revolution-

19

aries. Of course, they were executed by the new, rational, instrument of death, the guillotine, a clean, sharp, and heavy blade suspended between wooden runners. None of those sloppy bloody executions by individual axemen as in the old regime. Now, death came clinically, impersonally, reasonably, from the force of gravity, just like Sir Isaac Newton's apple. Mobs roamed France killing, raping, burning, and drowning priests in full exercise of their freedoms. Charles Dickens, the English novelist long praised for his attacks on the social structures in England which allowed heartbreaking extremes of poverty to exist in the midst of plenty, has given us a blood-curdling picture of these "democratic excesses" in his unforgettable *A Tale of Two Cities*.

It was at this time that Edmund Burke, the "Father of Conservatism," wrote what is to this day the most widely applauded scholarly attack on the mentality of the Age of Revolution and its propagandists, the Enlightenment men.

In his brilliant *Reflections on the Revolution in France*, Burke refused to be hypnotized by the noble rhetoric and self-professedly charitable aims of the *philosophes*. (Which is a good example to keep in mind. The liberal does have all the "good intentions"—verbally at least—on his side. The conservative opposition always seems less concerned about the "needs of mankind," and "progress," and "brotherhood." It is always difficult to argue with the idealist who has his dreams of limitless pie in the sky. It is very much like telling a house-hunting friend that his newly discovered dream home has rotten timber in the basement. He will hate you for it.)

Burke realized that the basic errors of the revolutionaries revolved exactly around this lack of realism—their refusal to see man as he was in historical perspective, and their resulting failure in judgment about how men would behave once they were removed from the social disciplines built up by society through trial and error down through the ages. Burke realized that men were not like the bubbling liquid in a test tube which the men of reason could make behave as they wished by changing the environment. Man's capacity for evil, for behaving in an aberrant way distinguished him from apples falling from a tree, house plants, and the planets in their regular orbit. It also made him the noble creature he is, for without the ability to sin, there is no ability to be virtuous. It is only noble to be brave, to risk one's life for a friend, if there is a possibility of behaving otherwise. They only give medals to soldiers because it is easier to cut and run.

Burke called the *philosophes* "alien metaphysiks," men who had lost contact with their people, men who looked at man's capacity to reason in a vacuum, cut off from his passions and inclination to evil—what in the Judaeo-Christian tradition is called "original sin." He realized that man was, as Aristotle argued four centuries before the birth of Christ, a social animal, and that only through the learned virtues of life in a civilized society would he become capable of true virtue. Aristotle actually argued that man separated from social discipline would be the worst of animals since his intellect would enable him to plot and plan his savagery unlike a wild animal's simple instinctive attack.

Society, then, for Burke was the check upon man's worst instincts, and the teacher of his best. Through fine literature, elevating music, active church groups, good laws, and even a fine tradition of fairy tales and village folklore, man could learn civilized behavior. The wisdom of the ages, man's vision of God's will, tested and transmitted through time, would make man a creature worthy of political freedom—of the trust of his fellow men. Without this process—barbarism, a "Reign of Terror" such as the one going on in Burke's time in France.

Burke argued fervently for man to disown this exaggerated view of the individual intellect, and to trust instead the wisdom of his people as reflected in their customs, national heritage, church doctrines, and law of the land. By coming to understand how these social forces combine to make life decent and livable, men would be able to defend their country from the menacing abstractions about how things "should be" made by the social disrupters. For as Burke insisted, where the individual is foolish, the "species" is wise. Or as he put it more poetically:

> Because a half-a-dozen grasshoppers under a fern make the field ring with their importunate chink, whilst thousands of great cattle, reposed beneath the shadow of the British oak, chew the cud and are silent, pray do not imagine that those who make the noise are the only inhabitants of the field; that of course they are many in number; or that, after all, they are other than the little shrivelled, meagre, hopping, though loud and troublesome insects of the hour.

You cannot help but wish for some kind of law that would make school administrators think long and hard about that quote, especially before their next confrontation with a list of non-negotiable demands presented by trouble-making, would-be student revolutionaries.

It was this civilizing process that Burke felt the Enlightenment

21

"We've called this faculty meeting to discuss the decline of the academy image—causes, solutions."

men were casting aside. When they blamed society for holding back man's development, they were letting their unrealistic dream of a perfectly free, perfectly rational man—Rousseau called them "noble savages"—blind them to the less grandiose but real good done for mankind by society's revered institutions.

It is this naive Enlightenment confidence in the natural goodness of man, and the accompanying denial of the Biblical revelation of man's inclination to evil, that inspires the modern liberal's contempt for customs, rules, laws, and regulations of every sort in our own time in history. When a liberal gets in charge of anything, whether the Cub Scout Pack or the American Presidency, he, in what has to be the most reflex action this side of the way your knee jerks when the doctor hits you with that little hammer, starts "putting people on their own." Students are given free time to "pursue independent study." Schools are put under "community control." Welfare checks are distributed with less "bureaucratic meddling" into the lives of the recipients. Athletes are taken off curfew. Susie is allowed to pick out her own dresses. Junior is given the keys to the car. Dress codes are dropped, mandatory courses dropped, entrance requirements dropped. And all of this is done to the accompanying rubric of "the only real discipline is self-discipline," as if self-discipline grew on a person like tocnails.

It is this confidence in human nature which also makes the liberal a "social engineer." Since the liberal is convinced that man is naturally good and naturally reasonable, he has to explain somehow why people do steal, cheat, rape, kill, plunder, torture, act promiscuously (for those liberals who believe there is such a thing), and act in the ornery way common sense tells us people in such great numbers on this planet act. Well, the liberal's answer, of course, is that society is to blame. The environment must be constructed improperly, unreasonably, in an unenlightened way. The liberal takes to government programs and social betterment schemes like a pig to slop. And when the schemes do not work—as they usually do not, since they attempt to change a part of man which is not subject to change, his inclination to evil—the liberal looks for a new scheme, a new tax-supported program, a bigger program, more taxes, more bureaucrats. And if that does not work, then he tries another program, more taxes, etc. It is ironic to hear many modern liberals complaining about bureaucracy and red tape, the standardization of life in America, government snooping, computer banks, and all the other apparatus of big government, when they have been so responsible for the growth of the bureaucratic mess in government—in the name of helping their fellow man, of course.

What is far more menacing about the liberal from the modern point of view, however, is the zealous and constant promotion of the proud self-doubt called "relativism." The dictionary defines relativism as "a view that ethical truths depend upon the individuals and groups holding them." A relativist holds that men and societies cannot know truth, only opinion. It is also the theory that a society, quite simply, cannot have the ideals which are required for its survival. Perhaps that sounds a bit extreme, but bear with me for a moment.

First of all, it is easy to see how relativism flows from liberalism's Renaissance and Enlightenment background. If the Bible and the teachings of the Church are "medieval" superstitions, if national cus-

23

toms are narrow-minded presumptions, if laws are chains which bind man's development, if the great books from the past are only antiquarian excess baggage, if all change is progress, and social stability mere stagnation, then we just do not have any knowledge, any idea whatsoever, of what is worthy of our love or our sacrifices. We do not know truth. Certainly, if you follow this logic, there is nothing we can be sure enough about to make us willing to take up arms in its defense.

That is the deadly legacy of liberalism: a malignant self-doubt that makes us very willing to bend on every confrontation with enemies at home and abroad. After all, "they might be right," says the liberal. "How do you know?" "How can you tell?" And that is right, how can the liberal tell?

About the only "noble" act a modern liberal can perform confidently, and in good liberal conscience, is a dignified surrender. You might be able to recall what I mean in the proud bearing with which many college deans allowed themselves to be tossed from their offices by student revolutionaries in the late 1960's. Or the way your own school principal led the hoods who were rampaging through the school halls into his office for a "rap session" peace conference. You could almost read their minds. "Do with me what thou wilt, my students. I will never, never, bring the police to this campus." Maybe you have seen it, too, if you have ever viewed the old films of Neville Chamberlain leaving office in despair after Hitler double-crossed him by ignoring the Munich agreement not to invade Czechoslovakia. Chamberlain was dejected to be sure, but he seemed to be saying "Well, at least I did not behave like that crass German bully boy."

What makes this loss of national confidence in our ideals most disturbing in our modern age is that it infects us just at the time when we are forced to deal with an enemy that shows no signs of succumbing to the same loss of purpose. The Communists have their faith. They have their goals. They have a sense of mission. They believe that there are things worth dying for. And killing for. But more of that in a later chapter.

A young person genuinely concerned with being an intelligent conservative, or with defending his liberalism, must deal with this question. It is the great question mark staring America in the face. It hovers over every conference our leaders have with the Communist superpowers, over every confrontation our police have with revolutionary groups in our streets, over every court where judges mete out sentences to protestors and draft dodgers. Do we have anything worth protecting in this country? Anything worth a military campaign? Anything worth sending a young man to jail? Or keeping him in exile because he refused to serve in the draft?

Unless history tells us nothing about how the world will turn in the future, it is clear from past example that only a country with a strong sense of unity and purpose can survive as a major power. Only countries capable of inspiring their citizens to sacrifice—to be willing to die if necessary—survive as great nations.

Only authorities who are convinced of the dignity and virtue of the way of life of their people, in the social order they are sworn to defend, can act decisively enough to maintain public order.

Only school authorities who are convinced that the job of defending, preserving, protecting, and extending our cultural heritage, is a sweet burden—since our cultural heritage enshrines the history of a virtuous people—will be able to summon the energy to run a healthy school system. Those who are not convinced of anything, those who are good liberals, will let the students have their heads, to "do their thing."

Those who want to turn the tables on liberalism must turn somewhere to find the social premises, "our truths." Either to a reinvigoration of Christian religious truths, or to a renewed respect for our heritage through a renewed affection for our past, and our national unity.

In the opening lines of the Declaration of Independence, Thomas Jefferson writes "We hold these truths to be self-evident." That is the question. Liberalism denies the possibility of holding any truth as self-evident. They deny the existence of truths, holding that no one can know truth. What is puzzling is that they do not shudder when they tell us.

In each of the chapters that follows there is a discussion of one or more liberal arguments about the issues facing modern America. Young people are likely to come across these premises in a favorable light in their schools. Each is an example of what liberals and radicals might call an "enlightened" or "progressive" attitude.

It is not my claim that a significant number of American teachers actually try to brainwash their students into accepting these positions —although some of that does go on. After all, a teacher's job is to expose the student to "correct thinking" on many of these matters—as it were. On some of the issues, many teachers do try to give both sides, but, naturally, since most social studies teachers seem to be liberal or radical, they tend—perhaps subconsciously—to make their opinions come out a little bit better than the opposition's. That is to be ex-

25

pected. Conservative teachers are just as likely to do the same. (Although one might ask why so few social studies teachers reflect the more conservative sentiments of much of the community where they teach.) On others of these issues, especially among young teachers, there simply is a belief that there is only one acceptable point of view —theirs. That is not at all surprising—I guess—since that was the only point of view they heard in their own classes at college. These young educators naturally feel that it is their job to promote the "progressive" viewpoints they learned at college. (Kind of a conservatism about liberalism, no?) After all, why else did Daddy pay all that tuition?

A confrontation between these "radical-liberal" ideas and the opposing conservative viewpoints, should, in the short run, show the reader that there are responsible arguments from respectable sources that run counter to the liberal disposition. That in itself is worthwhile. But in the long run, it should point out a deeper question whose answer lies beyond the scope of this book. It is the one posed above. If *you are not a liberal, what are you?*

2

Patriotism Is Not "Mindless Jingoism"

You might think that someone with an attitude which represents a scholarly perspective on historical change, on the validity of religious and national beliefs, on the potential for unleashing man's capacity to reason out and rationally direct his future—such as a liberal—would make known his philosophical convictions only as a result of deep and thorough scholarly questioning. You would not think that you could spot a liberal, pick him out from the crowd, as easily as you could spot a Marine drill instructor at a glitter rock bar. But you can.

There are certain cultural touchstones, so to speak, which can be used to spot the liberal as confidently as you can use litmus paper in a lab. If there are exceptions to the test, they pop up infrequently enough to prove the rule. Let me give you a few examples of what I mean. Pass out flag window decals at a local picnic and see who turns you down with a bemused smile. Give away some free American flag lapel pins and watch for those who do not come around to take advantage of your generosity. Call for volunteers to carry the flag at a parade and see who eases toward the back of the room. Watch in a ballpark during the playing of the national anthem and see who seems either uncomfortable or bored by it all. Bring up the subject of encouraging students to consider the benefits of a military career and see who snickers or leaves the room. Mention a John Wayne movie, and see who expects you to be making fun of the characters Wayne plays, and who raises his eyebrows disdainfully when he finds out that you are not.

Of course there are many non-liberals who might not want, say, decals on their new car, or who feel that flag lapel pins are a little corny, or that John Wayne is a lousy actor. You obviously cannot push an analysis like this too far. To be honest, I feel like making a little fun of it myself. But there really is something to it. If you can get a liberal when he has his guard down, when he does not see you as one of "those conservatives" who are always accusing him of being a Communist, he will admit to the uneasiness he feels in situations where he is asked to make an open show of love of country. Not that he is above open shows of his dedication for other causes. He will march for peace, for clean water, to protest the treatment of the American Indian, for civil rights groups. He will wear the peace insignia around his neck, put peace decals and "ban the bomb" bumper stickers on his car, wear "make love not war" sweatshirts, and sit down on principle in any hall anywhere, anytime, for the "right reasons." No, it is not an innate shyness which holds him back. It is patriotism which makes him uncomfortable.

It is as if an open show of love of country is a childish or boorish type of behavior that all sophisticated, educated, and generally "with-it" people learn to transcend somewhere along the line.

"Well, how can you expect someone to love a country filled with poverty and racism and ghettos, and which fights wars like the one in Vietnam?" That is the question with which young liberals, and those liberals who have not thought through their position, and those liberals who do not want you to know their true position, will answer your questions. But, no, that is not it, either. There is more to it. Much more.

If America followed every one of Abby Hoffman's, and William Kunstler's, and Joan Baez's suggestions, you can bet dollars to donuts (which might not be such a bad deal nowadays) that they would not end up making patriotic speeches in front of their hometown American Legion Hall next Memorial Day. Oh, they might praise the policy decisions as being wise, and charitable, and in line with the better instincts of better people around the world. But they would not let loose a torrent of rhetoric (on the same level that they used to encourage protests, for example) designed to make the American nation feel good about itself. They would not talk of America's "destiny" or America's "greatness" as a nation. They would not heap their praise upon the American nation as a separate entity in the world. They would go out of their way, in other words, to avoid catering in the least to the kind of group-consciousness, and love of country, we know as "nationalism."

THE ONE WORLD DREAM

It is difficult to tell when it all started. Certainly during World War II and the years immediately preceding it, being educated and sophisticated did not mean being insensitive to a strong feeling of national consciousness. Actually, many of the most admired leaders of the American intellectual community during those years were unabashedly proud of the American national experience, and eager to praise the thinking of the average American. Robert Frost's poetry, parts of John Steinbeck's and John Dos Passos' novels, Charles Ives' music, Carl Sandburg's historical essays, and John Ford's movies come to mind.

But certainly, by the mid 1960's the anti-national strains in the life of the American intellectual, and would be intellectual, community were pronounced. It was the age of faculty-led students strikes, of poets reading anti-government poems on the White House lawn when they were invited to speak at cultural gatherings, of movies like "M*A*S*H," and "Easy Rider," of books like *The Greening of America*, of songs like "Bring the Boys Home," and "The Times They Are A-Changing." American movie stars became anti-heroes, Dustin Hoffman and Elliot Gould instead of John Wayne and Randolph Scott. Jane Fonda could be called the high priestess of it all, as she went from moderately talented pop-actress to a spokesman for an enemy regime, as she made announcements over Radio Hanoi encouraging American soldiers to desert in Vietnam.

Dr. Henry Paolucci, an American professor, historian and political scientist, makes the case in his difficult, but rewarding book, *War, Peace, and the Presidency*, that it was the birth of the nuclear age, and the unthinkable war which the nuclear weapons made possible, which brought these anti-national feelings to the surface. But he insists, as well, that the urge to rise above regional loyalties, and to construct a "world order" to insure the peace, is one which goes back far into recorded history—and that intellectuals have had a tendency through the ages to be especially vulnerable to the appeal.

Because in the recent past all wars have been fought by one nation-state against another—England against France, or France against Germany, for example—the logic is that the way to stop wars is to end the independence of these national groupings. If there is no such thing as an individual who feels a strong loyalty and a special sense of duty towards, say, France, or Germany, then it will be difficult to imagine a war between these two groups. The liberal, who tends to accept this proposition, then, feels that "nationalism" is a curse on mankind since it sets the stage for a world-destroying nuclear war, Armageddon.

From the liberal point of view, you must purge yourself of the national sense of exclusivity, and do whatever else is possible—in the classes you teach, the books you write, the movies and television shows that you direct—to break down this feeling in others. The liberal becomes the "enemy of patriotism."

The world must be prepared, instead, for a new structure of government, a world government, a strengthened U.N. perhaps, which will have the strength to take away the war-making power of the individual nation-states. And, of course, individuals must be made ready for this glorious day by being "educated out" of their strong love of country, their love of America.

This fits into the overall liberal vision of the ultimate nature of "rational man," as well. Without national groupings—the powerful and the weak nations, the rich and the poor nations, developed and underdeveloped nations, etc.—man will not be held back by the accident of birth. Just as human freedom and full individual development demanded the end of privileged distinctions between lords and peasants, it demands now an end to the distinctions between, say, America and Ethiopia. Man will not be what he should be until all the world can know the advantage of a proper liberal environment, so that all the world can grow to adulthood properly—like the student body at a typical American college, I guess. The poor Ethiopians.

Liberal teachers share in this anti-national missionary zeal. They call it promoting "international understanding," or breaking down "ethnocentric assumptions," or simply promoting the "end of war," and "world peace." And, once again, this is not some kind of sinister conspiracy. Seminars, summer classes, and weekend institutes for teachers, are run by respectable, above-the-board groups to assist teachers in preparing their approach to "Teaching Peace In the Nuclear Age." Surely, even those who have tasted only the popular

30

edges of cultural life in America, those who have seen the movies "Fail Safe," or "Dr. Strangelove," as opposed to those who read Kurt Vonnegut, have learned that the prospect of nuclear destruction is menacing enough for us to face up to "new realities" and to cleanse ourselves of "old myths" (as Sen. Fulbright used to put it) about the desirability of an independent America.

And, without a doubt, anyone who says he is in favor of ending America's independence (which, once again, the liberal reminds us will not be so bad at all if you do not have a very special nationalist affection for the place in the first place) has some very prestigious company, in very high places indeed. It almost looks like a *Who's Who* in American politics and educational circles. Ex-Senator Fulbright, as we just mentioned called the idea of national sovereignty (self-rule) one of the most dangerous of the "old myths" we must destroy in his book *Old Myths and New Realities*. Walt Whitman Rostow, the chief foreign policy advisor to both John Kennedy and Lyndon Johnson, was no less emphatic. In his influential book *The United States in the World Arena*, he says it as clearly as you could want: "It is a legitimate American national objective to see removed from all nations—including the United States—the right to use substantial military force to pursue their own interests." And, just in case you miss the full implications of that statement, he adds, a bit later in the book: "It is, therefore, an American interest to see an end to nationhood as it has been historically defined."

In 1962, our own State Department, under the influence of men like Rostow, through its Arms Control and Disarmament Agency, issued a plan known as "Blueprint for the Peace Race." In it, was the proposal that separate states hand over to a United Nations-type organization all their military strength except for that required "to maintain internal order and protect the security of its citizens."

In a speech delivered at the American University in June of 1963—which raised many eyebrows at the time—John Kennedy came as close to making statements reflecting an American willingness to surrender national independence as any President in history. Kennedy spoke of a willingness to create a new world order, a "new effort to achieve world law, a new context for world discussions" by working to establish a "genuine world security system—a system capable of resolving disputes on the basis of law, of insuring the security of the large and the small, and of creating conditions under which arms can finally be abolished." Of course, if Kennedy, or whoever was his speechwriter on that occasion, meant these words to mean what they

31

say, he would have been recommending an overtly treasonable, unconstitutional action, since the President takes an oath of office upon inauguration which entrusts him with the responsibility of defending our national union and its constitution, not handing us over to some world government. It is difficult to determine, now that Kennedy is dead, how much of the academic liberal's willingness to surrender our sovereignty Kennedy shared. He could have thought of the speech as campaign rhetoric, or words which he felt were suggestive only of increased cooperation among the world's independent nation-states. He might have read the speech without much thought at all about its ultimate meaning as he went through his busy day—taking his speechwriter's word that it would get a favorable message about peace across to his audience.

But a good example of what liberal "internationalists" felt and hoped that Kennedy meant can be found in the way all those books and movies—"Rush to Judgement," "Executive Order," "Parallax View"—try to make a case for a right-wing, super-patriot assassination conspiracy against Kennedy. All of this swamp-fever brand of left-wing paranoia uses the Kennedy willingness to talk turkey with the Communists as the reason for their villains', the "patriots'," determination to kill him. You see, the left-wing internationalists in America know full well that their "one-world" dreams for our future run counter—in a truly revolutionary way—to the patriotic aspirations of the great mass of the American people. They are saying, in effect, that if those who are eager to preserve America as one nation indivisible knew what was being planned for them by their enlightened, internationalist, leaders—as the better-educated assassins in these movies do—they would rise up in full wrath.

Who else? Americans for Democratic Action. The World Council of Churches. The League of Women Voters. James McGregor Burns, Franklin Roosevelt's biographer, who claims that Roosevelt had a new world order—a U.S.-U.S.S.R. partnership in mind—when he gave in so compliantly to the Russians at the Yalta Conference near the end of World War II—that conference which gave U.S. assent to the Russian domination of the Eastern European "satellite" nations.

And Dr. Henry Kissinger. People tend to forget that long before Kissinger became a world-hopping diplomat, he was a teacher of politics at Harvard and MIT. In book after book, during those years, Kissinger made clear his vision of how peace should be structured in the nuclear age. In his *Troubled Partnership*, written in 1965, he says that "institutions based on present concepts of national sovereignty are not enough. The west requires a larger goal: the constitution of an Atlantic Commonwealth in which all the peoples bordering the North Atlantic can fulfill their aspirations. Clearly it will not come quickly; many intermediate stages must be traversed before it can be reached. It is not too early, however, to prepare ourselves now for this step beyond the nation-state."

When Kissinger returned with Richard Nixon from Russia in early July 1974, he talked suggestively to the press of how the arms control agreements which were being worked out with the Russians would have to be explained patiently to the American military, and large segments of the American people, in order to calm their apprehensiveness. When you take that statement in the context of the books written over the years by Kissinger and his like-minded internationalist colleagues, you cannot avoid getting the impression that they have a determination to push for the end of national sovereignty irrespective of the patriotic longings of the American people, and that the intellectual architects of this new order, who seem devoid of all national attachments themselves, realize that they must proceed cautiously lest the American people come to see, too soon, what is being done, and, as a result, rise up as ferociously against this assault against their homeland as they would against an invading army.

The fact that American statesmen are negotiating with a willingness to surrender sovereignty should become even more troubling to the American citizen-patriot when he considers the fact that we are dealing in the modern world, not with a traditional nation-state, but with the Communists. For the Communist vision of the world also calls for the end of the nation state.

Karl Marx and V. I. Lenin—and every Soviet Party Congress since the first—have made this point clearly. The Communist movement is by its supporters' own definition an "international brotherhood." When the Russians or the Chinese define their aims in foreign policy, they speak of "spreading the revolution," not of increasing the scope of Russian or Chinese military power in the world. Whether they mean it or not is another question.

They claim to be operating selflessly in the name of Marx's united "workers of the world." In the Communist scheme of things, a Communist world would be run by a kind of council of Communist leaders who would view the world's resources and creative industrial and agricultural capacity, not as the exclusive domain of any one "nation" but as a shared wealth to be administered as "commonwealth" by the representatives of the international working class.

At first glance it seems far-fetched, but Communists would give you Russia as a miniature example of how it would work, if you asked for an example. Remember, the official name of Russia is not "Russia," but the "Union of Soviet Socialist Republics." In other words the socialist workers republics of Eastern Europe—Georgia, Latvia, Kazakhskaya, Ukrainskaya, etc.—under the "benevolent tutelage" of the mother of Communism, Russia, have joined in a working Communist brotherhood for their "mutual advantage"—as the Communists might put it. Why not, then, the other national groupings around the world?

As you can see, it puts us in a most troubling situation—especially when our foreign policy is being conducted by our "one worlders." For not only can the Communists pose before the neutral nations of the world as generous workers for the good of mankind, but they also can frame their desires in a way that is most attractive to the American liberal. The vision of a world government pushed by our liberals, in many ways, is identical to that pushed by the Communists. The liberals, of course, do not like the idea of a world government run by Russian commissars, and they are perceptive enough to know that Russia has used its position as leader of the Communist nations of the world to its own advantage, rather than that of the international working class. They do not want a Russian empire. (If they do, we have to use a much harsher word for them than "liberal.") But, nevertheless, for the internationalist, much of what Russia wants in the way of a world government is commendable. If only those Russians could be persuaded to allow American professors and writers and gentle scientists to run the thing instead of their Communist party bosses, they would be on the right track, from the liberal point of view.

What a stew! To be working for your supposed enemies' goal, with just some modifications, but clearly against the aspirations of the patriotic masses in America.

The Russians can sit back and watch American liberal leaders push for the liberal internationalist version of a world government. They know, too, how similar it is to Communist aims. If the American liberals cannot move America fully over to the world government, well, they will have to deal with us as powerful nations have dealt with other powerful nations down through the ages. No big loss. And if the American liberals can convert America, then, it should be pretty easy to deal with the soft American professor types who want to cooperate with the Soviets in the new world government, and run the thing right, the way they did in Czechoslovakia, Poland, and Hungary.

The liberal, of course, being a liberal, does not really fear that kind of an outcome. Remember that to a liberal all men are rational and basically good, including the Communists. If Communists have acted aggressively and in disregard for the human freedoms of the countries around them, it must be because of a bad environment. It must be our fault. They must be afraid of us. Their poverty must make them unnaturally assertive. So if we would only stop making weapons and scaring them, and help promote their economic growth instead of allowing our capitalist corporations to try to dominate the world economy, why they will become cooperative, less assertive militarily, and will want to have the new world government run by gentle and decent men, instead of their generals. (I am not trying to be snide. This is exactly the analysis which is receiving the widest support in the American academic community. It is called "New Left Revisionism." We will have more to say about that in a later chapter.)

Most conservatives reject all of this as being wishful thinking, at best, and a dangerous flirtation with disaster, at worst.

For one thing they tend to see the nation-state system as a legitimate and workable solution to a problem which has plagued Western man since the days of Ancient Greece—that is, how to provide *both* freedom and security for man in an organized social structure. They also argue that the liberal internationalists' lack of concern for America's national success, because of their overriding concern for world peace, makes them decidedly unfit to play important roles in our government and its dealings with foreign powers, and with revolutionary groups at home.

THE NATION-STATE IN HISTORY

Anthropologists and historians study the way man has organized his life in both ancient and modern times. Man has basic needs—food, clothing, protection—but has organized the way that he provides for them in different ways. Studies of primitive man seem to indicate that early tribes passed through different stages in their development, but that all around the world pretty much the same progression took place. From roving, hunting, and gathering tribes, to horticultural societies who depended upon the bounty of nature in one particular

35

area, to agricultural societies who worked the soil and managed nature's cycle in order to increase productivity, and on and on through commercial, industrial, and technological ages of man.

They have also been able to tell that more complex ways of organizing for these basic needs led to more complex systems of government. As the needs of society increased, the power and size of government did as well. Ironically, the improvements in productive capacity, which required more powerful government, also led to a greater self-consciousness on the part of the individual (as a result of increased leisure time) and a greater desire for political freedom—and a resulting resentment of the powerful government under which he lived.

They say that you cannot have your cake and eat it, too, but mankind, especially Western man, has refused to accept the analogy in this case.

It was not only man's needs within his social grouping which determined the size and extent of authority given to his government. The likelihood of invasion and conquest by other groups also determined whether a group would have a large standing army, and an authority centralized enough to direct its command. The difficulty, obviously, in this situation is that an army large and powerful enough to protect a country would also be powerful enough to enslave it. The question? How do you make a country and its arms of government large enough and powerful enough to protect the country without, in the process, destroying human freedom.

All down through the history of the West, you can see countries struggling with this issue. The ancient Greeks, mostly because of the string of mountains dividing their country, organized themselves into relatively small geographic areas. History has given them credit, as a result, for solving one part of the problem. In their various city-states—Sparta, Delphi, Syracuse, Athens—the citizenry was small enough for a very personal type of government—a government of neighbors. Areas a stone's throw away from each other by the standards of modern nations, developed lifestyles thousands of miles apart in structure and purpose. Sparta and Athens became examples of the extremes of difference—one a military state, the other a democracy with an intense interest in the life of the mind. The governments were not faced with coordinating the conflict of interests of separate and opposing groups. Men knew their governors, and shared their view of what was a good life. Voluntary obedience—political freedom—came relatively easy to these quite homogeneous peoples.

But what do you do with a city-state when an invader, lured by the

36

riches built up by the social cooperation between your small band of brothers-citizens, decides to make it his own? The Greeks were faced with just this problem when the Persian Empire swept across the Aegean Sea in large fleets and multitudinous armies under leaders like Xerxes and Darius in the early fifth century B.C. The Greeks, seeing this menacing common enemy, smoothed over their differences. Athenians fought in cooperation with Spartans in the legendary Delian League, and after a series of reversals in which thousands of Greeks gave their lives—including the legendary Leonidas and his three hundred Spartan warriors in their suicide mission to block the pass at Thermopylae—they stopped the invader. The names of the battles used to be part of every schoolchild's heritage: Marathon, Salamis, Thermopylae. With the defeat of the Persians, however, the Greeks returned to their old ways, and the Delian League became a mere formality. Now Greeks battled Greeks.

At first, it did not seem to matter too much. Athens especially flowered under the wise leader, Pericles, in a period which has come to be called "The Golden Age." Great playwrights—Aeschylus, Euripedes, Sophocles; sculptors—Myron, Praxiteles; philosophers—Plato, Aristotle—made life in Athens a joy to the intellect and artistic senses. Who needed powerful armies and strong political unity with other Greek states when there were these more important things to think about—so they thought.

Later in that same century, the Macedonian "phalanx," the armies of Philip in battle formation, swept down from their kingdom just to the north of Greece. They conquered all of Greece, from the largest theater to the smallest book of poems. Aristotle, the greatest philosopher of the time, became the private tutor to the son of this crude barbarian. The boy's name was Alexander. He was later known as Alexander the Great.

It could be said that the Romans erred in the opposite direction. Instead of being too small to defend themselves, they grew too large to maintain freedom.

At its peak the Roman Empire stretched from northern England to the Middle East. Instead of facing the problem of providing a defense against their enemies, they crushed all their enemies. They created the so-called "Pax Romana," the Roman Peace. Their problem was that in the process they destroyed the political freedom, the government by discussion, which was the glory of the Roman Republic. Remember, Rome went through many changes in its system of government. Sometimes high school students who have studied Rome (those few who still do) speak of Roman ways, Roman beliefs, Roman government, as if there were only one Rome.

Actually, the history of Rome covers a period of nearly a thousand years, from the legendary founding by Romulus and Remus, the wars with the Etruscans and Samnites, down through the wars with Hannibal, the establishment of the Empire, and the eventual collapse in the fifth century A.D. Rome was first a kingdom, then a Republic, then an Empire. When you hear stories of Roman senators engaged in spirited debate of public policy- and large-scale participation in the competition for power between opposed candidates, and the rotation of citizens in public office, you are hearing about the glory days of the Roman *Republic*. But that did not last forever.

As Roman conquest piled upon Roman conquest, Rome eventually became an *Empire,* a patchwork of separate nationalities supposedly living as equals under Roman law. In fact, they were equal only in their forced submission to the might of the Roman legions, and the distant Roman emperors.

In truth, how could it have been otherwise? How could a spirit of brotherhood and mutual trust develop in a conglomerate like that? What could provide the reason for social cooperation and civic self-sacrifice among this collection of distinct and different peoples—these strangers? Certainly not the fear of being crushed by a common enemy. The Romans had destroyed all their enemies. By the time the Germanic tribes to the north were united enough to present that kind of a challenge, Rome was so far gone in an orgy of drinking festivals and spectator sports that about all the Romans were able to do in unison was whimper as one at the devastation of their cities. They so memorialized the name of one of their plundering enemies that we use it today—Vandals.

The modern nation-state is an ingenious answer to this problem. How big? How small? Big enough to defend yourself. Small enough to maintain a sense of brotherhood.

By using national loyalties instead of village loyalties, men are given a brotherhood based not on personal acquaintance, but on a shared historical experience. Love of country and love of fellow countrymen give men noble motives for self-sacrifice, and a generous and spirited sense of public duty. We Americans, for example, can feel free when obeying laws made in Washington, D.C. even though we live in Caribou, Maine, or San Diego, California, because these laws were not made by strangers living thousands of miles from us, but by fellow Americans. A sense of belonging, participation, and

38

worth develops from the role we see for ourselves in this social organism containing our national brothers.

Correspondingly, how could anyone feel any degree of "voluntariness" about the obedience he would have to give to a world government . . . how could the liberal feel it especially when he cannot even develop a sense of belonging in his relationship with the American people? World government, simply, would be world dictatorship. Those who push for world government somehow always manage to avoid this conclusion by imagining that if there is a world government it will be run by people like themselves. But it ain't necessarily so.

Of course, you could take the opposite tack and argue that an even more intense degree of freedom would be felt if our governments were smaller than nation-states. But remember the Greek example. Could we defend ourselves successfully if we made our state any smaller? Could a smaller state create the international balance of power, make other countries refrain from attempting to dominate us? Could it give us the peace required for the civilizing process of enjoying and creating music, poetry, literature, and creative play. You cannot paint the "Last Supper" on coffee breaks in a foxhole.

Whatever the reason for the liberal internationalist's sense of "alienation" from his nation, those of us who are determined that America should survive as a free and independent nation "one nation indivisible" cannot allow them to continue to direct our public policy. It is very simple. If someone is not dedicated to serving the best interests of the American people, except when they coincide with what is "best for mankind" as he sees it, he will end up making decisions that run against our own national needs. Perhaps that is why so many international confrontations between our diplomats and those of other countries end up with the United States coming out second best. Perhaps that is why so many people seem to feel that our fighting men win wars, and our politicians lose the peace treaties. To someone with a grand scheme of insured world peace, the loss of individual nations—Poland, Hungary, China, for example— might not be too great a price to pay for increased cooperation with the Russians.

Perhaps this is also the reason why going to college in our country seems so often to mean learning to dislike the customs, history, and religious beliefs of the American people; why being sophisticated seems to require a contempt for "flag-wavers"; why Archie Bunker, the carefully prepared network-TV image of what is wrong with

39

America, wears a flag on his jacket; why a significantly greater percentage of the faculty at Princeton University in 1968 gave their votes to Dick Gregory, a radical internationalist, rather than to Richard Nixon or Hubert Humphrey.

In *War, Peace, and the Presidency*, Henry Paolucci puts it very precisely. "America is not a civil society for transients on their way to membership in a 'rationalized' world community." Transients owe little more to their hosts than a few bucks for lodging. And they have been known to take an ashtray and a towel in return for that. America deserves more, especially from her leaders.

The burden of maintaining national independence is a heavy burden. But it is an exhilarating one for free men, since the alternative is the carefree irresponsibility of the slave. For Americans the choice is that clear—even though some of our learned news commentators fail to see that. James Reston for example, the dean of columnists for the *New York Times*, wrote early in 1974 of the joys he anticipated when America became a second-rate power, like the happier Swiss, Swedes, and Dutch. No more wars, taxes for the military, protests. No more worries about Vietnam, the Middle East, or Panama.

But what he fails to include in this rosy picture, is that these countries do not have to worry about those things because we do. They do not have to worry about Russian expansion, because we do. Who will do it for them when we become second-rate? Who will do it for us when we become second-rate? Although Reston, being a liberal, probably feels that Russia would not succumb to the temptation of getting a bit pushy if there were no opposition. It would be great fun to let the Restons of the world see if they are right, except for the fact that we would all have to pay the price with them.

One final note on this subject: America cannot build a world government without the cooperation of the other nations of the world. Unless we want to bomb them into surrendering their independence with us. (The war to end all wars?) And it is clear that the rest of the world is moving in the opposite direction. This is the age of emerging nationalism around the world. From the Middle East to Northern Ireland to Bangla Desh to Angola, men are waging wars for the kind of national freedom our liberals want us to surrender.

Attacks on national loyalties and patriotism do nothing for world peace—unless you see a weakened America as a step toward your version of world peace.

3

Capital Punishment Is Not "Institutionalized Murder"

From all the righteous indignation—the sense of shock—that pours from those opposed to capital punishment, it is hard to believe that it is only very recently, as history measures time, that there has been any real opposition to the idea that a society has a right to execute those judged to be guilty of heinous crimes. The same cultures that produced a Socrates, a Dante, a Shakespeare, or a Florence Nightingale, executed their criminals without much hand-wringing at all. The great minds of the past, with very few exceptions, accepted the death penalty, not as the high point of their cultural life to be sure, but as a "necessary evil," as natural to life in organized society as a police force.

Interestingly though, if you go back far enough into what is usually called "ancient" history you find the death penalty used less frequently than in more modern times. It was not the more primitive man who punished with a state-organized death sentence. Records of early tribes in what we now call Europe indicate that these barbaric people did not bother with it much. There were penalties for certain crimes—robbery, adultery, treason—and sometimes these penalties were very severe. You might have your hand cut off at the wrist, or your forehead branded if you met with a more merciful judge. But if someone killed a member of your family, or a friend, you —not your government—were expected to force the murderer to pay for his crime. You were supposed to seek "vengeance," by killing him. Or you could take a pay-off instead (blood money) if the murderer had enough wealth to make it worthwhile.

When death penalties were established, it was a step forward in the direction of fairness, and equal rights. The flaws in the older system were obvious. What if the murderer were very wealthy—say if he had a large herd of cows? He could kill half the people in the village and still never feel the penalty of the law in any real way—a cow or two for everyone he felt like bumping off. Or what if the murderer were a fierce and brawny warrior, and the survivor of his victims a twelve-year-old child? And a puny one at that? What would the chances be for vengeance against those odds?

The ancient Hebrews are remembered by history for many things— most of all their covenant with the one God. But they also were one of the first peoples to recognize the value of the written law. The first thing that Moses did after his meeting with God on the mountain was to carve the Ten Commandments on stone. One of the most remembered of all their ancient laws was the famous "An eye for an eye, a tooth for a tooth." No longer would individuals have to strike out on their own in justice's name—and hope for the best. Their people, their society, would establish a standard of justice for them.

The Romans used the death penalty infrequently. But their reluctance was not based on the modern liberal claim that a death sentence would not actually "deter" anyone from the act of murder, or that it was cruel and immoral to execute a murderer. No, the Romans were no bleeding hearts. They just thought that would-be criminals would be more frightened out of committing crimes—deterred —if the penalties of the Roman law were an ever-present reminder. You see if you killed the criminal, only those who were actually present at the execution to see the blood and guts spilled would be frightened by the prospect of appearing before a Roman court. The Romans decided that people roaming the streets with missing hands or feet, eyes, fingers, and noses would be a far better deterrent.

During the Middle Ages the death penalty was used frequently—as it was during the early years of the developing monarchies of Europe. And the number of offenses meriting the death penalty grew. In England at one time there were over one hundred and sixty such offences. Of course treason was a capital offense, and kings in most European countries proved more than willing to behead those considered to be traitors. Often the heads would then be placed on spikes in prominent places for the birds to pick at, and the people to see. Henry VIII is just about everyone's favorite virtuoso.

Decapitation (beheading) was not the only way you could be sent to your eternal reward, however. Boiling in oil, being stretched on a huge wheel until your bones separated, drawing and quartering (having the ends of four ropes attached to your arms and legs, the other ends to four horses, and giddyap!) were some of the more common and ingenious ways. And yes, witches were burned, or drowned, as in America.

By the sixteenth century hanging became more and more commonplace, and remained in vogue right up until the modern time when "improvements" such as the gas chamber and the electric chair were introduced.

Admittedly, when you look at the death penalty in this kind of historical context, it does seem barbarous, a leftover from periods in history when people thought that the earth was flat, and that the stars were holes in the sky through which the light of heaven shone in the darkness. There are many conservatives, too, who see things in this way and who are in favor of abolishing the death penalty. But not, if they are thinking conservatives, for the same reasons as the liberal, as we shall see.

The liberal resistance to capital punishment usually makes use of one or more, or all, of the following propositions:

a) Someone who is angry enough to kill will not take the time to think about being punished for his act. The death penalty is no deterrent.

b) Only someone who is insane would commit a murder if he were not angry beyond control; and the insane should not be punished for their "sickness."

c) There is always a chance of error. An innocent man might be executed.

d) The rich can hire skilled lawyers to protect them. Only the poor die.

e) If the society "kills a killer" then it is as bad as the killer. It is doing the same thing.

f) The murderer might be reformed while in jail.

As we examine each of these arguments, it is likely that, in the process, the reader will find himself vacillating—*for* capital punishment at certain times, *against* it at others. I must admit that when I look at certain of these arguments I, too, have my doubts. At times I feel that a sentence of life imprisonment, without the chance of parole, might be adequate punishment.

However when you look at the doctrinaire liberal's approach to these positions, you find yourself in the presence of the kind of fuzzy thinking which has been so destructive of our social order. The purpose of what follows then is not so much to defend the death penalty to the death, as it is to show the liberal-relativist at work in the cause of making it impossible for society to make standards for human behavior.

a) *Someone angry enough to kill will not take the time to think of being punished. The death penalty is no deterrent.*

Well, to begin with, there is some substance to this argument. A man who has been cheated out of his week's salary in a game of poker just might smash a beer bottle over the head of the man who cheated him, and kill him. A jealous husband or boyfriend might shoot his competition in a bar some night. There was a case in the newspapers not too many years ago of one man shooting another to death over a parking space in New York City. In cases like these the shooting or knifing, or whatever, takes place so quickly that the assailant does not even think about what he is doing, much less about the severity of the penalty he is likely to face. I am sure that every reader has experienced anger welling up within himself to an extent that gives at least a hint of how, in a sudden flash of rage, a person can commit an act of violence.

But the liberals are building a straw man here—an argument they make just for the purpose of cutting it apart with ease. For no intelligent supporter of the death penalty would argue that capital punishment can stop crimes of this sort. Obviously it cannot. If a person is not thinking at all because of inflamed passions, he cannot be thinking of the death penalty. Nothing can stop violence when it is caused by this kind of consummate rage. It would be a very good argument, indeed, if all murders were of this sort. But they are not.

Take the case of two men planning a robbery next week. One suggests that they get some guns in case things get rough. The other says no, that if they have to use them, and kill someone, they might get the electric chair. He suggests toy guns instead—just enough to frighten the storeowner into complying. (And criminal confessions have given us many records of such discussions.) Or what about a man

44

whose wife has run away with another man to a city a few hundred miles away. He thinks of getting a gun and going after them—and killing them. If he had the gun in the room with him, and the two lovebirds were there as well, he would kill them without hesitation. But as he thinks about it on the way to buy the gun, he thinks of what the gas chamber might be like. He remembers how his wife used to nag him all the time anyway. He thinks of all the other fish in the sea. He thinks of the gas chamber again. He goes out and gets drunk instead.

We could go on and on with examples like this. Anyone with some imagination and some understanding of human nature could come up with hundreds at least. It is obvious. Not all murders happen in a flash of anger. Some are planned. Human beings—normal human beings—are quite capable of enough anger, or greed, or hate, to consider and plan a murder. The death penalty is there to help these would-be murderers (you and me) understand the seriousness of taking a life; and to help them overcome their rage. Anyone who has any touch at all with the way men think and behave (and with himself) knows that the fear of execution will enter into the decision-making process in cases like these. Granted, there will be times when hate or avarice will be strong enough for a person to risk his own death. It will not deter in a case like that. But in many others the would-be murderer will reconsider his plans based on the fear of being executed.

When liberals advance this argument they usually point to murder statistics in certain areas when the death penalty was in effect as support of their claim. "If all these people committed murder when there was a death penalty, how can you say a death penalty deters a murderer?" Even radio hosts and television news commentators, who should know better, make silly statements like that. It is so obvious when you think about it. All that these statistics show you are how many people were either too angry to think of the death penalty, or willing to risk it—and so committed the murder. It tells you who was *not* deterred. It tells you nothing of the numerous men and women who sat in lonely rooms, and decided that killing their hated enemy just was not worth the risk of going to the chair themselves.

It will help you here to remember what we said about the liberal mind in an earlier chapter. The liberal mind insists that men are basically good and rational. And that only a bad "environment" (in this case the surrounding anger) makes him behave improperly. The liberal denies the existence of the great drama of moral choice. Men's lives are merely the victims of circumstance to the liberal. He

45

denies man's capacity to sin—to deal with the decision of whether to commit an evil act, or not, and at what price. He denies the greatness of man, his ability to act and behave as a responsible individual. In other words, he cannot picture anyone sitting down and making the kind of a decision about whether to kill or not that we have just described.

The basic question is then, who is the realist? Who knows human behavior?

Well, children are seldom "liberal" on this point. They know the need for some kind of external discipline in most people's lives. They know what happens when the teacher leaves the room during an exam. They know what would happen if you did not have an usher to check the ticket stubs at a movie house. They know that some would cheat and that some would not. It is difficult to disagree with them.

What is most confounding is that the liberal in denying this reality, denies his own inclination toward evil, dishonesty, and violence; and thus his own capacity for acting freely, as a moral agent. He dehumanizes himself.

b) *Only someone who is insane could commit a murder. And the insane should not be punished for their "sickness."*

This is, of course, a topic very much related to what we have just discussed. Here it is not the temporary insanity caused by anger which causes the murder, according to the liberal, but a more lingering disorder. When the liberal hears of someone killing a child, or torturing a young girl, or setting fire to a derelict, he, at first, like the rest of us, is outraged by the act. But, after a while, he tends to forget the dead victim, and turns his sympathy instead toward the poor murderer in his jail cell. "He must be insane. No sane person could commit horrors like that. Maybe poverty did it to him."

Because of this outlook the number of criminals included in the category "criminally insane" grows by leaps and bounds with each passing year. If it continues at this pace almost everyone who commits a crime will be considered insane. Maybe their mothers didn't love them enough, or something about where their desks were placed in the first grade.

More and more perpetrators of the most foul misdeeds are being sent to hospitals for psychiatric care, instead of to prison or the electric chair. And they are released from those hospitals in amazingly short time. In a survey made in Washington, D.C., a few years back, 16% of all murderers judged insane were back on the streets in less than five years.

In the past a man was judged to be criminally insane or not by a

46

fairly simple test. One of the earliest and most famous statements of the guidelines came in 1863 in an English case known as the Mc-Naghten case. In that case it was decided that to be judged insane "it must be clearly proved that, at the time of committing the act, the party accused was laboring under such a defect of reason from disease of the mind, as not to know the nature and gravity of the act he was doing." These guidelines were not really all that different from those found in another English case about a hundred years earlier which demanded that "a man must be totally deprived of his understanding and memory so as not to know what he was doing, no more than an infant, a brute, or a wild beast." Note those words—like an "infant, a brute, or a wild beast."

The liberal, however, was not pleased with that definition. For if a man is naturally rational and good (as the liberal insists), and still murders and rapes, and does not act like an infant or a wild beast, then something must be wrong. If he behaves shamefully, he "must be" insane even if he shows no obvious signs of what the average person knows as insanity. There must be things deep in his subconscious that lead to his criminal behavior, things over which he has no control.

Sharing this view, and giving it respectability, are numerous members of the twentieth-century field of medicine known as psychiatry. Psychiatrists who accept a view of human nature called "determinist" are moving in the direction of calling the criminal act in and of itself an insane act. Of course, there are many other psychiatrists who reject this view completely. But they are not the ones who are very much in demand by lawyers for the accused in murder trials.

In 1954, the so-called Durham case gave great impetus to this tendency in the United States, by setting a new standard for what constituted insanity in a criminal trial. According to the judge's decision in this case, the accused murderer was exempt from punishment, even if he knew right from wrong, as long as he could trace his behavior to some mental disease or defect. As you can guess that really threw the doors wide open.

Once again, the liberal has the noble slogans on his side. He is asking us to be forgiving, to understand why the criminal behaves the way that he does, to see his "problems".

But once again the liberal has actually besmirched the dignity of man by treating him as little more than a plant whose growth and vitality are dependent upon forces beyond his control.

Think of what it means if the criminal act, by definition, becomes an insane act. Think of what it means if the criminal is not to be blamed for his actions. Great heroes in history—Moses, John the Baptist, Francis of Assisi, Joan of Arc, Abraham Lincoln, Congressional Medal of Honor winners, Jonas Salk, the defenders of the Alamo, the Dutch boy who held his finger in the hole in the dike—would really be no more worthy of praise or blame than Nero, Herod, Caligula, John Wilkes Booth, Pontius Pilate, Jack the Ripper, Charles Manson, Adolph Hitler, Al Capone, Sirhan Sirhan, Rapunzel's witch. The human notions of courage, loyalty, perseverance, become "hang-ups" or "lack of hang-ups" which can be explained away on a psychiatrist's couch.

What we must take time to consider, too, is the fact that even people with genuine mental difficulties in many cases can differentiate between right and wrong clearly enough to know that they should not commit acts of violence. After all, a philosopher might understand why he committed a murder more completely than would a bellhop (although I would not bet on it anymore). But that would not make the bellhop (or the philosopher) exempt from the consequences of his act, and free from the burden of punishment. The "knowledge" of right and wrong exists on many different levels.

In addition, even those with severe psychological disorders are capable of knowing fear. Animals can know fear. Dogs can be taught not to bite. The threat of a death penalty certainly would enter the minds of a great many of those judged to be criminally insane today. As long as that threat were not an idle one.

This is not as heartless a thought as it sounds on first hearing. The laws are formed to protect the innocent. It does a victim and his family little good to know that the murderer was not "whole" psychologically. If a disturbed person, who would have been frightened into not committing a murder, or terrorizing a child, by the knowledge that in his society that kind of behavior leads to severe punishment, commits an atrocity because he does not know that fear, then our laws have failed in their purpose—disgracefully so.

It is not possible for the law to right all wrongs—to cure every mentally unbalanced person in the country for example. It serves a more limited, but nevertheless noble, purpose if it protects us as much as possible from the dangerous elements in our society. If it fails to do that by not "threatening" sufficiently those who are likely to do us harm—whether from criminal or psychological disorders—we have a right to be genuinely angry.

Certainly the genuinely insane should be committed, not executed. If they are dangerous, however, they should be committed forever.

But the thousands being excused from the full force of the law today are not all in that category. We have a right to be protected from them—by the threat of death.

c) *There is always a chance of error. An innocent man might die.*

The thought of executing an innocent is one which has to chill the bones of all decent men. A society with a death penalty must do everything within its power—everything—to avoid making such an error. That is not up for debate.

When people try to deal with this question it almost always sounds like a question of mathematics. "Would you be willing to allow ten murderers to receive lesser penalties than kill one innocent man? A hundred killers? A thousand? Every killer in the world?" But this kind of thing misses the point—at least partially. It concerns itself only with prisoners already in jail awaiting punishment. I am sure very few people would be willing to execute ten or twenty or a hundred-thousand criminals accused of murder if they knew that one innocent man was in the group. Most people would just recommend that they be kept in jail indefinitely until the innocent man could be found. You don't have to execute them before dawn.

The bigger question is: What about the *potential* murderers, and their potential victims out on the street? If you accept the idea that the death penalty is going to deter certain would-be murderers, you have to ask yourself (again like a math problem): "How many of these murders are you going to allow, during the entire course of a country's history, because you have abolished the death penalty in fear of executing one or ten or a hundred men?" When you phrase the question this way it is not a question of executing murderers or not, but of saving innocent lives or not.

Actually, the chances are remote of executing even five innocent men over the course of a country's history. Now, remember, that is not like saying that you are *willing* to kill an innocent man to protect a certain number of potential victims of murderers. You are not *willing* to kill *any* innocent men. But knowing the remote possibility exists, should you be willing to live with this possibility in order to safeguard the lives of those who would be killed by murderers if there were no death penalty?

In our society, especially in the last fifty years or so, it is hard to imagine an innocent man being executed. First of all there is the trial, the presentation of evidence, the cross-examination of witnesses, and the requirement that *all* twelve jurors agree that the accused has been proven guilty "beyond a reasonable doubt." Then there are appeals, stays of execution, reopening of cases because of additional information. If someone is convicted after all that, it has to be considered a fluke, an oddity, or a Hollywood script.

If death penalties are abolished because of the remote chance that this kind of thing could occur, something is out of balance somewhere.

To put it simply: If you agree that a death penalty would deter certain potential murderers, but you are against it because of the miniscule chance of executing an innocent man, you show a remarkable degree of indifference to the lives of the potential victims.

d) *The rich can hire brilliant lawyers to protect them. Only the poor die.*

Well for one thing, being stricter with the rich could take care of that. But that is avoiding the issue.

It is true that if you go down through the lists of those executed in our country, you will find very few wealthy men. Part of that can be explained by the fact that the rich do not kill as often—not because they are more virtuous but because they lack much of the motivation. They lack poverty, slums, and criminal neighbors. This is just a fact of life, not the way things should be necessarily, but the way they are.

There are no intelligent conservatives who make the case that a poor man does not have certain disadvantages when he goes on trial; or when he goes house-hunting or into a restaurant. There is very little conservative opposition to the idea that a poor man should be given an attorney to handle his defense if he cannot pay for it on his own. (There is conservative opposition to the idea that we have to turn to the Communist version of "equality" to take care of this problem.)

True, chances are that the attorney he will end up with might be young and inexperienced. But, let's face it, there are only so many "top" attorneys to go around. If the ability to pay did not determine who would get the services of the "best" what would? Whether or not you know the clerk who passes out the lawyer assignments if all the lawyers in the country were government employees? Whether or not you were a good-looking girl with the right kind of smile? Whether or not you got lucky if they assigned lawyers by a lottery of some sort? Then you might get the very best for a parking violation; and the worst if you were accused of murder.

Our society is filled with certain inequalities. Some people are brighter, stronger, prettier, richer, than others. All societies have these disparities, and some unique to themselves. In a Communist society, being in good with the party leaders would be the way to get yourself the best attorney around. Although if you were in good with the party leaders you probably would not need an attorney.

It is not hard to feel angered at the fact that a millionaire can afford to hire a team of top lawyers to defend his son on a murder charge, while a ghetto youth goes to legal aid for a young and inexperienced lawyer. But, like everything else, it is easier to spot the problem than to devise the cure. Millionaires drive Cadillacs and eat caviar too.

Even if these extremes of wealth and poverty within a society are wrong, it simply does not follow that poor would-be murderers should not be burdened with the knowledge that they will be punished in a most severe manner for their crime. The ideal would be to have an effective deterrent for both rich and poor. Deterring the poor is better than deterring neither. Remember, all that can be said about the opposition to the death penalty because of the advantages of the wealthy, is that the wealthy are not receiving justice, not that the poor are not.

e) *The murderer might be reformed in jail.*

The argument is the most persuasive of all. As all Christians know, man can overcome his temptations, he can defeat the psychic scars of growing up in a bad environment. He can overcome his inclinations toward evil. Man is not a houseplant.

The most vicious of murderers—in enough cases to make us think about it—have reformed and become decent men. Christians call it grace, repentance, and redemption.

Handling this argument becomes almost like some of the number games we needled earlier. How many reform? How many people will be murdered because there is no death penalty? Which comes first?

For those who believe in the Christian promise of eternal life there is some room for maneuvering here. You can tell yourself that when you execute a man who might have reformed, you are not really ending his life. But society, even the most Christian societies, never answer questions that way on other issues, so it does seem to be a cop-out.

Perhaps the only answer to the dilemma, is that society can only do the good of which it is capable, and avoid the evils that it can control. Society can provide suitable punishments for grievous crimes. It cannot see into a man's future.

f) *If a society kills a killer, it is as bad as the killer. It is doing the same thing for which it is executing him.*

The argument is liberal-relativism flying high. It would be nice to

51

think that intelligent liberals shy away from this one, but they do not as clearly as they should. It keeps coming up.

Before a society takes someone's life, it obviously must be convinced that the criminal has done something evil, something *wrong*; that he has violated certain codes of behavior that are *right*, virtuous, honorable.

But, you will recall, the liberal insists that all any society knows are its opinions, superstitions, myths, prejudices, and nationalistic "ethnocentricities." There is no such thing as truth. An execution of a human being in the name of "those things" is not much different from someone killing the guy in the gas station to get enough money to buy some reefers. Actually, for many liberals it is worse, because society does not kill in blind anger or desire, but after thought and full consideration of what it is doing.

Since the liberal rejects the idea of divine revelation, he also rejects out of hand the idea that a murderer might have violated God's law as well as man's, and have done something as evil as the acts for which the Old Testament God burned and drowned out entire cities.

The initial temptation for a sane man when he hears this argument is to throw up his hands and walk away. Really, if someone cannot admit to the difference between beasts who throw gasoline on a girl and light it just for the thrill of watching her burn to death, or someone who joins in with a mob that gets its kicks by stoning an old man fishing in the river (two recent cases in Boston), and the jail guard who would be given the job of turning the switch on the electric chair during their execution, it might be time to give up.

There is a way, however, of handling the morality and permissibility of capital punishment that is often effective with people who have not traveled that far off the deep end of liberalism. It goes like this:

Just about everyone agrees that an individual has the right to defend his own, and his family's life. In more primitive times—and even in recent periods—a man had to be a warrior. He had to possess and know how to use a club or a spear, a sword or a gun, or he would not be a proper "husband" ("one who provides for another"). Weapons were carried on the person in prominent, well-advertised places. Spears were often adorned with ribbons. Swords had elaborately carved handles, shields elaborate heraldry. In the American West, hand guns sat in fine leather holsters. It was common knowledge that these weapons were carried to be used if necessary. They could be used legitimately and honorably in defense of property, family, or person. In fact, great shame was heaped upon a man who did not use them when he should.

In those simpler times, would-be assailants *knew* that they would have to take the risk of being killed themselves if they attacked another man. They knew that he was entitled to run them through, or blow their brains out, if they harmed a member of his family. They knew that surviving relatives would try to hunt them down, by any and all possible means, and kill them. They had to take all of that into account before they undertook their attack. That is why large and powerful cattle barons were not as likely to have to face up to nighttime raids as were poor, one-mule sodbusters.

As populations grew, as society progressed, as law and order became a more common demand, the state began to take over this "protective" function. Who would want to go for a Sunday stroll, or a picnic, where shoot-outs were the order of the day? Handguns eventually were regulated. (In addition, as mentioned earlier, there was a need to bring justice to these conflicts, so that the fastest gun was not always "in the right.")

Men no longer carried their own weapons. Sheriffs and cops did it for them. They no longer executed those who harmed them in a grievous way. Their government did. They surrendered their arms, and the security (the power to frighten—"to deter") those armed offered, for the greater security of an organized police force. *Greater* security was the assumption.

A society with a police force, then, must do for its members at least as much as pistol-packing men could do for themselves. It must frighten would-be wrongdoers at least as much as they could. And it must be repeated that they were supposed to do *more* since not everyone with a gun on his hip was all that frightening. That was supposed to be the big improvement of a law-and-order society. You did not have to be Buffalo Bill to get justice.

A society, then, has as much right to kill as the individual used to have. When a government renounces that responsibility, it is betraying its trust.

If a man cannot walk the streets of his neighborhood, if his wife must tremble in fear in her own home at night—even more than a frontier wife in an isolated cabin near Indian country—if his children are not safe in their playgrounds, that is a clear indication that his government has betrayed its trust.

The applications for pistol permits are skyrocketing in American cities.

4

Capitalism Is Not "Institutionalized Exploitation"

Conservatives do vary in the intensity of their support for capitalism and of private ownership of business in general in America. But they never come close to the total rejection of the idea of decentralized property ownership displayed by socialists. They reject the notion of "totalitarian economics."

Some conservatives see the right to free ownership and operation of private business as being absolutely essential to the preservation of political freedom. They see any increase in government's scope which comes from allowing the government the power to manage the economy as being an unacceptable increase in the government's control over the lives of free citizens, and a dangerous step in the direction of socialism, and totalitarian dictatorship. They battle government interference on principle; they see it as a violation of individual liberty. They find it difficult to see how you can call a country "free" if the government of that country can tell an individual how to administer his own property, including his shop, farm, or factory.

Conservatives of this stripe, sometimes called economic libertarians, classical liberals, or supporters of *laissez-faire* economics (a term used by the eighteenth-century British economist Adam Smith who first defined this theory of the economy), also argue that government interference, even when well intentioned, destroys the natural flow of an economy, thereby holding down productivity. Instead of helping the poor, or spreading out the wealth, government regulation only makes it more difficult for those individuals who know how to make a profit to do so. And without profits, there are no businesses—and no jobs. Profit, from this point of view, is not the result of one man "exploiting" another. It is a sign that a farmer, or manufacturer, or entertainer, has managed to prepare and deliver a product that the public wants. And the more profits you have, the more people you will have to hire to satisfy the public's demand for what you are making. The more profits you have, the more money there is to pay those workers higher salaries. Without profits, no new factories, new farms, whatever, can be started. You have to pay for a new business with *something*.

These conservatives argue that there are natural laws, as essential to a healthy economy as water and sunlight are to a flower. They are *competition and supply and demand*. Without them, the economy becomes distorted. People are forced to pay more than they should, or find products not to their liking, find themselves unable to buy what they need at all.

"Competition"—more than one producer trying to sell the same product or service—keeps prices at their "natural" level, and forces the quality of the product to improve. If someone tries to make an excessively high profit on, say, the shoes he sells by charging too high a price, he will soon find out that people will shop in the other shoe store down the road. The shoe store owner, in order to keep his customers, will tend to drop his prices to the lowest point at which he can still make a living for himself. This point, according to *laissez-faire* theory, will be the "natural" and fair price. Competition will also force our shoe store owner to look for the best possible shoes on the market, the color, style, and quality most attractive to the buyer, in order to keep his customers, and maybe even get some new ones.

Socialism and communism—where the government owns and operates all the factories and stores—lack this stimulus towards greater efficiency and better products, and lower prices. They have no competitors. As a result, people end up buying products which the government decides they "want," and at prices the government thinks "fair." The best argument that conservatives have going for them when trying to make this point is a simple, common sense comparison, an "eyeballing" as carpenters put it, of the standard of living in Communist countries as compared to our own. In the so-called "workers paradises" built by Communist theorists and technicians, the average worker has to wait for years for the "privilege" of buying an automobile (only party favorites get the chance), and that privilege will cost him two or more years of total salary. In our country, cars could not be sold like that—the car companies would go out of business. Our car manufacturers, like all our businessmen, *must* make a product that people want and at a price that people can pay, or they will have no sales. Communist manufacturers have no such worry. They cannot go out of business.

A good case to use to make the point is a comparison of the subway system in New York City with Greyhound buses. Greyhound is a privately owned company run for "its own good," for profit. The New York subways are run by a city agency for the good of the people of New York—no nasty profit-hungry owners here. The subways have gotten dirtier, slower, less dependable, and more dangerous in recent years—while the prices have skyrocketed. Greyhound buses get bigger, roomier, cleaner, more comfortable, all the time—while prices climb very, very slowly. Why? Well, Greyhound has competitors. If their buses were dirty and slow, people would take Trailways. If you do not like the subways, you still have to ride them, or walk.

Early in American history it became clear that not only would businesses which had no competition (monopolies) be able to charge whatever price they wanted for whatever quality of product they cared to turn out in the short run, but that they would go out of business altogether in the long. Competition, it was discovered, was good not just for the consumer. It was good for the companies. As a result laws were passed which outlawed monopolies and "price-fixing" (where business competitors agree not to compete, but agree on a price that they will charge, and split the market evenly). When critics of American corporations, by the way, argue that big business in America is engaged in this kind of activity, they are arguing *with*, not *against*, conservative economic libertarians. Conservatives do not support American businessmen without reservation. Businessmen, too, can violate the natural laws of the economy.

The free operation of the law of *supply and demand* is essential, too, from this viewpoint, in order to insure that the price paid for an object or service is a fair one. It is easy to imagine the philosophical difficulties which would develop if a group of "experts," or housewives, sat down one afternoon and tried to decide if bubble bath should, on principle, be considered more "valuable" than a paperback edition of a best-selling novel. One comforts the body, one the mind. One takes a scientist to produce it, one an artist. Who is more important, the scientist or the artist? By allowing supply and demand to operate, this endless debate is avoided.

If a thing is scarce (supply) and wanted by people (demand) its price will be high—diamonds, silk, the Allman Brothers. If it is plentiful, and few people have any need for it, the price will be low —dandelions, twigs, the rock band that played at the last school dance. Most other things sold in this world find their value somewhere in between. If you do not interfere with the operation of the economy, and if there is genuine competition, prices and wages should be "harnessed" by supply and demand, and placed in the best possible balance. Not everyone will be able to afford diamonds. But not everyone in a Communist country has diamonds either.

People who take professional training, thus making themselves part of a scarce supply, will be fairly confident that they will be repaid for their investment of money and time. Investors who gamble fortunes in a search for scarce oil or gold will know that they will be repaid if they find what they are after. Consumers will find a decrease in the price of their bread, or their whiskey, if there is a bumper crop in wheat and corn. They will share in the prosperity. Farmers and industrialists will have reason to learn exactly what the public wants to buy (demand) and to come up with a product that fills the bill.

When the government upsets this delicate balance in the name of "the public good," they do tremendous harm instead. Any informed economic libertarian could give you hundreds of examples: Minimum wage laws that either force up the price for the consumer (the higher salaries have to be reflected in the price of the product), or put workers on the unemployment lists when owners can't afford to hire them. For as Henry Hazlitt, the noted economist, puts it, "We cannot make a man worth a given amount by making it illegal for anyone to offer him less. We merely deprive him of the right to earn the amount that his abilities and opportunities would permit him to earn." Or price controls which end up forcing farmers to kill baby chickens rather than raise them and sell them at a loss.

(When the sight of farmers killing baby chickens proves revolting, remember that if a farmer's electric bill, his costs for fuel, feed, and transportation, to say nothing about taxes, go up, and he cannot raise the price of his chickens—or whatever—he just might find himself actually losing money that he needs for his family by keeping the chicks alive.) And government import quotas, and tariffs on foreign products, which force the consumer to buy more expensive goods. Government regulations forcing a man to hire only union workers, thereby making it impossible for him to hire non-union workers at a lower rate, thereby depriving the non-union worker of his right to work and raising the price the consumer must pay for the product. Farm parities (government payments to farmers *not to grow* certain crops in order to decrease the supply and keep *up* the price that you pay for farm goods. And this really only scratches the surface.

There are other conservatives who are less enthused about American capitalism, and the "naturalness" of Adam Smith's *laissez-faire* system.

For one thing, the birth of the large "multinational" corporations has made those whose "conservatism" is primarily their "nationalism" feel more than slightly uneasy. The suspicion is growing in certain circles that these corporations would be willing to sacrifice American military and economic security for the sake of profit. Henry Paolucci, for example, the American nationalist historian and political theorist mentioned in an earlier chapter, edits a monthly newsletter called *State of the Nation*, in which he regularly devotes a section to the anti-national activities of certain large corporations and their leaders. The eagerness with which some large corporations have pushed for closer cooperation with the Soviet Union seems especially ignoble from the nationalist point of view.

Many nationalist conservatives nearly exploded when certain oil company executives admitted to holding back oil supplies from American ports on orders from Arab leaders, just to keep healthy their profitable working relationships with the Arab states. One such executive said point-blank at a Congressional hearing that "we are not an American company. America does not have a priority claim to our product. Our first responsibility is to our stockholders and they are not all Americans."

Similarly, the increasing size and power of many American corporations and conglomerates, whether multinational or not, have forced other "conservatives" to rethink their support for *laissez-faire* economics. These conservatives, often called "traditionalists," whose conservatism is to a large extent religious in nature, dislike what they see as the social irresponsibility of the major corporations. The medieval, church-dominated economy, the *Res Publica Christiana*, had always been more attractive to these conservatives because of its emphasis on order, social harmony, and economic responsibility. But they were willing to buy many of the *laissez-faire* theories because they seemed to work so well—and because they seemed a much healthier alternative than the kind of socialist dictatorships in operation in Russia and Red China. Prosperity was on the rise. Opportunities were opening up for the poor. More and more of the working class seemed on its way into the middle class.

Recent developments, especially the just-mentioned growth in power of the large corporations, have given some of these traditionalists second thoughts. In many cases they have become as critical of American capitalism as people on the left. *Triumph*, the well-argued Catholic journal, in trying to reflect a posture consistent in all ways with papal pronouncements on the economy, is a good example. In one article, Robert A. Miller, one of their editors, stated:

> Two international powers, which resemble more than any others the "great piracies" that St. Augustine said all political powers are at bottom, are the multinational corporations and the media of communication and entertainment. In *Octagesima Adveniens*, the Holy Father singles them out as new and oppressive powers, the more dangerous in that they are free from effective political restraint. He is very close, in holding this view, to the Catholic populist oracle, Rev. Charles E. Coughlin, who has warned recently that the most formidable enemies of Christians and of all men are not to be found in the Kremlin, but on Wall Street, on Madison Avenue, on Fleet Street, and in Zurich where opposition to traditional social values is most potent.

The main points these critics make is that the size and efficiency of computer-assisted corporations have made it impossible for people to escape their influence. People cannot play a productive role in a country without being willing to become part of the corporate structure. Competition and free enterprise cease to exist, except on the level of competition *between* the major corporations. If you want to make shoes, or raise cucumbers, or build furniture, on your own, you would not be able to do it with much chance of supporting yourself because the corporations with their technology have "closed the field." You could not compete as an independent—except if you wanted to live as a hermit, and on the pauper level. You would have to play the game, become part of the corporate structure—work for them—if you wanted to stay in business. And having to become part of the corporate structure seems to these critics to be a dangerous loss of freedom and an unhealthy substitution of a "materialist" way of life for older religious outlooks. The corporation becomes more of an influence on the culture than churches, fine books, family ways, and the heritage in general.

These criticisms, however, never quite reach the all-out level of opposition of the liberal. They are criticisms of specific "abuses," not an overall ideological preference for another modern economic system.

THE LIBERALS AND SOCIALISM

The liberal's opposition to our economic system is usually based on an ideological rejection of the very foundations of capitalism and the free enterprise system in general. For most liberals, socialism—or some modified version—comes much closer to the healthiest way of running an economy. Maybe the American liberal would not want to push America all the way to socialism, but he certainly wants us to rework our economic system to get us closer to the overall socialist outlook. When the socialist system fails, it is a failure in administration for the liberal. Socialists have their hearts in the right place. Capitalists, even when they succeed, are operating on faulty premises, and succeed only because of "circumstances."

The standard textbook definition of socialism is "government ownership and operation of the means of production."

The fatal flaw in private ownership for the socialist, is the "profit motive". It causes one man to seek his private advantage by "exploiting" his fellow men. The owner of a factory, for example, tries to pay the lowest possible salaries, and to force workers to work as hard as possible for as long as possible, in order to increase his profit. It tempts the owner to make his product with the cheapest of materials—to lower his costs—but to charge the public the highest possible price to increase his "take." It leads to deceptive advertising, pay-offs to government officials to get them to overlook unsafe or unsanitary production techniques, and bribes to politicians to get laws passed favorable to the owner's concerns irrespective of whether or not they hurt the community. It makes industrialists pollute rivers, strip-mine hills, and in general destroy the American environment in search of the quickest, most effective way to a buck. It convinces companies to buy and develop machines to replace men, to "automate," thereby increasing unemployment. It leads to brutally monotonous assembly lines on which men are turned into mere appendages of machines, machines themselves.

And socialism would cure all these ills, say its supporters. Since the government is the representative of "the people" it would run the farms and mills and factories for the "good of the workers and the community at large." Since there would be no private owner there would be no one seeking a profit. The total amount of money coming into a business as a result of sales could be split up among the workers on the basis of their needs. The workers would not be driven to work as brutes for long hours at a time; profit would not come before human values. The product would be designed to be the best possible for the buyer—no short cuts—since there would be no need to cut corners in order to increase the owner's "net." Advertising would be unnecessary. The representatives of the people who run the factory would not want anyone to buy anything that he did not really want and need. If the production of a certain product did damage to the surrounding countryside, production would be stopped, since the factory is run for the best interests of the community. Automation would never be instituted if it resulted in men being fired. The factory is run to produce work and wealth for the workers, not to end their jobs.

When a young person hears a persuasive socialist, or socialist-leaning liberal, go through this kind of analysis for the first time, he usually is impressed. It sounds so logical.

One way to handle this pitch for socialism is to use what could be called the "wise guy approach." Just keep repeating "Look at Russia . . . Look at Russia . . . Look at Russia." On one level it is not an unsatisfactory argument. It does not deal with the substance of the socialist claims. But on another, very legitimate level, it makes quite a bit of sense. For an economic theory cannot be analyzed the way you do a poem. It is not enough for it to be beautiful on paper. If it cannot be translated effectively into practice it makes no sense at all no matter how high-minded its intent. And certainly the socialist regimes of the world have a pretty poor track record. They have not matched the standard of living in the capitalist countries, and their economic control has been accompanied by political despotism ranging from "pretty offensive" to "downright tyrannical."

But what about the theory? The liberals can argue that socialism just hasn't been given a fair try, and that under the right leaders it can

**"It's great to split from city pollution and congestion
and reconnect with the Environment."**

achieve a truly just distribution of the work and wealth in a country. It is necessary then to deal with the "theory of socialism," too, and its flaws as a theory. What about the "evils" of the profit motive?

It is interesting, first of all, that the liberal who wants so much freedom in the way we run our schools, in the choice of books we can sell, the kind of movies we can see, and the kinds of speeches we can make in public, wants the government to control so much of the way we run our businesses. It seems as if "freedom of choice" should be maximized everywhere but there.

Those attracted to the idea of governmental control of industry somehow seem to find it very easy to make the assumption that men who work for the government are going to be more virtuous and concerned for the welfare of their fellow man when they run a factory or a mill than a man working for a private owner. Even though the fact is that some of the worst things ever done to man by his fellow man in the history of this planet have been done by governments to their citizens. (If, for example, you ask someone to name the ten most cruel men in all of history you can be pretty confident that he will come up with a good many leaders of governments on that list.)

The liberal makes the same mistake here that he makes when he envisions a world government. He always pictures someone that he likes—like himself—in charge of things. But think of the possibilities—a government controlling all the industry of a country also controls all the jobs in that country—quite a level of potential tyranny, no? If you do not like your boss at the Ford plant, you can quit and go to the Chevy plant. What do you do in Russia if you do not like your employer. There is only one employer—the all-powerful state. The only path to success in Russia, or any Communist country, comes through doing everything within your power to please the party bosses. The best jobs, the best houses, promotions, vacations, are distributed by the Communist party to their favorites—those who live closest to the standards of the dictators in power. In Russia they even have a medal which they pass out to the outstanding workers. It is called the Stakhanovite award, after Alexei Stakhanov, a kind of Paul Bunyan of Russia.

It is hard to figure out how anyone concerned about human individuality, independence, and freedom could feel comfortable pushing a system like this for America. Of course, the liberal will argue that socialist systems do not have to be run by men who will use their power over people's livelihood to tyrannize them. But you have to agree that it is quite a gamble. Lord Acton, a famous English historian and statesman, put the problem quite succinctly in one of history's most quoted statements: "Power corrupts; absolute power corrupts absolutely." The control over how and when and where a man makes his living might not be absolute, but it comes pretty close. Those people who voted for Richard Nixon in the 1972 election should picture a George McGovern in charge, those who voted for McGovern, Nixon, when they picture their ideal socialist state.

The socialist argument that eliminating the owner means that you can take the money the owner used to keep as his profit, and use it to raise wages, improve working conditions, and lower prices seems logical mathematically. If an owner is making a thousand-dol-

63

lar profit per week, you have an extra thousand dollars to split up fairly in the best interests of the workers.

The question of whether a redistribution of wealth like this would be just, and whether or not a man who risked every penny, and dedicated his life to building his business should have his profit "expropriated" is one consideration. Elementary justice would seem to demand that this businessman—the entrepreneur—deserves to make substantially more than someone who comes around afterwards and asks him for a job. But that need not be a major concern of ours just now, for liberals could argue that there are very few of these "pioneers of industry" around anymore, and that most of the people making big money today have inherited their wealth, or earn high salaries because they are in "management" and on the good side, so to speak, of the corporation leaders, rather than because of their skills, dedication, and sacrifice.

All of that might make some sense, but it becomes an endless discussion with the only available proof of your position being a study of the rich in our country in which you try to analyze "how" they got that rich, and whether or not they deserve it. A far better approach is one which concentrates on whether it would be good for the country *as a whole* to eliminate profits—whether the worker really would have higher wages if there were no owner getting his profit at the end of the month.

Let us remember what a profit indicates. It is a sign of a well-run business—a sign that a product is being made which pleases the buying public; and being made efficiently.

It is the drive for profit which makes a man in charge of a factory or farm look for better ways of doing things. If the owner is making a profit, if his product is selling, then, his workers have jobs and salaries —not as much as the owner, but more than if he were out of business.

If you eliminate the owner—and the profit motive—what will be the new motive for making better products in the most efficient way? The good of mankind? Maybe. But I keep thinking of the New York City subways which are run for the good of those lucky New Yorkers.

There might be something unsatisfactory, by heaven's standards, in a situation where one man makes a thousand dollars a week when his workers earn only two hundred dollars or so. But is not that better than everyone in the factory making an equal thirty-five dollars? Without the incentive to improve things—the profit motive—a business, any business, is likely to founder, drop down, stagnate—lose money. The owner, in making himself very rich, makes his workers fairly well off. An equal share of the net income of a business that is losing money is not much of a deal.

The quality of the product is also more likely to improve under an owner striving to make some loot. Sure, there are numerous examples of products made by privately owned firms in our country which are of shoddy workmanship and design. Although it must be remembered that in many cases people do not mind that at all. That is often the way the public wants it. If, for example, people had the choice of toys which would last a lifetime at a very high price, and cheaply slapped-together gadgets at a very low price, they would choose the junk at least part of the time. They might prefer to give their children more toys more often, than buy one toy which would last longer than childhood. The same could be said of the twenty-nine-cent ball point pens—you lose them all the time anyway—children's play clothes, furniture for a guest room that you hardly ever use, work shirts, certain stationery, tools—almost everything.

In general, however, the need to capture the public's imagination with "something new" and "something better" in order to maintain and increase sales will lead to a constant search for product improvement. As Lincoln said, "You may fool all the people some of the time; you can even fool some of the people all the time; but you can't fool all of the people all the time." A product which gets a bad name, or which was designed in a mistaken estimate of public taste, will go under eventually. The manufacturer will have to redesign his product or fold, and lose money. A socialist system does not have people facing up to this problem. The Russian women have been complaining for years, decades now, about the style of clothing available; and certainly it was not the Chinese people who insisted upon Mao jackets. They get what the government thinks best for them—like it or not.

Frequently this argument is countered by liberal spokesmen with an argument based on the power of advertising. John Kenneth Galbraith made a reputation for himself by the thorough and sometimes entertaining way that he pushed this theme in his books *The Affluent Society*, and *The New Industrial State*. The power of advertising, he argues, can be used by manufacturers to actually "create a demand" for the product that they sell. Advertisers, he insists, can convince people that they need and want a product whether they do or not. In a television debate with Galbraith, William Buckley fielded Galbraith's charge along this line by telling the story of the Dupont company's difficulty with their CORFAM shoes. CORFAM was a synthetic product which Dupont executives felt eventually would replace leather as the most-used material in the manufacture of shoes. It was waterproof, durable, and never had to be polished. Dupont invested millions of dollars in their production techniques, and millions more in their advertising campaign. But the public just did not like CORFAM shoes. The whole plan collapsed, and Dupont lost millions.

There are many CORFAM-type failures in American business. Most businessmen would give their eyeteeth to anyone who could let them in on the secret of making a product that will always succeed the way Mr. Galbraith's products do in his books.

It would be wise, however, for people to keep their eyes on the advertising industry—even if it is nowhere near as powerful as Galbraith suggests. With the use of advanced psychological techniques, and the skillful use of the media in general, just could come close to having more influence over us than is healthy in a free society. The possibility that the time will come when we will be sold political leaders the way we are sold toothpaste is not a pleasant thought.

But even that power would not approximate the power that the governments hold in the socialist states. The socialists do not have to convince you to buy their product—or in the case of the Communists, their leaders. You have no choice. What makes Galbraith's thesis puzzling is that Galbraith suggests a powerful centralized government with control over the economy (in his newest book, he openly suggests socialism) as a way of curbing the private businessman and his advertising aides. He is willing to give openly to government the kind of power that he *warns* us businesses might be attempting to get for themselves through advertising techniques.

Pollution and the "environment questions" in general are issues of much current interest—and not only to liberals. American sportsmen's magazines—for example *Outdoor Life, Field and Stream, Sports Afield*—which are usually conservative in tone on other issues, have come out strongly in favor of the need for some drastic reevaluation of what we are doing to the natural beauty of America. You would have to be pretty insensitive to see oil-stained beaches, rivers floating with dead fish, strip-mined hillsides, and smokestacks belching their acrid wastes into the air over our cities, and not feel that something has gone wrong somewhere. There is much room for intelligent criticism of the "freedom to pollute" which we appear to have given to certain industries in our country. But that does not mean that you have to end up making the ideological pitch for a socialized economy as the answer.

And there really are liberals who think that way. You see, they argue, if socialists were in charge of those polluting industries and mines, their primary concern would be the good of their fellow man, not profit. And as soon as a socialist saw how he was polluting the countryside with his factory, why he would close it right down for the good of the people. American capitalists, on the other hand, being profit-hungry exploiters of the people, try to get away with as little pollution control as possible, since pollution control costs money and hampers their operations—and reduces their profit.

Once again, the wise-guy approach is pretty effective. You can lean back again and give out with a few "Look at Russia . . . Look at Russia . . . Look at Russias."

In the Russian socialist economy, where the profit motive has been eliminated, the rivers around their factory towns are as dirty as any in America. There was a case in the paper a year or so back of a Russian lake, near an oil refinery, which caught fire—the lake not the oil refinery. There was so much waste from the refinery in that lake that it was covered with flames for days.

Once again, though, it is just as effective to make the case against the liberal's theories as theories, for once again their arguments display a marked inconsistency. It is this simple: In a capitalist economic structure, chances are far better for some real pressure being applied effectively against polluters because the government and industry are separate entities. *In a socialist system the government would be the polluter.* They would have to be their own pollution policeman. There would be no one applying pressure on them from an outside viewpoint.

On this whole question of ecological balance sincere critics must seek a reasoned and realistic view of what a country like America is up against. One thing is certain: we cannot be an industrialized society *and* a country with air and water as clear as it was in the days before Columbus. We have to ask some difficult questions, and make some difficult choices. Do we want cars and stereos and air conditioners, and clothes made of easy-to-care-for synthetic fabrics? If we do, we must pay the price of having more wastes in our air and water than if we all moved back to a life of small self-sufficient homesteads scattered around the countryside.

We can live with *some* level of pollution. We have had it since the mid-1880's. As a matter of fact, it has been said that air pollution around factory towns might have been worse in the early years of this century than now. How many of us would be willing to really live the simple life in order to get the air and water clean? How much in tax dollars would you be willing to spend in order to make the river that runs through your part of the country as clean as it used to be in colonial times? How many men would you be willing to force out of work to clean up the sky around your city? There are no simple answers. If the air pollution is damaging to your city's health, for example, you would have to close as many factories (and unemploy as many men) as it takes to clean it up. Even all of them. But what if it is just a question of making the countryside more pleasing to the eye? These are intelligent questions, which can be discussed intelligently without resorting to the mindless clichés of the liberal about the government being able to run industry without pollution.

There is one area where socialist governments can prove to be attractive in comparison to American capitalism. They can guarantee work for those willing to work. There are no unemployment problems in a socialist country.

American companies, in order to keep their profit margins, sometimes resort to tactics which are menacing from the working-man's viewpoint. If there is a drop in sales for example, in the automobile industry, the manufacturer will "lay off" sometimes hundreds of workers—even if in the five previous years or so sales have been record-breaking and profits high. The worker can get the feeling that he is viewed by his employers as a machine which can be closed down when not needed. Unfortunately the worker cannot close down his rent or his food bills.

Or companies might buy machines which take the place of dozens of workers—"automation"—in order to increase profits. Conservatives can argue that now that men are not needed doing the work which is being done by the machine they are needed to build the machine which took their place. But that is not a very consoling argument from the fired workers' point of view since they are not likely to be the ones hired in that new industry. All they know is that they have been discarded like an old worn-out drill bit.

Capitalism must find some way of making the workers feel more secure—even at the price of reduced profit. But enlightened capitalists know that, and they know that you do not have to turn to socialism to come up with an answer. In the give and take between representatives of labor unions and management, business leaders have been able to come up with answers to many of the problems of the working man in the past. It would not be surprising if this one were just around the corner.

But most conservatives would insist that the best thing that can happen to the working man is to be employed in a well-run, *profitable* business. Profits hold the key to more and better-paying jobs. If too many obstacles are placed in the path to profits, even if in the name of job security, it could lead to a stagnation which will make things worse. The profit-seeking owner is the goose laying the golden egg of fairy tale fame. And everyone knows what happens if you demand too much too soon from that bird.

5
Pornography Is Not
"Just a Matter of Taste"

Just as conservatives differ on the degree of "freedom" which should be tolerated in the operations of American business, they differ on how much control the American government should have over the behavior of its citizens. There are conservatives (the libertarians) who feel that the government has no business "legislating morality." They emphasize the importance of freedom, and are willing to tolerate the presence within society of a wide range of taste and conduct. They see it as the price of freedom. Other conservatives argue, in opposition, that the government has a responsibility to promote a healthy moral atmosphere for its people, and to discourage, through law and appropriate punishments, behavior which is destructive of public virtue. These "traditionalists" emphasize the reliability of the ideas about virtue which have been handed down to us from our ancestors—revealed religious truths, customs, inspiring books, folk tales with a "moral" of decency, honesty, self-discipline and courage. They argue that the behavior of our citizens must be judged by this accumulated wisdom of the past, and as much as possible be brought into line with it.

Both traditionalists and libertarians, however, refuse to accept the current permissiveness in society—the "do your own thing," "if it feels good do it," "different strokes for different folks" view of what life is all about. The libertarian conservative does not want the government to get too active in controlling the books that people read, the movies that they see, or the places they frequent, but that does not mean that he is opposed to "other agencies" within society acting energetically against immoral behavior.

Remember, there is a vast difference between what the word "society" denotes and the word "government". Society includes hundreds of different non-governmental associations and organizations—many of which exert more influence on the country than the government. Churches, youth groups, businessmen's associations, men's clubs, fraternal associations, professional associations, ladies' clubs, social clubs in operation in every village in this country have a great deal to do with forming the public opinion about what is "acceptable" in American life—and most libertarian conservatives do not mind that at all. Think of your own community and the role played by the Chamber of Commerce, the Elks, the Daughters of the American Revolution, the League of Women Voters, Holy Name Societies, B'nai B'rith, Knights of Columbus, American Medical Association, volunteer firemen, rod and reel clubs, Boy and Girl Scouts, etc.

THE LIBERTARIANS

The libertarian conservative position is one which denies a) the legitimacy, and b) the capability of the government's claim to have the right or power to enforce morality. The libertarian conservative applies the same standard to sexually oriented books and movies that he applies to the operation of business. *Laissez faire*—the less government has to say the better.

As the libertarian looks back on recorded history he sees a consistent record of tyranny imposed upon people by their governments in the name of protecting public virtue: the Athenian court sentencing Socrates to his death, the Romans executing Christians, medieval tribunals torturing and killing heretics who refused to accept the religious truths of the authorities, the burning of witches, the French revolutionaries under Robespierre sending to the guillotine "enemies of the people," Henry VIII having St. Thomas More beheaded for his "traitorous" opinions, Russian Communists murdering millions of small Russian farmers to "protect the revolution," the Nazis attempt-

71

ing to save the Aryan race by committing genocide on the Jews. He sees as well numerous cases of great writers and thinkers condemned by their short-sighted governments—the Socrates and Galileos of history.

Consequently, the libertarian argues that it is essential for human freedom and human development that the states's activity and involvement in individual lives be kept as small as possible. The individual should be left with the final say about what is moral or immoral for himself. Only when it is shown, and convincingly, that a certain activity is damaging to others, or that other individuals are forced to participate in an activity which they consider immoral, does the libertarian agree that the government should step in and enact and enforce a prohibitive law.

This guideline, naturally, leaves much room for disagreement among libertarians. Some libertarians end up being more permissive than others. *National Review,* a journal edited by William F. Buckley, Jr., generally thought to be one of the outstanding forums for intelligent conservative thought, occasionally features articles in which scholarly conservatives argue about whether or not certain activities cross the line and become subject to government prohibition. It has featured debates over pornography, homosexuality, and abortion along these lines in recent years.

The questions surrounding pornography give a good example of some of these differences of opinion. Should a movie which features open and explicit—even perverted—scenes of sexual behavior be allowed to be made? Where? In a basement movie studio? Whose right would be violated? Who would be hurt by the filming? Should people be allowed to show it? In their basement for a few friends? In a certain section of the city known for that kind of entertainment—a section where people who are repulsed by pornography know that they should not go? In a local theater, right next to the supermarket and the soda fountain? On television?

In each of these cases there is a different degree of likelihood that people who do not want themselves or their children to see the movie, will have it thrust upon them. It would be very easy to argue, for example, that the government would have no right to break into a man's basement where he and a few of his friends were satisfying their taste for pornography of the grossest sort, but would have a right and a duty to outlaw that same movie, and much milder versions, on home television, where children are likely to come across it while flicking the dial from "The Flintstones" to Walt Disney's show. The television is a permanent presence within a home.

By these standards the local movie house, or drug store magazine rack for that matter, becomes a questionable site for sexually related material, since its presence "in public" is an open invitation for young people. Movie ratings, or "adult only" warnings on books, do little to satisfy complaints of this nature since young people find it fairly easy to get around these controls; and because most parents feel that even at seventeen (when these codes no longer prohibit anyone) people are still "young enough" to be hurt by the influence of obscene matter. Many—including many psychologists—would argue that people can be influenced in the wrong way at sixty by certain kinds of obscene books or movies. Some libertarians, as a result, would argue that books and movies of questionable taste should be restricted to certain clearly designated areas of a city, far from the flow of family life. Some libertarians would be willing to include prostitution within these areas since that too, it could be argued, would not offend anyone, or violate anyone's rights, if it were going on in an area where he and his family would never go. Nevada has set up something like this in trailer parks, of varying degrees of comfort, a half-hour's drive away from centers of population. Others would argue that even the most residential of neighborhoods—whether the majority living there likes it or not—should be open to at least pornographic books and movies, since they could not exist profitably in a neighborhood if there were not a sizable number of people who wanted what they had to offer; and that if one group of citizens wants to seek these pleasures for themselves—and do not in the process harm anyone else—they have a right to do so as free citizens of a free country.

William Rickenbacker, a libertarian columnist for *National Review*, agrees with Dr. Thomas Szaz, a noted psychiatrist, that narcotics use should be treated in the same way. They argue that what a man does with his body should be his concern, and his alone.

This approach to law is called *secular*—a belief that no Church-interpreted version of what is right and wrong should be reflected in the laws of a country, and that independent citizens should be free to decide for themselves, according to their own conscience, what is moral and immoral. (Again—as long as it does not injure anyone else.)

What separates libertarian conservatives from most liberals on this issue is that the libertarian conservative usually does not go so far as to say that there should be no right and wrong recognized by a society in the matter of sexual behavior. He is not, like most liberals, a relativist. He believes in right and wrong. But he does not want his government to define them for him.

At least this is true of the average conservative American. Among those intellectuals who accept the label "conservative" there are some "moral relativists," although they usually end up calling themselves "libertarians" or "individualists" instead. In the introduction to his book *American Conservative Thought in the Twentieth Century*, William Buckley has some interesting things to say about this breed of "conservative":

> Can you be a conservative and believe in God? Obviously. Can you be a conservative and not believe in God. This is an empirical essay, and so the answer is, as obviously, yes. Can you be a conservative and despise God and feel contempt for those who believe in Him. I would say no . . . If one dismisses religion as intellectually contemptible, it becomes difficult to identify oneself wholly with a movement in which religion plays so vital a role.

Vital role? How can religion play a vital role for conservative libertarians? Especially for those who would allow pornography, homosexuality, prostitution, and drug use? Well, this is where those "other agencies" of society are to play their role. Many libertarian conservatives in their personal lives display a marked religious orientation, a deep love and fear of God and His rewards or punishments after death. And they do want a healthy moral climate for themselves and their children. But not with the state in charge. This is the difference. Their historical analysis leads them to believe that state power in this area means tyranny and little resulting virtue. Giving the government the power to close down pornographic movies is giving them the power to close down churches—if you accept this logic.

The libertarian conservative is confident that his country's families, churches, and community groups, fine novelists, poets, and playwrights will be able to teach the great moral lessons, and win over so many people to a virtuous life that even if "anything goes"—it won't, so to speak. Our culture and religious teachings will create a social milieu in which so few people will take advantage of the "permitted" vices that it will not be a social problem of any magnitude for the great majority—certainly not a problem worthy of the dangers of a too-powerful government and a loss of freedom.

If a free-thinking liberal were to suggest to conservatives of this stripe that sexual promiscuity, homosexuality, drug addiction, and prostitution were just a matter of choice, and that it is just society's backward prejudices which prevent people from accepting them, he certainly would get an argument. But the libertarian conservative, at the end of the evening, would agree that since not everything which is immoral should be illegal the force of government should not be used to stop anyone from engaging in any of these "preferences."

There is one way, however, of arguing against the presence of pornography in a community, on what could be called "libertarian grounds." If you argue for the "right" and the "freedom" of certain individuals to see or read off-color movies and books, you must handle the claims of those who demand the right and freedom not to have to live in such an atmosphere. It has long been accepted in American law that communities have a right to "outlaw" certain kinds of industry, certain sizes and styles of houses, cars with certain kinds of mufflers, billboards—even old cars and pickup trucks parked in driveways. They are considered "eyesores" which can be forbidden by "zoning" laws. Individuals who like loud mufflers, or old pickup trucks, or who would want to live in a building ten stories high are forbidden to do so by many local communities. Their "freedoms" and "rights" are taken away in the name of community taste and local standards. Why not apply the same standard to a drugstore where you have to pass a magazine rack full of pictures of nude cuties in order to buy some cough drops? Or to a movie marquee that blares its suggestive titles into people's faces on their way to the supermarket or church? Are not these things far more offensive to tastes than old pickup trucks in a driveway? Or, at least, should not a local community which has the right to outlaw one have the right to outlaw the other?

Minority rights are important. But so are the rights of the majority. Those who demand the right to have full access to obscene movies or off-color magazines demand the right at the expense of those who wish to live in an atmosphere with a moral tone more to their liking. The fact that court decisions have been made in recent years which make this kind of censorship difficult reflects the blatant liberal bias against religion. Think about it: liberal judges allow a community to make laws against styles of houses that do not meet community standards of taste, but not against behavior the community finds to be offensive by its moral standards.

THE TRADITIONALISTS

The real battle over the "censorship issue" takes place between the liberals and the traditionalist conservatives. Here it is not just a question of balancing contesting "freedoms"—the freedom of those who want to see porn against those don't want it in their neighborhoods. The traditionalists deny the "right" of anyone to immoral pleasures, and assert in opposition the community's responsibility to provide the proper moral climate for its people. They also argue—since they almost always believe in God and their own responsibility to do His will—that a society has a duty to create a climate which will help men to save their souls. Obviously, for anyone who believes in God, this is a serious responsibility. The kinds of behavior which are tolerated in society are not just reflections of taste. The toleration of immoral behavior means a toleration of temptation—what old books of religious training used to call "occasions of sin."

This outlook is called a *sacral*, as opposed to *secular*, view of society. It is a belief that the way we organize our lives is not just a matter concerning one fellow citizen and another which can be refashioned at will, but a contract between men in our time in history, and our ancestors—and God. Gilbert Keith Chesterton called it "the democracy of the dead":

> Tradition may be defined as an extension of the franchise. Tradition means giving votes to the most obscure of all classes, our ancestors. It is the democracy of the dead. Tradition refuses to submit to the small and arrogant oligarchy of those who merely happen to be walking about. All democrats object to men being disqualified by the accident of birth; tradition objects to their being disqualified by the accident of death. Democracy tells us not to neglect a good man's opinion, even if he is our groom; tradition asks us not to neglect a good man's opinion, even if he is our father.

Not surprisingly, it often seems as if the traditionalists argue more with their "fellow conservatives" over this issue—the libertarians— than they do with the liberals. The traditionalist knows that the liberal has no standards. He knows that the liberal can do little more than shrug and maybe shake his head in bewilderment at the widespread growth of seedy movie houses, and gross, unnatural, filthy magazines. After all, the liberal admits that morality is just a matter of taste, and that if someone likes to see movies in which the expression of love between a man and a woman—the act which God has designed to enable man to share with Him in His loving creation of life —is depicted as a souless and selfish pleasure-seeking manipulation of one human being by another, so that the wormy guys in the neighborhood can get their jollies—well, the liberals tell us "do your thing," whatever your thing is.

The traditionalist knows that the liberal is defenseless in the face of moral decline. (The liberal calls it "changing tastes.") He knows that the liberal cannot define why there is anything all that wrong in the frightening growth of "skin flicks," massage parlors, creep magazines, prostitution, drug addiction, homosexuality, and assorted perversions. (It is amusing in a sad way to watch liberals deal with this kind of moral decay when it comes too close to them. It is as if common sense tells them one thing, but their relativist convictions another. A group of New York actors and actresses formed a committee in 1973 to deal with the growth of prostitution and massage parlors and open homosexual solicitation in the Times Square area. They demanded a police crackdown. People were beginning to refuse to go to the theaters in those areas if it meant crawling in the gutter of life to get there. About six months later, after the clean-up had done its job, the New York *Daily News* carried a story called "SHOW PEOPLE GIVE COPS FOUR STARS." The movie stars were overjoyed by the success. "There are far less evil-looking people around," said one actress. "I used to be scared working in New York, but I notice a huge difference," said liberal-radical Lynn Redgrave. What is ironic, though, is that if you put these same actors and actresses on a television or radio talk show where the topic for discussion was something like "Personal Freedom in Modern America" they would all be good liberals in favor of doing your thing. But I guess that means as long as you do it where it does not interfere with *their* lives.)

The traditionalist tries to convince the libertarian conservative that he (the libertarian) fails to grasp the flow of history. He argues that if the libertarian conservative genuinely wants a healthy moral atmosphere for himself and his children and his countrymen, he must begin to abandon his reluctance to use the force of law in defense of his way of life.

For the traditionalist, you will recall, what is healthy about our way of life can be traced to its Christian origins. During the Middle Ages, the Christian framework of society was highly visible. People lived their lives by the conviction that proper behavior was not just demanded by society, but by God; and the laws of the society, and the customs of groups within society, were constructed in an attempt to give man as clear a picture as possible of what was God's will. The teachings of the Church (at the time there was only one Church, the Roman Catholic Church) became most influential as a result.

Ever since the Renaissance (perhaps) and from the Enlightenment (to be sure) this religious mooring of our way of life has been under attack. The liberal belief that man could live by reason alone, without reference to Church teachings, challenged the right of those with religious convictions to "push" their ideas about God's will on anyone else. The traditionalists might not want to go all the way back to the government structures of the Middle Ages, but they do argue that the idea that reason alone is to be the guide to acceptable human behavior is faulty in design and destructive of society. For what is "reasonable" to one man might be "unreasonable" to another. The liberal who relies on unaided reason, through the ages, has proven to be susceptible to more and more ideas about what is "reasonable." More and more moral codes have eroded under this rubric of "reasonableness." More and more has become tolerable, until we end up with the anything-goes atmosphere of today, where drug users and prostitutes and homosexuals and pornographic movie stars can sit on television talk shows and discuss the reasonableness of their behavior. And the liberal hosts of these shows, of course, being "men of reason" end up smiling meekly and saying "well, to each his own."

The traditionalist warns the conservative libertarian that things have deteriorated too much to go on with a *laissez-faire* approach to public morality. *Laissez-faire* morality might have been a workable posture in the past when most people were a decent, virtuous, self-disciplined sort, when they still had in their hearts the influence of Christian codes of behavior. Then, their inner discipline, their fear and love of God, made them capable of handling a permissive atmosphere. Now that those inner disciplines are crumbling under the assault of liberal relativism, the time has come for those determined to stop further social decay to stand firm and to outlaw those vices which are destroying the moral atmosphere of the country. Or, the traditionalist warns, sit back and watch the deterioration continue.

In addition, the traditionalist refuses to accept the proposition that what goes on in the society, in "public," will not adversely affect those whose standards of behavior are stricter than society's as a whole. What you allow for "others" you allow, by inference, to those near and dear to you. Society is a great teacher. The most liberal and radical of classroom teachers push this view endlessly and convincingly. They take students on field trips, bring newspapers into class, stress the use of other "media," bring to their classes outside guest speakers. "The world is a classroom," you hear them say. And they are right.

There is no way for a person growing up in a society which permits pornography, open homosexuality, or drug use not to get the idea that these things are acceptable forms of behavior, no matter what he hears at home about how evil they are. "Everybody's doin it, ma!" It is near to impossible to cordon yourself off from the influences of society unless you are willing to live in almost total isolation, like the Amish. Look how many generations of Americans tried to preserve their "old ways" by teaching them to their children, and giving a good example by living the old ways at home. And look how what society tolerated, in opposition, eventually won over the young people. Skirts below the ankle—out. Not smoking in public—out. Going to church regularly—out. Chaperoned dates in the early teens—out. Never drinking excessively—out. Respect for elders—out. Respect for property—out. Prohibitions against drug use—out. Love of country—out. "Do your own thing!" Right on.

(Of course, the liberal will say now, "See you closed-minded conservatives would have kept women in skirts beneath the ankles, too. You are always afraid of change and progress." Which just shows the liberal's moral bankruptcy—not being able to see the difference between modern pornography and skirts above the ankles. Relativism at work.)

It is obvious. Privately taught virtues cannot survive, except in rare cases, when the society as a whole is teaching something else. The ideal situation for parents is to find the values they teach at home reinforced and supported by their public institutions—schools, courts, laws in general. In this way the home values and society's values are corroborative, not enemy, ways of life.

The libertarian conservatives sooner or later are going to have to face up to the fact, argue the traditionalists, that if they want to protect themselves and their children from the growth of the "counterculture" they are going to have to reassess their ideas about the nature of the relationship between a society and its laws. They are going to have to look at the question of whether or not a society has any great lessons to teach its citizens, and whether or not these lessons should be defended by the force of law.

L. Brent Bozell, in his book *The Warren Revolution*, attempts to argue this case by referring to what he calls "the unwritten constitution" of a country—an understanding among the society's members about the kind of society it is. What are the society's purposes? Or does it have any purpose beyond merely surviving? What does it "believe in?" He goes on to argue that in our Founding Fathers' eyes much of American life was to be governed by this unwritten constitution, and that even if the Federal Constitution contains no references to promoting a virtuous way of life, it does not mean that the Founding Fathers did not expect local governments to be active in defining what kind of behavior was to be tolerated in the individual states. The fact that there were local ordinances against vice in those days far stricter than anything in modern America, and that not one of our Founding Fathers wrote in complaint against that practice is a clear indication of their state of mind. The much-discussed separation of Church and State found in the First Amendment did not mean, then, that religious beliefs could not be put into law. They were put into law, in each of the states—without, I repeat, opposition or condemnation from the Founding Fathers. The First Amendment was more concerned with preventing any *one* of the different Christian religions of the time from becoming the official "state religion" of the country as a whole. It had nothing to do with a local Christian community's making laws for its area from a Presbyterian, or a Methodist, or a Catholic point of view. These local communities, it was understood, would have the heavy responsibility of protecting public virtue.

The Founding Fathers, simply, had little difficulty in accepting the proposition that men needed well-constructed laws to guide them toward proper behavior. As James Burnham puts it in his *Congress and the American Tradition*:

> The Fathers did not believe that men were continuously both rational and good. They believed, rather, like John Adams, that "human passions are unsatiable" and that "reason, justice, and equity never had weight enough on the face of the earth to govern the councils of men."

When you look at the utter degradation around us you cannot help but shake your head in bewilderment at the liberal naïveté over the persuasive power of reason, of their faith in the beauty of the new way of life which would be built once men were free enough to behave as they wished, unimpeded by religion, custom or law. You cannot help but wonder about an outlook on life which stresses, according to J. Salwyn Schapiro, a proud liberal, in his book *Liberalism: Its Meaning and History* "that all opinions, even erroneous ones, should have freedom of expression." Those sentiments might have seemed noble and generous in the America of thirty, or a hundred, years ago when we were a country without the squalor of places like Times Square in New York City, and the affluent, preening "swingers" of Sunset Strip in Los Angeles, and the topless bars in the most residential neighborhoods, and *Deep Throat* and its imitators, and *Play-*

80

boy and its imitators. But do we want a country where that kind of "entertainment" is going to continue to flourish and spread, and get worse in the process? Do we want to excuse it all as a form of freedom of expression which we have no right to control? The traditionalist would call that idea national suicide.

John Lukacs, a prominent historian and professor of history from the Philadelphia area, in his book *The Passing of the Modern Age*, focuses in on what a place like Times Square means to the society which tolerates it. He hints that America has more Times Squares to look forward to in the future because we have lost our ability to define for ourselves what is virtuous and what is not—because we have accepted the influence of liberalism for so long. He has to be quoted at length. If the evocative power of his words does not arouse readers to the dangers we are facing, perhaps it is already too late.

What Lord Elgin wrote about Old China a century ago: "the rags and rottenness of a waning civilization" have seeped into our very midst. It may be seen around Forty-second Street and Times Square in New York, within the once throbbing and triumphant heart of America's steely civilization, in the very place where twice during this century millions of the masses of democracy poured out to celebrate the victorious end of a world war.

It is not an especially filthy place—physically that is—although even at glistening noon hours the street is littered with the paper and metallic refuse of the new world, whirled about in a wind; even on the bluest of days the air has poisonous yellow and gray streaks in it, and there is the repulsive smell of hamburger grease wafting over these enormous cold Northern thoroughfares just as in the hot kitchen of a disreputable and sleazy household. What is filthy, beyond the imagination of the gloomiest visionaries of the past, is the imagery of the place: the lettering and the pictures, what their forms and combinations represent, and what they evoke: not so much the commerce with the human flesh but a sort of commerce with the Devil. It is not so much the material abundance of pornography as the cheap ugliness of its presentation that is pervasive: it is the spirit, not the matter, of the place that is horrid and depressing. It crawls onto the countenances of the loitering people, a frozen grin rather than a carnal leer. Contrary to the liberal belief, the dissolution of authority and censorship has not lifted burdens off minds. No one can close his mind to the imagery of Forty-second Street, no matter how he wishes to pass through it; a low kind of diabolical interest burns and scratches on the bottom of his brain, like a pebble at the bottom of a shoe. It is this vile imagery that is unavoidable, it clings to the mind just as bad smell clings to clothes. It is no longer in the material slums of large cities that the depths of modern degradation are to be found; it is in this

81

slum of slums of the Western spirit. This most crowded of streets of the greatest city of the greatest country of the greatest civilization: this is now the hell-hole of the world.

True, societies have always had their fleshpots, their red-light districts. But what Lukacs describes is so different. People who frequented the Tenderloin area in New York or the Barbary Coast in California knew that they were leaving society when they went on a spree. There was a sense of shame about it. (I just recently heard a would-be sophisticated liberal disc jockey in New York laugh at how only ten years ago he used to wear dark glasses and look about with embarrassment when he went in to see a pornographic movie. Now he has been freed from those hangups—as has our society. He takes his dates to see them these days. Progress!) The vices were underground, behind doors needing paint, or in dark alleys. Now they challenge you, taunt you, stare you in the face. A walk through Times Square, or its counterparts in other cities, has to leave psychic scars. Hideously painted creatures of both sexes and in-between stride the sidewalks menacingly offering their bodies like a slab of meat; the streets are theirs. Creatures of a twilight world of sick pleasures—for whom you would offer prayers if you met them in a hospital—taunt you with cold smiles, invite you to enter the new world, where religion is dead and pleasure an end in itself. Young boys in sequins and chains, old women in perfumed rags, gaudily dressed muscle-men; elaborate hairdos, smeared mascara, massage parlors offering "cheap thrills," movies featuring "All Male Casts" and "mixed combos"—they all offer you a taste of the future. Yours and your children's.

"A healthy society would never slide in that direction." That was always the libertarian conservative faith. And America is a country of virtuous people. The "marketplace" would drive the filth off the streets. No one would buy it. Immoral lifestyles will never catch on we were told, except in the kind of off-beat communities, the bohemias, which society has always had down through history. That way of life never could take hold in America. America is a country of virtuous people.

What do we do now when the opposite seems to be true? When the Times Squares and Sunset Strips seem to be setting up annexes in every village and hamlet in America.

The traditionalist says close them down. It is that simple. Act energetically against immorality in public. And most of all, do not be afraid to call the immoral what it is, immoral. (This does not mean that you have to have underground cops in every section of the country, peeping into people's homes. Vice cannot be wiped out. Sin is part of life. But it can be driven underground. It can be made an unacceptable sort of behavior, and people can be forced to feel the full weight of our disapproval when they act immorally. And we can live our lives without stumbling across immorality at every bend in the road.)

America did not spring to life yesterday like a day lily. We do not have to operate as if mankind has not learned anything in the last three thousand years of our civilization. We have a heritage. We have a Faith. There was a Moses and he did receive Ten Commandments. Jesus Christ did walk this earth. Great writers have left us in written form the legacy of their struggle with the great moral issues. Great philosophers have studied the meaning of life. Great religious leaders have interpreted the Gospels for us. We might have little minds ourselves—but we have giants of intellect to assist us in our defining of truth. When we forbid certain activities, we do not force "our opinions" on others. We apply the standards of civilization, of our Western heritage, of our Judaeo-Christian culture. If we doubt the wisdom of that heritage, if we are afraid to work with its teachings, then we too are nothing but liberals, and we might as well "do our thing," and like the Romans, go out in one last orgy.

These are most serious issues. Perhaps the most serious raised in this book. Americans intuitively want to respect the rights of others. We grow up with slogans like "every one is entitled to his opinion," and "it is a free country." Talk of censorship and control over what individuals do for kicks might seem offensive at first glance. It might seem un-American.

Well, for one thing, it can't be very un-American, because Americans, up until very recently, would not tolerate the filth we are expected to live with. Public surveillance over sexually oriented books and movies is as American as apple pie. You do not think that they could have shown *Deep Throat* in Boston, or New York, in 1800 do you? Or in 1950 for that matter? Those who push for greater permissiveness in these matters are the ones pushing something "anti-American" judged by the historical standard.

If "freedom" means more and more Times Squares in our country, then that definition must go—say the traditionalists. Malcolm Muggeridge, a famed British essayist and critic, has warned us of what is happening: "Sex has become an obsession, a mania, a sickness. Never, it is safe to say, never in the history of the world has a country been as sexridden as the United States of America." G. K. Chesterton, too, in the early years of this century recognized the danger in an unhealthy preoccupation with sex: "All healthy men, ancient and modern, Eastern and Western, know that there is in sex a fury that we cannot afford to inflame, and that a certain mystery and awe must ever surround it if we are to remain sane." Times Square is insane.

The ultimate solution, of course, is not in the hands of the government. The most government can do is stem the tide for a while. Religion is the only solution. A country without religious convictions will never be able to substantiate its claim that certain activities must be forbidden. Even the most rigorous and extensive use of our "cultural heritage" will prove inadequate in the long run. Our modern liberal world has spawned a crop of writers and movie makers who are pushing, as actively as anyone, a relativist, and "anything goes" approach to morality. How do you handle the argument that what an Andy Warhol, or a John Lennon, or the current best-selling novelist has to say about what is moral is just as valid as what Dante or St. Thomas said? I once heard someone say that if St. Thomas Aquinas were alive today he would be writing for the ultra-liberal magazines—with all the other modern intellectuals.

This is the great despair of the modern world. The eighteenth-century liberal was confident that "objective truth [was] discoverable though reason, according to the scientific method of research, experiment, and verification," to quote J. Salwyn Schapiro again. The modern liberal is convinced of just the opposite. There are so many conflicting opinions about what is "reasonable" today that colleges build their social studies curriculum around this confusion, proudly. They hire a positivist, an empiricist, a semanticist, a Marxist, a Marcusite, a New Left Marxist, a historicist, a spiritualist, an ambiguist, a pragmatist, a utilitarian, etc., in order to give the student a taste of the variety of truths; and graduate him when he has seen enough of the conflict of opinion to be a good liberal— confused and uncertain.

Reason alone will not do the job. People have to make the "willing assertion" to truth that can only come from faith and love. Unfortunately most religious bodies in Europe and America have succumbed to the Zeitgeist, the spirit of the age—liberalism. Many modern ministers and priests and rabbis seem more determined to make people "feel good"—not guilty—when they are doing their thing, than teaching them the need to repent. Christ was forgiving they tell us. But they forget to tell us that he also commanded man to "go and sin no more."

L. Brent Bozell, whose book *The Warren Revolution* we mentioned earlier, has come to the conclusion that Christianity must be made a more prominent part of our law-making process. Bozell was a high-placed assistant to conservative Barry Goldwater, and co-editor with William Buckley of *National Review*. He has left behind his old concern with defining the proper conservative governmental structure in America, and has launched the magazine *Triumph,* and a new organization called *The Society for the Christian Commonwealth*. Both are dedicated to the proposition that America can only hold back the social decline we are experiencing through a commitment to make America Christian. Our laws will be firmly based, he argues, only when they are designed to conform to Christ's teachings—not to the standards of the intellectual currents of the age. Bozell is a Catholic. But it might be that Protestant Americans will be making a similar decision in the near future.

6

Traditions Are Not "Shackles of the Past"

If a man of the late nineteenth century, or mid-twentieth century, were made invisible through the chemical reaction described by H. G. Wells in his science-fiction classic *The Invisible Man*, and if he were allowed to roam unnoticed through the halls of a modern high school or college he would be surprised by many things. The deliberate sloppiness of dress would puzzle him. He probably would see it as an expression of contempt for the standards of the world outside the school, where neatness and cleanliness were still viewed as a way of showing respect for others and the high purpose of their institutions. He would be amazed by the widespread vandalism, the ever-present spray paint smears on the walls, sometimes right in front of the building, near the entrance where students in the past would have their pictures taken on graduation day, with their parents smiling proudly beside them. Imagine the backdrop the graffiti would present for that picture now! He might want to rush to call a doctor for the students sprawled disjointedly along the halls or on the lawn in front of the building. After all, only sick people, or mental patients, sprawled that way in public in his day. Or maybe a drunk, when, in the "enlightenment" that comes just before you pass out, he realizes that plopping like that would be a great way to show near-ultimate disrespect for those in his presence. Certainly the people who run a pizza parlor, a barbershop, or a gas station would never allow anyone to treat their premises that way. Obviously, our invisible visitor would assume it would not be an acceptable way to behave in a school. He might be surprised, too, that many of the teachers seemed to share the "style" of the students. He might not know what to think when he sees a teacher flop his dirty blue-jeaned self onto the floor to "rap" cross-legged with his students. But maybe he would think that it was one of those school spirit weeks they used to have, when teachers and students would dress and behave outrageously—to suggest by the comparison how different and how much more noble and serious was their "normal" activity in school during the rest of the year. All of that would surprise him. But not as much as what he would hear—or not hear—in the classrooms.

It would not be the math classes, shops, science labs, or the home economic sessions which would capture much of his attention. Or he might smile sadly, or shake his head disappointedly at the way the students lounge across their chairs or carve their initials and obscenities with ballpoint pens on the desktops. But, after all, in his day some students would have done the same thing if their teachers had let them get away with it. "Kids are kids," he would tell himself. They are immature; that is one of the reasons why they go to school. He would assume that he must have run into a string of weak-kneed teachers who did not know how to keep kids in line. There were a few of those around in his day. But then he would think of the halls. And the graffiti. Well, maybe it was just this school. Bad neighborhood or something, where they couldn't keep the critters in line.

But once he listened to the teachers and watched the kids at work in these classes he would feel better. In math they were still determined to get the students to the point where they could add up a string of prices on a shopping list, or determine the perimeter of a rectangle. In auto shop they were still working to set their points at the correct gap and get enough grease into the ball-joint fitting. In science you either knew what photosynthesis was or not. In home economics the cake was still considered a failure if it came out of the oven as flat as a waffle. No personal liberal interpretations of "right" here.

But when he got to the history and English classrooms, and

floated his invisible self to the back of the room . . . well, he would drop his teeth.

In his day those classes were dedicated to teaching students "their heritage," to make them proud of the political, intellectual, artistic, and moral legacy passed down to our generation by the great minds of the past—to defend, preserve, protect, and extend our way of life. In history, the stories and legends of the past—of Washington, Jackson, Daniel Boone, the Alamo, the Rough Riders —were used to make the student aware of the blood and sacrifice and heroism upon which our way of life depends. In English classes, the lessons about virtue and vice, cowardice and courage, developed through story and song by the great minds of European and American literary history—Shakespeare, Tennyson, Hawthorne, Cooper, Melville, Steinbeck—were presented as a loving gift from one generation to another. Certainly many of his classmates didn't respond all that well, he would recall. But you might not like the knit cap your grandmother made for you, until it snows. The fact that the students did not respond enthusiastically did not seem to surprise his teachers. If kids enjoyed great literature by instinct— like a cool dip in the river on an August "scorcher"—they would not need English teachers. Not everyone would respond. That was understood. But not everyone in biology became a doctor either.

But now . . . in English class they were studying the lyrics of rock songs, reading paperback books about rock singers, analyzing the writings of rock critics, talking about last night's television shows, or pondering the "heavy" message in the movie playing down on main street.

In history . . . they were not talking about history. They seemed more interested in what was going on "now"—they kept repeating that word, "now". They talked about proper attitudes on sex and racism and super-patriotism and ethnocentric values. When they mentioned history it was only to make a point about these modern issues. "Was George Washington a male chauvinist?" "Was Teddy Roosevelt a fascist pig?" Our invisible man would quietly float to the door to see if he was in the right place. Perhaps he was in a drama class where they were putting together one of those student-written parodies of school life so popular in the old days.

EDUCATION AND NORMS

Russell Kirk has long been considered one of the major conservative writers of our time. His influence might not appear to be as great just now as some of the conservative columnists and personalities who appear every so often on radio or television, but in the long run it will likely be far greater. He has spent much of his time researching and writing scholarly books on conservative themes and conservative writers who deal with ideas of lasting value and importance. He first received widespread recognition in the early 1950's with the publication of his book *The Conservative Mind*. It is still considered by many to be the "bible," so to speak, of conservative thought.

One of the themes that has occupied much of Dr. Kirk's time is the importance of great literature in our educational systems as a teacher of the "norms" of human behavior. By norms he means "an enduring standard . . . a law of nature which we ignore at our peril. It is a rule of human conduct and a measure of public virtue." They are the "enduring standards superior to our petty private stock of rationality."

Kirk is convinced that these norms of behavior are essential to the preservation of our way of life. Without them, we will return to what we were before the Greeks and Romans, medieval theologians, and the literary giants of the modern age developed our ideas about nobility, heroism, and piety—barbarians. These lessons of the past, found in the great books, poems, songs, and drama of the West, should not be forgotten, he argues. We forget them at the risk of uprooting our entire civilization, our way of life, our sense of stability. We open ourselves to the most radical of social and moral transformations—which is why the liberal has labored so diligently, and successfully, to remove all traces of them from our schools.

First of all, let us not confuse the gung-ho liberal ideologue, who has pushed determinedly for these changes in school curriculum, with the teachers or professors who have "gone along" with the changes in despair, or resignation. There are thousands upon thousands of teachers of literature across the country who are saddened by the deteriorated state of what is, after all, their great love. These teachers, although they might never think of themselves as conservatives, are conservative in the noblest of ways. They know what Kirk means by the "norms" of fine literature. They know that the lessons found in the masterpieces of our past are essential to man, and that our society will be greatly damaged if they are not conserved. They, too, are disappointed that they are no longer teaching Milton, Dickens, and Thackeray. But they have decided to go along with the changes to preserve their sanity. For when the schools are not providing overall discipline, or expelling known troublemakers, it is insanity to expect a teacher to explain the intricacies of poetic inscape, or the beauty of a passage from Joseph Conrad, to a typical class. That class very likely will contain hoods and punks who would have been in jail, or perhaps straightened out by a tough master sergeant in the army, years ago. Before anyone is critical of a teacher who has decided not to fight the change in curriculum from Coleridge's "The Rhyme of the Ancient Mariner" to the lyrics from an Alice Cooper record, he should try to teach Coleridge to a group of sullen, mean-spirited, disruptive, and violent twelfth graders.

The convinced liberal, on the other hand, is all for these kinds of changes. He applauds them in the name of "liberation." For the liberal, the great books are the signposts, the identifying characteristics of a civilization which he rejects. The moral complexities of adultery explored by Hawthorne in *The Scarlet Letter* are old-fashioned, middle-class hangups to him. The religious fervor of a man's encounter with his God in Francis Thompson's "The Hound of Heaven" is an example of an irrational, medieval superstition. The image of Sir Galahad as the ideal knight—honest, pure, willing to die to live up to his code of honor, chivalry—is just too corny for the pleasure-seeking young liberal educator who finds his heroes more in people like Mick Jagger. Alfred Lord Tennyson's love of country and heritage shown in poems like *Idylls of the King* comes across as "super-patriotism" and dangerous "nationalism" for the liberal who refuses to be bound by loyalty to his own country. Shakespeare, most especially, can be a narrow-minded, fascist type when you get down to it. I mean what right-minded person could talk of battle and love of country the way he did in *Richard II* and *Henry V*:

> Once more unto the breach, dear friends, once more;
> Or close up the wall with our English dead.
> In peace there's nothing so becomes a man
> As modest stillness and humility:
> But when the blast of war blows in our ears,
> Then imitate the action of the tiger,
> Stiffen the sinews, summon up the blood,
> Disguise fair nature with hard-favoured rage . . .
>
> Now set the teeth and stretch the nostril wide,
> Hold hard the breath and bend up every spirit
> To his full height. On, on, you noblest English . . .
>
> Be copy now to men of grosser blood,
> And teach them how to war. And you good yeomen,

Whose limbs were made in England, show us here
The mettle of your pasture; let us swear
That you are worth your breeding; which I doubt not;
For there is none of you so mean and base,
That hath not noble lustre in your eyes.
I see you stand like greyhounds in the slips,
Straining upon the start. The game's afoot:
Follow your spirit and upon the charge
Cry "God for Harry, England, and St. George."

You can almost hear the moans from the liberal: "Oh! What non-sense! Like I swear you would get laughed out of any place where progressive people get together if you said things like that. Really!" And you would.

The liberal is in pursuit of a new standard of virtue, one without the "blemishes" of old-fashioned love of God, country, strong family ties, respect for property, hard work, and self-sacrifice. The liberal is more concerned with immediate, earthly self-realization, international man, freedom from middle-class notions about sex, family life. He sees hard work as exploitation, even if you are being paid well for it. Self-sacrifice is a reactionary idea. The self-denial of a woman for her family becomes "male chauvinist oppression." The sacrifice of a father for his children becomes "inhibitive of personal growth." Sexual fidelity of husband and wife becomes just a "preference"—if it's your thing, O.K., if not, that is O.K. too. "If it makes you feel good, do it." His mind never allows for the notion that it is just and honorable and beautiful—and "self-fulfilling"—to do things which are not the easiest and most pleasurable. There is no room for the great books of Western man in the courses they teach.

For them the past is a shackle, a burden which inhibits them in their pursuit of a life of pleasure. It makes life too narrow, binds man, ties him down—to God, family, and country.

Russell Kirk, once again, warns us of what this means:

> In a time like ours, when the political and religious institutions which kept some continuity in civilization are weakened or broken, the responsibility of the writer and teacher of literature is greater than ever, it is possible that the only tie with the past which will survive in our century may be a literary continuity.

And:

> When the old order of civilization reels and falls, it is because the keepers of the Word no longer are confident in their truth. I am inclined to

think that human learning has been terribly injured in our time because the people who are entrusted with the conservation of human letters have forgotten the true meaning of humanism; and I believe that English literature has been treated with contempt in our schools and colleges because of what a friend of mine calls "The treason of the English teacher."

It seems a strong word—"treason." The dictionary calls it "the betrayal of a trust." It does not seem to be too strong a word when you think of it that way, does it? The people who pay the salaries of teachers and professors—most often the parents of the students—pay that money under the assumption that the teacher will be the bearer of the finest standards of our civilization, that he will do for the student that which the parent has not the time, or perhaps the ability, to do for himself. He does not see the teacher as a member of the vanguard of a new way of life designed to replace the older ways of the parent. The teacher's trust, especially the teacher of literature, is the responsibility of transmitting to the young the noblest aspirations of our people, as expressed by our greatest minds. The teacher who decides for himself that these aspirations are "outdated" and that he has found a new and better way of looking at things in the trendy journals and magazines that he reads, and the television debates and movies that he sees, and the parties he attends, and that he will teach that "new way" to his students—to liberate them from the past, too—is engaged in a betrayal of his trust: treason. But that is what is going on in classrooms taught by liberal ideologues and secularists all over America.

The most surprising thing is that changes of this sort have not raised more opposition. Perhaps that can be attributed to the fact that many adult Americans, having little formal education themselves as a result of poverty or the fact that they are the children of immigrants, do not really know what the literary heritage of our country and Western Europe is supposed to look like. That does not make the betrayal any more acceptable. Just more hucksterlike—like the guy in a gas station who puts used oil in your crankcase when you pay for an oil change.

It could be interesting, ten years or so from now, to watch the anger and bitterness pour out from many of today's students when they realize how cheated they have been by their schools. You can almost make the point with a silly wisecrack: "How is anyone of America's teenagers ever going to be able to do crossword puzzles?" Pretty silly—but not its full implications. For even the slickest of newspapers, magazines, and television commentators make certain assumptions about the level of knowledge of their readers—to say nothing of fine novelists, essayists, and playwrights.

Walter Cronkite on the evening news, Jack Anderson in his newspaper columns, Peter Bogdanovich in his movies, Truman Capote in his books, all perform with the idea that their readers and viewers have had some schooling. They make humorous asides, remarks, comparisons, explanatory contrasts, by referring to the history and literature of the European and American people. And these are not the kind of public figures whose works are designed only for an educated elite, a well-educated few. Their work is for the masses.

Will today's high school students be able to understand and share in this adult communication? Not unless they work at it on their own.

Perhaps I can give you an example. Below are just some of the phrases which have become part of every writer's and commentator's "tool kit." They are used regularly, without explanation most times, in modern newspapers, books, and television shows. They are dropped into paragraphs, used as adjectives and wisecracks. The user expects the hearer to get his point. How many of today's students will?

draconian	Renaissance man	ante-bellum
"crossing his rubicon"	"march to Canossa"	Faustian
ostracize	Anglo-Saxon	status quo
a Caesar	Puritan	Napoleonic
a solon	a Star-Chamber	"reign of terror"
spartan	utopian	imperialist
oracle	an Inferno	mercantile
Delphic	Divine Right	laissez faire
oedipal	bourgeois	capitalist
Olympian	Falstaffian	Marxist
medieval	philosophes	Trotskyite
chivalrous	protagonist	proletariat
quest	antagonist	reactionary
Machiavellian	Victorian	empirical
a Fagan	Fascist	Victorian
a Romantic	nihilist	lilliputian

You could go on and on with a list like this—really. There must be hundreds more. And remember these are not the concepts you have to be able to work with in depth in order to be an averagely intelligent person. These are just items you have to know a little about so that you can read a daily newspaper. I am not exaggerating. Of course, there are many people who do not know these terms, and who can still read their newspapers—but not at the level of understanding a bright young person should want for himself as an adult. Even if it is true that a school should not be expected to give a person all his knowledge, it should set him on the right path. The fact of the matter is that a fairly bright student just fifteen or so years ago, if he were fairly conscientious about his school work, would come from high school with a working knowledge of nearly all of these terms. Nowadays? Kids—as they say—you are being ripped off.

Look: it is a pretty simple idea. Most adults could not read a copy of *Rolling Stone* magazine. When their writers make jokes about the performance of the Beatles on the Sgt. Pepper album, or Janis Joplin's favorite nightspot in St. Louis, or complain that Chicago's latest album is no match for their second album, adults cannot get the point. They have no "rock tradition." The "past" is unknown to them. The present is not a result of anything. It just is. They have no way of judging quality. Or being patient with shortcomings. An adult cannot get what you mean when you play a new Stevie Wonder album and comment on his improvement over his early records.

Today's teenagers will be in the same boat as a member of adult American society.

"But people our age will be the newsmen and writers when we are adults!" you might say. "They will talk on our level." Maybe—although that slide into cultural rootlessness should frighten you. But chances are it will not be that way. A man of thirty today listened to Walter Cronkite, Eric Sevareid, and David Brinkley on the newscasts when he was fifteen. He saw movies directed by David Lean and Stanley Kramer. He read newspaper columns by James Reston and William Buckley and Art Buchwald. Chances are that today's fifteen-year-old will find many of them around when he is thirty. Today's teenagers just will not find themselves in control of things all at once when they reach twenty-five. The way people talk and write and make movies is not going to drop to today's teenager's level. If a young person intends to be a thinking and reading member of the community, he will have to develop the skills required. The only difference between today and the past will be that today's teenager will have to develop them with far less assistance from his school. But he will have to do it—or not know what the heck is going on.

Should all of the above be taken to mean that only old things are worthy of study? Should we ignore great modern writers just because they are modern? Not at all. But it does mean that a course which concentrates on books written in the last ten years is a course which is very likely to feature not even one substantial work of literature. That does not imply that there was "something wrong" with the last ten years or so. (Although there certainly was. They might have been the most culturally disruptive ten years in history since the Huns rode to Rome.) It would be true of most ten-year spans. Genius is not produced in broods. How many great writers come along in a generation?

For a work to be considered "great" it has to stand the test of time; prove that it is of lasting value. There are works that stand up to this test. No English teacher twenty years ago would have denied that. He might have denied that each and every one of them was suitable for a high school audience. Some were too difficult, some too dull—when judged by teenage standards. But the works of Chaucer, Dante, Shelley, Keats, Shakespeare, Browning, Thackeray, Dickens, Trollope, Conan Doyle, Chesterton, Dos Passos, Steinbeck, Jack London, Hemingway, and dozens of others, certainly presented a large enough selection to keep any group of high school and college students busy for four years.

If you think of all the "works of art" which have received so much attention in the last few years—and of how forgotten they are in so short a period of time—you almost want to laugh. Only the fact that so much money was spent by the schools in covering them, and so many young people, on their teachers' advice, spent so much time reading them, holds you back. It was not long ago that some high school teachers were talking about Simon and Garfunkel's lyrics as poetry of the first order. (Not that those lyrics are not pleasant—but ten years from now they will be remembered, if they are lucky, only in the way that the words to songs like "Night and Day" and "Stardust" are remembered. Fine songs, pleasant, but certainly not poetic masterpieces.) Bob Dylan's folk rock was called by one college professor "the finest poetry of the modern age"—an age which included Yeats, Auden, Eliot, and Pound. Social studies classes were analyzing in depth Charles Reich's *The Greening of America* for weeks on end. Only a few years later hardly anyone remembers what it was all about— which is fortunate for Reich. Movies like *The Strawberry Statement*—really—were talked about as meaningful comments on our time. Now it does not even make it on the late-night movies.

O.K., O.K., these are all honest mistakes. Anyone could make them. No one can tell for sure how important a new book or movie will be over the long run. *But that is why you do not waste your time includ-*

ing it in a school curriculum! There are important books which students are *entitled* to learn about, and they are being smothered under this deluge of pop-culture. The great lessons from the past should not be tossed aside in favor of the intellectual fads of the present, especially since the so-called intellectuals pushing them display such a sheep-like tendency to go along with whatever they hear from the *in* "guru" of the time—a Charles Reich, for example; and most especially since these intellectuals seem to have developed such a contempt for the rest of us—us "Archie Bunkers." As John Lukacs puts it: "they (the intellectuals) came to depend on each other, especially in countries such as the United States (they) felt that they were a small, indeed a misunderstood, minority among the large mass of their countrymen." All the poor educated liberals, "freed" through education, living in the midst of people who cling stubbornly to their love of God, family, home, and country.

When a course is not constructed with the great works of literature as its framework it degenerates into a course in "right thinking"— which ends up meaning a course dedicated to introducing the students to what ideas are "in" this year in liberal and radical circles. The same can be said of history courses which no longer talk about anything that happened over two years ago. All the claims about "doing your thing" and "independent thinking" to the contrary, the modern liberal is abjectly subject to the intellectual fads of the time. If you have to spend a good portion of your day teaching high school or college classes in order to put food on your table, you cannot read another eight or ten hours a day. Not everyone can be a scholar in the true sense of the word. As a result, the liberal would-be intellectual is continually in search of the "right opinion" about things, the right columnist, right magazine, right movie, and right television show. Even the books which are most popular with the liberals are more about opinions than about topics. They tell you *how to think* about ecology, sex, women's lib, styles of dress, food, religion, psychology, entertainment, politics.

The most free-wheeling, rap-session-type courses become, as a result, the most restrictive of all courses. In the name of a spontaneous, uninhibited exchange of ideas, a dictatorship of the radical-liberal "now" is established. The student loses one of the most important freedoms of all, the freedom to become acquainted with his heritage —the great minds of the human race over the last three thousand years.

You cannot be "free" without this heritage. It would be like the freedom you would have if you tried to drive cross-country without a road map. It is the freedom to be lost and confused. But instead of wandering aimlessly through dreary backroads, and decaying ruins of old villages, you wander in confusion in search of the nature of God, and the meaning of life, unaware that these questions have been handled by scholars, poets, and tellers of tall tales of the first magnitude at least as well as the guy who makes road maps. For over two thousand years now men with a taste for learning have spent their lives trying to preserve this treasure for us.

There was a time in history, not that long ago, when these men of intellect were respected and admired for that service. There was a time when going to school did not mean going to an institution which saw itself at odds with the community around it, as a bearer of a new way of looking at God and life. As a matter of fact, even the word "intellectual" did not exist a hundred years ago. People who read and studied in depth were called scholars or bookmen. Notice the difference in implication. These terms indicate one who is familiar with the great ideas, with the achievements of the human mind. "Intellectual" indicates more a state of mind, an outlook, an interior disposition based on a certain amount of brainpower or "sensitivity." The term intellectual indicates a separate group in society, different from the mass of men. Scholar does not. The scholar learns, and then preserves for us, the traditions and achievements of his people. The intellectual is a liberal, a member of a group determined to break the "superstitions," and "antiquarian bonds" of that tradition. He is by self-definition different, a separate class, a social disrupter.

This can end up sounding too negative, as if the main danger were what the liberal teacher will include in his course rather than what the student will miss as a result. After all, reading books of narrow, topical interest is probably—only probably—better than reading nothing at all. And listening to much of modern rock is a pleasant and rewarding experience. Parents who dislike the "sound" should not necessarily condemn it for that reason. William Allen White, the well-known editor of the *Emporia Gazette*, called Glen Miller's music "syncopated savagery" when he first heard it. He wanted the authorities to ban it in his area. Now Miller's music is thought to be the best example around of the sweet and wholesome music of the 1940's. Tastes in pop music do change. Much of the early rock and roll music people are listening to today for its child-like innocence, its "Happy Days" sound, had a wild and primal sound to those who were its greatest fans back in those times. (This should not be taken as an approval of the overtly immoral and degrading side of modern rock, the vulgarities of some of the Rolling Stones music, and glitter rock). Even comic books can be quite harmless fun. Their use in a school curriculum would not be that bad at all (especially in after-school discussion clubs) if it were not that it forces out so much else.

Our age is one which is crying for answers about the mystery of life. People are asking for "meaningful" experiences, for "authenticity." Thousands of people are seeking psychiatric care because they find themselves "depressed" over the purposelessness of their lives. People with fine houses, trendy clothes, new cars, money to spend in fine restaurants, the time and money to go on lengthy vacations abroad, just "can't put it all together." The psychiatrists and psychologists tell them they are not "whole"—and they agree. But, sadly, they end up going to more and more psychologists and more rap sessions and more physical pleasures for the answer. They fail to see that they are not whole because they are living like particles in space thrown off from some passing meteorite with no past, no meaningful future, no reason for going on. They have no God, no sense of community, no sense of continuity with the past, no heritage. They live in vast and impersonal apartment complexes, or sprawling suburban tracts, where an independent sense of inner worth is so much more essential than in the communal life of a medieval village or colonial American town. They have no answer to the question "Who am I?" "What is it all about?" Medieval men, who had so few pleasures, could take great satisfaction in the feel of a well-strung bow, a new pair of boots, a warm fire, a glass of wine, a soft blanket on their shoulders. Modern man in air-chilled rooms, drinking carbonated beverages, stereo earphones in place, anticipating irresponsible sex after a night of movies and nightclubs and all the booze and drugs you could want, feels "empty," "unfulfilled," "alone."

He does not have lyrical passages from the Bible telling of Christ, Dante telling him about the mysteries of life, Chaucer about the comical frailties of the race, Cervantes about the unquenchable human quest for nobility in life, Malory about the courage of Arthur and his Knights of the Roundtable, T.S. Eliot and William Butler Yeats about the dangers of the modern Godless world, Dos Passos about the stormy, proud history of the American people.

You know, he really does have a good reason to be unhappy. Even a snort of cocaine only lasts for so long.

We must remember that. We must resist the temptation to boil over in anger or scorn in our dealings with the liberals—even when they are openly arrogant in their attacks on our most-hallowed beliefs. They are sad and lost and lonely people.

7

Education Does Not Mean Learning "How Wrong Your Parents Are"

The teacher vs. parent confrontation creates one of the most puzzling questions a person has to deal with during his adolescent years. Why should his parents be constantly at odds with his teachers—especially some of his history and English teachers. After all, the young person has seen all the movies and television shows about bright and dedicated young teachers—*Room 222, Lucas Tanner*—and has come to the conclusion that teachers are seen by his society as pretty noble individuals who usually end up battling the narrow and bigoted forces "out there" in society. And his parents are not narrow and bigoted. Or are they? Is that the message? (Just in passing—the entertainment industry's treatment of typical classroom activity has to be the least realistic presentation of all that they offer for public consumption. Policemen will tell you that certain police shows and movies give a "pretty good" picture of what the job is like. Teachers, on the other hand, never fail to show amusement and disappointment, and sometimes anger, over how their jobs are portrayed. A typical class just is not composed of curious young athletes; intense, poetic, aspiring writers; and sensitive and socially aware blacks. And a typical teacher just does not come in, smile sincerely, lean back and say "Well folks, do you think there are any lessons for today to be found in your last night's reading assignment about Atlanta during Reconstruction days?" And then nod intently, and ask a brief question or two as the eager young learners rip apart the full implications of the issue. *Blackboard Jungle's* combat zone conditions are a far better representation for many schools, and closer to the truth than a *Room 222* for all. If people base their opinions about how easy teachers have it on that kind of hogwash, they have some soul-searching to do. There are many valid complaints that can be made about the teaching profession in America; that they work in a genteel, country club atmosphere is not one of them.)

Students are aware that their parents pay for the support of the schools through their tax dollars. They know that the teachers' pay comes from those dollars, as well. Why should there be such a difference between what their parents want them to hear, and what the teachers think appropriate? Why should what they hear from their parents during the week and their pastor on Sunday come across in classroom discussions as examples of what is wrong with the world, as obstacles to a new and better life for mankind? Why is it that almost all the teachers in the social studies department vote the opposite way from his parents?

EDUCATION AND SOCIAL CHANGE

In order to come to grips with this struggle of values you must work your way back through the history of the American public schools. The harsh and visible clash between teacher groups and parents is a fairly recent phenomenon, but its roots are buried deep in the nineteenth century.

Public education was not very controversial in the early third of that century. It did not exist to any significant degree. Private tutors were used by those who could afford them. Some churches ran schools for their members. Other communities might hire a "schoolmaster" to teach the "3 Rs" to twenty or thirty local children. Washington Irving's unforgettable fictional character, the bumbling Ichabod Crane, was a caricature of the type. Each of these teachers was viewed as an employee of the parents, in the strictest sense of the word. The parents, in accordance with Christian tradition, were seen as the "primary educators." It was their job to raise the child

100

properly, to make him a gentleman and a Christian, or as Cotton Mather, the famous eighteenth-century Puritan minister from Massachusetts, put it: "I would make my Children apprehensive of the main END, for which they are to Live; that so they may as soon as may be, begin to Live, and their Youth no be nothing but Vanity. I would show them, that their main END must be To Acknowledge the Great God, and His Glorious CHRIST; and bring Others to Acknowledge Him: And that they are never Wise nor Well, but when they are doing so." Obviously any teacher working for individuals or communities with such an outlook was expected to mirror this religious conviction. The school was a secondary agency.

By the middle of the nineteenth century, however, a movement known as "The Free School Movement" was well on its way toward providing "free" (tax supported—nothing is free) schools for all children up to a certain grade—what we now call the public schools. These new free schools soon developed a new philosophy of education too. Much of the new philosophy was necessary and commendable. If you were attempting to educate rich and poor alike, you could not run the schools as if they were only for the relatively rich, the way they were when only those with money to spare could afford to hire a teacher. The skills required to be the absentee owner of, say, a Southern plantation just are not the same as those needed to survive as a factory hand.

Well-meaning and intelligent "educational reformers" sought to define a suitable program for this new clientele. Vocational training, for example, was stressed rather than the study of Greek and Latin.

The more perceptive of the reformers, however, went one step further. They looked not only at their young students' academic needs, but at the world they would enter upon graduation as well. The mid- and later eighteenth century was the time of the greatest excesses of the Industrial Revolution: sixteen-hour workdays, six- or seven-day work weeks, children ten or twelve years old working to an early death in mines and mills. To these reformers it made little sense to educate the child for a purposeful and rewarding life if that life was to be lived in squalor and degradation, or come to an early end pulling coal through a tunnel. For them, the school became a vehicle of reform, a way of developing new attitudes in young people. They hoped that their students would leave their schools with a commitment to change their society's standards. They turned the tables, an educational flip-flop. The schools, instead of preserving, protecting, and ex-

101

tending the values of society, were to attack, to undermine, to subvert.

Even if you grant the correctness of the analysis of society's ills made by these educational reformers (I do), you have to marvel at what can only be called their "arrogance." What they were suggesting for themselves was control over the *ultimate directive thrust* of society. The teaching profession would decide for themselves what was right and what was wrong for their fellow men, package this new message in an educational curriculum, and then go out and preach it to the natives—whether the natives who were paying their salaries liked it or not.

Samuel Harrison Smith, for example, in his 1798 book, *Remarks on Education*, argues that "Error is never more dangerous than in the mouth of a parent. The child, from the dawn of its existence, accustomed to receive as undoubted every idea from this quarter, seldom, if ever, questions the truth of what is told."

You can see the developing attitude—as early as 1798. The teacher is beginning to reverse the relationship. The society, even the parent, becomes an agent you often must work against for the good of truth and justice, not someone whose values you preserve. The teacher is becoming a social missionary.

These "missionaries" were to attack the "system" with their new "gospels." They were the enlightened, the chosen, the elect, the bearers of new truths about how society was to be constructed. No longer would teachers push the beauty and wisdom found in the great books of the West, and hope that young people exposed to these ideals would absorb them and carry them as adults, as citizens, into the discussion of public policy. No longer would the schools hope to influence society in this indirect way. Now, schoolmasters would offer specific criticism of social injustice, act as engineers of correct social attitudes. They would play a direct role in educating society into the wisdom of specific reform goals. Stephen Simpson, in his book *The Working Man's Manual: A New Theory of Political Economy on the Principle of Production the Source of Wealth* (1831), insists, for example, that it "is to education, therefore, that we must mainly look for a redress of that perverted system of society, which damns the producer to ignorance, to toil, and to penury, to moral degradation, physical want, and social barbarism."

But there was a big difference between the reformers of the mid-1800's and the modern teacher-missionaries. Most Americans were willing to accept this new role for the teacher in the mid-1800's. They shared the reformers' outlook. The poor did want the schools to teach their children the skills required for economic and social advancement. The average American was convinced that society did have to be reconstructed in some way to end the abuses of the local mine and mill. The only parents likely to be offended were the rich and privileged who would see a challenge to their position in a socially mobile mass citizenry. And they probably wouldn't have their children in public school anyway. So even if these educational reforms contained propositions which were "anti-establishment" they were proposals acceptable to those connected with the schools. The teacher-parent animosity came later.

JOHN DEWEY AND PROGRESSIVE EDUCATION

In the early twentieth century, the educational philosopher John Dewey and the young graduate students and teachers who were drawn into his orbit pushed the reformers' ideas a few steps further. Their suggestions for American education reflect reformers' zeal, but also the fact that they had become thoroughly converted to liberal-relativism. They display a growing dissatisfaction with the "narrow" outlook of the American people. Where the earlier reformers championed the views and interests of the masses, these Dewey-ites show the first traces of what we could call an "elitist" view. They were not as interested in what the common man wanted as much as in what he "should" want.

Dewey himself, in his book *The Public and Its Problems*, discusses the common man's devotion to his country and its ways as a "problem," as backward ideas. "The belief in political fixity, of the sanctity of some form of state consecrated by the efforts of our fathers and hallowed by tradition, is one of the stumbling blocks in the way of orderly and directed change." Dewey, in fact, was one of the earliest American champions of anti-nationalism. He, as early as 1915, proposed that the schools be used to promote that outlook even though it was quite foreign to the wishes of the common man. "We have no right to cast stones at any warring nation" he wrote at the outbreak of World War I, "till we have asked ourselves whether we are willing to forego this principle [national sovereignty] and to submit affairs which limited imagination and sense have led us to consider strictly national to an international legislature."

Followers of Dewey, operating first at Teachers College of Columbia University, and later at almost every school of teacher education

103

in the country, made an understanding of this "social mission" of the teacher an important part of the training of future teachers. The student teacher was taught that his job was to bring the masses of men out of the "dark ages"—especially the recent immigrant groups living in the American cities in the late 1800's and early 1900's, who often came to this country with the strong religious convictions of their countries of origin. They had to be taught to be good, enlightened, liberal-thinking Americans. This was the reason why immigrant Catholics spent the enormous amount of time and money required to build the parochial school system. (If young students today think it difficult to live with the tension between their parents and their teachers, they can imagine the anguish that was brought to many Irish and Italian and Slavic families when, at great sacrifice to themselves, they sent their children to schools and colleges to learn to be teachers, and found their children learning from the American liberals that their most cherished traditions—the ideals for which they would die—were just "peasant Old World" superstitions.)

Boyd H. Bode, a disciple of Dewey, who went on to Ohio State University to spread the Dewey "truths," spoke freely of this great responsibility for the young, progressive-thinking teacher. For Bode the goals of progressive education recognized the need for "an extensive revision of our conceptions of property rights and of the function of government. As applied to organized religion it means a shift of emphasis from external salvation to progress through social control." Quite a job for a schoolmaster to take on—especially when it is self-appointed.

The ultimate questions about a society's reason for existence, its purpose, its goals, programs—questions that all societies have reserved for their highest councils down through history—were now to be defined by the country's teachers. They were somehow to become the visionaries, the uncorruptible who would be able to see the "right thing" while the rest of society was foundering about in confusion or mired down in corruption.

The children would be taught to see what their parents could not, but their teachers could. "The aim of education will be to help those of each period so to study its problems that they will surely act intelligently both in public and private affairs. All must come to expect social changes and adjust their thinking accordingly . . . The idea that education consists in the acquisition of stated subject matter must give way" says Bode, "to the study of problems vital within the lives of the young people, and to undertaking of enterprises significant with the community. Only in such a way can we hope to get the needed intelligent thinking about social affairs or build adequate social attitudes." Of course, "intelligent" and "adequate" in short order came to mean what liberal, free-thinking teachers said it meant.

In every movement for change there is always someone who says too much for the other members of the movement, someone who puts things too clearly, and frightens off potential converts before they have a chance to be "eased" into things. George S. Counts must have been someone like that in the 1930's as far as the more perceptive "progressive" school reformers were concerned. He made a speech in 1932 entitled *Dare the School Build a New Social Order?* The speech, like the title, pulled no punches. The schools for Counts were to get themselves "ready to lead society," to acknowledge that "in this union of two of the great faiths of the American people, the faith in progress and the faith in education, we have reason to hope for light and guidance. Here is a movement which would seem to be completely devoted to the promotion of social welfare through education . . . If the schools are to be really effective, they must become centers for the building, and not merely for the contemplation of our civilization."

Counts narrows in on the enemy:

> The important point is that fundamental changes in the economic system are imperative. Whatever services historic capitalism may have rendered in the past, and they have been many, its days are numbered . . . The times are literally crying for a new vision of American destiny. The teaching profession, or at least its progressive elements, should eagerly grasp the opportunity which the fates have placed in its hands.

Let us assume that Counts was right about the American economic system back in 1932 (the height of the Depression), and that his criticisms hold even today. As we mentioned earlier, you do not have to be a liberal in order to be critical of some of the tendencies in big business. The bigger question remains: Where do teachers like Counts get the idea that they have a right to make these decisions about what America needs, to choose sides in current political disputes, and to then proceed to teach that opinion to America's young people whether the parents and society as a whole like it or not?

And if you think that Counts might have been an isolated educational visionary, you are wrong. With the passage of time, it has become more and more common to find educators talking about their duties in such self-aggrandizing terms. In the July 27, 1974, issue of the prestigious liberal journal *Saturday Review*, Frederick L. Redefer, professor emeritus, higher education, at NYU, gives us a good example of the Counts-type educator in our modern world. Echoes of his words, in a much less polished arrangement, can be heard in faculty rooms all over the country:

> A new purpose for higher education must be directed toward the future, making students aware of the dangers of the present drift; the crucial shortages the world will face in energy, resources, foods; the effects of over-population; pollution of water and land as projected in the recent report by the Club of Rome . . . Such a purpose requires design and experiment *to create the kind of man* [my italics] needed by the world into which we are moving so rapidly. The traditional liberal arts are no longer relevant to this end. Rational thought needs to be applied to daily living, and a knowledge of the past must be applied to contemporary problems. An education limited to the study of the Western world is an anachronism. The traditional courses of the history of Western civilization, the appreciation of Western art, Western music, and Western literature omit more than half of the world of man . . . Before one becomes a lawyer, a doctor, a business executive, or a teacher, one needs to be a *man*—who knows himself and others, who thinks of himself as a man before he thinks of himself as a citizen of any particular country, or an example of any racial strain, or as a member of any religious or non-religious group . . . Is it not a time when a social purpose for education can be found and a commitment for an improved world accepted? Must we wait for society to change before colleges do?

Talk about arrogance! Mr. Redefer might be the gentlest, kindest man on the face of the earth, but his words are a declaration of war on the ideals of a significant majority of the American people—those Americans who cling determinedly to their belief in the uniqueness of the Judaeo-Christian religious ideals, the desirability of a special affection for the American nation-state, the magnificence of the cultural achievements of the Western world. His goal is to convert America into something it does not want to become, by working on America's young people—in schools supported by the very society he wants to undermine.

In times of political and social stability, when there are no great issues dividing the people of a country into opposed factions, it makes little difference whether a teacher or professor describes his job in such grandiose terms. The teaching profession is an important one. There is nothing wrong with someone describing it as one which is engaged in building a civilization. At its best, that is exactly what it is supposed to do when it preserves our cherished heritage for us.

In times of internal division, however, when the society has factions at odds with society as a whole it is presumptuous at best. Try to imagine some school authorities attempting to write acceptable textbooks for both the Union and the Confederate schools during the Civil War.

Many of the issues which divide us today are as deep and as wide as those which led to the Civil War. Is there a God? Do the Bible and Church-teaching have anything to say to modern man? Does the American nation-state deserve our loyalty and service? Do we have to be willing to fight in America's wars? Should Communism be seen as an enemy system? Should pornography be allowed? Is sex "free"? Is all truth relative?

What we are experiencing in our public schools today is an attempt by those who claim to have seen the light of liberal-international relativism on these and other issues to spread their version of the good life to the "rest of America." One bloc is attempting to convert the other through control of the educational system. It could be called "academic imperialism." The "rest" of America is seen as a culturally deprived hoard of selfish, uneducated bumblers, unable to see beyond their bourgeois opinions—their "middle-class standards." They have never had the advantages of studying under the right liberal professors, and rapping with the right student groups in the right student lounges at the right colleges—as have the liberal teachers, you see. Or they have sold out, forgotten what they learned in their concern for making a buck. They have sold out to the "establishment."

But the liberals feel there is still a chance with the young people. Maybe they can be reached. That is what "academic freedom" is all about, to them.

ACADEMIC FREEDOM AND THE LIBERALS

In order for a liberal or radical teacher with ideas far removed from those of the community where he teaches to fulfill his mission to educate young Americans out of their parents' "old-fashioned hang-ups," it became necessary to create some room for maneuvering. He could not function successfully if he was going to be bothered continually by those in the community with "backward ideas." After all it was the purpose of education to make sure that the children of the

**"You're very wise for your age. No one would ever guess
you're over thirty."**

community did not turn out like that—all that bourgeois nonsense
about God and Country and Duty and Decency. (And even if there
were little chance of converting the kids, the teacher's self-respect as
an educated liberal had to be protected so that he would not be forced
to "parrot" all those unenlightened ideas.)

As a result, teacher groups in colleges and local school-systems across
the country have pushed to raise to the level of an unassailable religious truth the idea of "academic freedom." It is almost always
spelled out specifically in teacher contracts.

Let us be blunt: academic freedom is a fraud in the truest dictionary
sense of the word—"intentional perversion of the truth in order to
induce another to part with something of value or to surrender a legal
right." It is an attempt to force the American people to sit by power-
lessly while their right and precious duty to raise their children properly is usurped by liberal academics.

William F. Buckley is perhaps the best known of all modern conservative writers. He has written numerous books, is editor-in-chief of the prestigious conservative journal of opinion, *National Review*; hosts a weekly television show, *Firing Line*; and writes a twice-weekly syndicated column for hundreds of American newspapers, in addition to appearing on many television talk shows and serving on committees and councils and conferences of every description. He seems to have disproved the old maxim about a day having only twenty-four hours.

Buckley first received public recognition just after his graduation from Yale when he published his first book, *God and Man at Yale* (1952), which he dedicated "For God, For Country, and for Yale . . . in that order." The book proved to be a sensation, going through over ten printings.

People applauded the book because it showed them that what they thought was going on in their schools and colleges—was going on. He exposed the extent to which liberalism had captured the educational processes at Yale, and by inference, the local junior high.

The fundamental assumption behind academic freedom, states Buckley, quoting Professor Edward C. Kirkland, is that "an academic institution is an arena. Into it ride different contestants. They may uphold different causes, some perhaps wholly or partially wrong. They may be differently armed. But all must meet the test of conflict, of argument, and of performance. We believe that in this free and open contest truth will be victorious and error defeated over the long time." Kirkland argues further that schools "do not possess or teach the whole truth. They are engaged in the quest for truth. For that reason their scholars must be free to examine and test all facts and ideas, the unpleasant, the distasteful, and dangerous, and even those regarded as erroneous by a majority of their learned colleagues."

The logic is perfectly consistent with the liberal-relativist view that nobody knows what they are doing: all ideas are mere opinions; all are of equal value; a school does not have a deposit of truths, and therefore cannot define beforehand what is acceptable subject matter; truth and justice will be served better by allowing bright and dedicated teachers to decide for themselves what they will teach in their classes and what their students will read. The only alternative would be to set some standard of truth beforehand, and that cannot be done since the liberal insists that no one knows truth—certainly not the community. Better, they tell us, to have an unending search for truth, as if the world's only acceptable truth is that there is no truth.

The result, says Buckley, is that the liberals have given themselves a field day. "Under the protective label 'academic freedom' one of the most extraordinary incongruities of our time (has come about): the institution that derives its moral and financial support from Christian individualists . . . then addresses itself to the task of persuading the sons of supporters to be atheistic socialists." Buckley was writing of Yale, of course, and things might not be that bad at the local college or high school (although they might be worse since many less-gifted liberal relativists lack the refinement of argument of the Yale professors, and make their arguments in a much more direct and blunt appeal). Perhaps the school you are familiar with is not actually "pushing" socialism and atheism. But it is making it difficult for anyone to learn intelligent standards with which to argue against socialism and atheism. Socialism and atheism become, in the *best* of classes run by liberal teachers, just a few more opinions that people around the world have come up with in order to handle their lives. No more, no less.

But I am not disagreeing with Buckley. He is on to something. As I have said, the "best" of liberal teachers promote a mere relativism—an atmosphere in which the ideas of Moses and Christ and Thomas Aquinas are treated as equal to those of Karl Marx and the LSD gurus of our time. There are others who display a marked bias in favor of left-wing and atheistic attitudes, and who operate freely under the banner of academic freedom.

Anyone who is even vaguely familiar with the operations of American school systems can spot the tendency. An Angela Davis, Herbert Marcuse, Bettina Aptheker—admitted Marxists all—will be allowed to address a student group. Or a teacher will quote from a Marxist historian to make a point about the corruptness of American life. If anyone protests that these people are using an auditorium or classroom, supported by the American taxpayer, in order to promote a movement openly hostile to the political system of the American people, he will be told that it is just a "free exchange of ideas"—academic freedom. If, on the other hand, an American Nazi, a member of the Ku Klux Klan, or a geneticist like William Shockley, who claims that blacks, as a group, by heredity have lower IQs than whites, tries to get permission to speak before those same audiences in those same rooms, he will be turned down. There are courses taught by admitted Marxists in public colleges all over this country. (In three of the four history courses I have taken in graduate school during the last few years I have had New Left Marxists—and I did not go out of my way to find them.) Can anyone think of any admitted Nazis working in an American school? Dr. Shockley is usually forbidden to speak at most schools and colleges, and when he does speak the academic freedom folks in the auditorium hoot and scream and holler until he gives up and leaves the stage.

Now the point—it goes without saying—is not that Nazis should be given audiences of American students and auditoriums built by the dollars of the American people in order to spread their ideas. And maybe Dr. Shockley should be hooted off the stage by those who believe his ideas are comparable to those of a concentration camp SS guard. Most Americans would hoot down an Adolph Hitler if he reappeared and came around spreading his plans for wiping out the Jews and the Slavs. (That is not meant to compare Dr. Shockley to Hitler. Shockley may be wrong—I think so—in his social advice, but he displays no Hitler-type race hatred.) The school systems can and should set standards. And they do—Nazis and Ku Klux Klan members and Dr. Shockley are prohibited. *But why are not Marxists and Maoists and other Communist sympathizers as well?* Why is their difference of "opinion" acceptable? Certainly by all objective standards the Russian and Chinese Communists are as offensive as the Nazis. They have persecuted and killed far more people than the Nazis. They have taken over more countries outside their borders—think of all the Russian satellites. They have a scheme for world conquest as clearly defined as anything found in Hitler's book *Mein Kampf.* Alexsandr Solzhenitsyn has become famous around the world for his many descriptions of life under Communist tyranny in Russia and its *Gulag Archipelago.*

We will have more to say about why the liberal has become so willing to compromise with the communists in the next chapter. For our purposes here it should be enough to note that academic freedom for the liberal means the freedom to promote liberal and left-of-liberal views. At best it is the freedom to operate as a free-thinking liberal in a community which rejects that kind of relativism. At worst, it is the freedom to promote ideas against American society, in favor of our enemy's society, while being paid by Americans.

One of the favorite liberal ploys in this argument is to appeal to what could be called the "power of truth" argument. After hearing someone tell students that America is to blame for most of the world's troubles, or that the "Catholic Church's leaders should be put on trial before a world tribunal because of their opposition to birth-control agencies in the poorer nations of the world" (as one pamphlet

111

used as a text in many high schools suggests), the liberal supporter of academic freeeom will say something like "Well, what are you afraid of? If you think those ideas are so wrong you must have good reasons for your opposition. Why not let the students hear the other side? If your arguments are so right, they will be so much more convincing that you will have nothing to worry about. Most of the students will agree with you, won't they?"

It is a remarkable argument. The person using it is either remarkably naive, or remarkably dishonest. It is an argument which looks at the world as if there were no yesterday—as if the *wrong* ideas of a Hitler or a Stalin never won over enough support to cause the persecution of the people in their countries. As if a Charles Manson, or a Symbionese Liberation Army, had never won over to their causes confused young people. Truth simply does not always win out. As Edmund Burke put it so well, truth needs help. "All that is needed for the triumph of evil is for good men to do nothing."

Perhaps a school system or college has no right to tell one of their teachers what he or she can do on their own. They cannot control what they say to friends, or what ideas they push in social gatherings of people their own age. The teacher or professor is free to read and research, and write articles and books which reflect that research. But what he *teaches* is not in the same category. There, it is not his freedom as an individual which is at stake, but his students' right to think as individuals. In the teenage years a young person is wide open to formative influences. What he hears and sees will have a great influence on the development of his character. And teachers unavoidably have a great influence. Especially on the better, more attentive students. After all, he has more time to actually *talk to* his students than any of their parents. What parent can sit down and talk to each of his children for forty-five minutes a day, five days a week?

When parents send a child to a school, they are choosing to have someone else teach the child in their place—*in loco parentis* is the term school system lawyers use. The education of the child is the parents' responsibility. Most Americans believe that one day they will have to stand before God and answer for that responsibility more than any other. And they don't believe that God will be happy with the answer that "we let him do his thing." Parents do not give that responsibility away to the schools any more than a homeowner gives away his ultimate decision-making power when he hires a carpenter to build a playroom in the basement. The parents have not only the right, but the obligation to make sure that the educational process

112

comes as close to their standards of truth and decency as they can get it. The teacher is hired by a community to provide that service. When he is teaching he is acting for the parents. What he does on his own time may be his own business; what he does as a teacher is not his own business. It is the parents'.

Of course the room for varieties of educational experience broadens in college. There a course goes by a name, and the student can choose to take that course or not. If he finds it offensive he can take another instead. The student is older too, and supposedly ready to hear many of the challenges to our way of life and accepted beliefs since he has received such a firm foundation in these things in grade and high school. (Which makes the grade and high school's responsibility as preservers of our heritage all that more important.) Chances are, too, that the student is paying at least part of his own way in college. You could argue that the *in loco parentis* responsibility ends here. But that does not mean that anything goes.

The society which supports the college has the right to protect itself from its enemies—even when they work in a college. Colleges do not just float down from the clouds on spring days. Professors are not just independent citizens who happened to stumble across a crowd of young people in a cafeteria somewhere and start talking about things.

The college was set up by state or private funds. The professor was hired by a state or private group. The classrooms were built with the dollars of that same group. The students were recruited from around the country by printed brochures and admissions officers paid for from the same source.

The people paying that tab must have gone to all that trouble to offer what they thought was a worthwhile service. It is not unreasonable for them to insist that that service stay worthwhile, by *their* standards. It would be unreasonable for them not to do so. If they are intelligent they will realize that a wide range of opinions is one of the most worthwhile experiences a college can provide. But that does not mean "anything goes." Encouraging a preponderance of ideas clearly hostile, such as Communism, to the entire social structure of which they are a part is hardly a noble aim.

In a short, but powerfully argued essay, the late Willmoore Kendall, onetime professor of government at Yale himself, stated the issue in his inimitable way. Below is a brief sample:

I accuse the educators of having for many years now used the schools for the purposes of sheer indoctrination—indoctrination, moreover, in ideas about equality, freedom of thought, collective security, socialism, that continue to be repugnant to the best judgment of ordinary people in most of our local communities. And I call upon ordinary people in all communities to serve notice on the educators that they will tolerate it no longer, that they wish, nay, are determined to bring up their children with beliefs and ideas and attitudes and loyalties as nearly as possible like their own, which they cling to because they believe them to be best, and the essence of a community is that it has a way of life it intends to perpetuate because it loves it.

The educators of course will at this point begin to make noises not about their expertise but about something called "academic freedom," but let our rebel's hands not be stayed by that; no community can afford a freedom for teachers to undermine its way of life, can afford it or will afford it once the community realizes what there is that is involved.

8

Anti-Communism Has Not "Become Obsolete"

You might not know the word "gnostics." (They were early Christian heretics who believed in their own power to construct an earthly paradise.) But you do not have to know too much about them to feel the impact of Brent Bozell's words.

Liberals are coming to understand, even if darkly, that the logic of their analysis and ambition points them down a road they cannot follow: that the gnostic dream of an earthly paradise can be realized (as the Communists know) not by changing society, *but by changing man,* by transmutative surgery on the soul. *It follows that if gnosticism is ever to triumph it will triumph in Communist form.* Yet liberals instinctively recoil from that prospect; their sense of humanity, their residual attachment to the values and norms of the West, forbid the Communist solution. What a pickle—to be possessed by a world view that demands the victory of your enemy! Men affected by such a neurosis go mad, and civilizations do also. And in the meantime they fight—stubbornly—but aimlessly, without hope and without purpose: a "twilight struggle."

A "twilight struggle"—a struggle without definable purpose, with-

115

out any real hope of success. It is a good description of liberals in their dealings with the Communists.

Bozell sees the issue clearly. The goals of the liberal, his vision of mankind's destiny, are so close to those of the Communists that the liberal has difficulty in treating Communists as an enemy. For the liberal, the Communist is a zealot whose heart is in the right place, but who is going about things in the wrong way—pushing for too much too soon. The liberal is more disappointed with the Communists than opposed to them. "Don't you folks see" he seems to say to the Communists, "that you cannot achieve your admirable goals through your clumsy dictatorships and war-like methods. You can win more flies with honey than with vinegar. Why not join with us liberals in our peaceful methods?"

As a result, the liberal is willing to bomb Germany into unconditional surrender in World War II, cut off all trade and military aid to Spain until they become more democratic, join in a boycott of all trade with Rhodesia because of the racial discrimination practiced there, march in protests before the U.N. every Sunday from here to eternity against South Vietnamese or South Korean "tin horn dictators" (as George McGovern referred to Premier Thieu of South Vietnam), make angry statements about the "authoritarian" and "oppressive" government in Brazil—while at the same time encouraging "cultural exchanges" and increased trade with Russia, praising the programs of Fidel Castro, going to poetry readings by Russian poets who call for the communization of the globe, discussing Ho Chi Minh as the George Washington of Vietnam, oohing and aaahing at the "heavy" insights found in Mao Tse-tung's little red book, writing angry letters defending the late Communist regime of Salvatore Allende in Chile, and calling the Viet Cong "freedom fighters." The Rhodesian government is evil because it denies full freedom to its blacks (although they can, for example, practice their religion freely and leave the country), but the Russian or the Chinese government is noble and worthy of our cooperation even though they oppress all their citizens (and none of their people can practice their religions freely or leave the country). Some dictators are to be excused, you see: The Communists!

THE COMMUNISTS AND THE LIBERALS: SOUL BROTHERS

It is not possible to summarize in a few pages the entire historical analysis and projections for the future which form the basis for Communist theory. What follows is superficial, but accurate and complete enough to give an idea of why the liberal finds it so difficult to handle the growth of Russian and Chinese power in world politics, and the presence of pro-Communist revolutionary groups in the streets of our own country.

Karl Marx, a German intellectual who did most of his writing in England after he was chased out of his own country for revolutionary activity, is known as "The Father of Communism." According to Marx, "the history of all hitherto existing social institutions has been the history of class struggle." Men all down through history, he claims, have been motivated by economic needs—the desire of those classes without money and power to get money and power from those classes with money and power: patricians against plebians in ancient Rome, serfs against lords in feudal Europe, middle classes (the bourgeoisie) against kings and aristocrats in seventeenth- and eighteenth-century Europe. The entire sweep of history is pictured as a movement in the direction of equality: political and economic power in the hands of one man (kings and emperors) breaking down into power in the hands of a few (aristocrats), then breaking down into the hands of the many (middle class)

The next and final step for Marx was to be a great revolution by the industrial workers of Europe—the *proletariat*—against the middle classes. The middle classes had overthrown the kings and lords in the revolutions in England in 1688, America 1776, and France 1789. Wealthy businessmen, farmers, and professional men now ran those countries—giving more power to more people than during the days of the kings and lords, which Marx applauded. But for an equal share in power and wealth, one more revolution was required—this revolution of the lowest class, of the proletariat. After that, all classes would be equal. The proletariat would be in charge; and since there was no class beneath them, there would be genuine equality.

The proletariat would be represented by a dictatorship—what Marx called "the dictatorship of the proletariat." This dictator would abolish private property. For Marx, private property was the villain. It forced men to "exploit" each other for their own economic good—the profit motive. It created a competitive mentality as men seeking more and more private wealth came to view their fellow men as threatening rivals in its pursuit.

Once private property was abolished men would have no reason to compete with each other since they could no longer make themselves any wealthier than their neighbors no matter how hard they

117

tried. All property was to be owned by the state (dictatorship of the proletariat) and would be administered by the state for the common good. The state would decide how much a person would earn—and according to Marx they would reward men who *cooperated* with their fellow men for the good of society as a whole, not those who tried to "use" their fellow men for personal gain. As a matter of fact, once they got used to the idea of living without having to worry about their personal wealth, once they became cooperative rather than competitive—they would be able to live by Marx's guideline: "From each according to his ability; to each according to his needs."

This maxim of Marx's foresaw the day when the brighter and stronger people would work their hardest for the good of their fellow man, but would not expect higher pay. The highest pay would go to those with the greatest needs. An unmarried brain surgeon, for example, would earn less than a mail boy with four children (greater needs). People would work for the community, not for themselves as individuals. All of society would operate like a family, each member contributing his best for the good of the group.

The dictatorship of the proletariat, then, would have the responsibility to do much more than just abolish private property and administer wages and prices for the common good. It would have to change human attitudes as well. It would have to eliminate the "self-interest" developed in men over the centuries of having to provide for themselves, and replace it with a "community interest"—make men see themselves "profiting" only as members of the community, not as individuals.

The dictatorship would control schools, newspapers, radio and television broadcasts—to make sure that only acceptable Communist ideas were circulated among the people. The old interest—anti-Communist interest—could not be allowed to hold back this dream of a perfect human brotherhood. They were "the enemies of the people" and had to be eliminated for society's sake. Marx admitted that many of them would have to be killed once the Communists took over since their minds were so set in the old anti-Communist ways. As a result in Russia and China, millions of "enemies of the people" were either executed or sent to the Communist concentration camps scattered across Russian Siberia—the *Gulag Archipelago* so frighteningly portrayed by Alexsandr Solzhenitsyn in his book of that name.

Religious groups had to be eliminated as well, either right away, or through slow attrition, whichever worked best. He insisted that religion was a medieval superstition and a tool used by the upper classes to keep the poor and the oppressed in line. The Christian religion was especially guilty, with its promise of rewards after death to the meek and humble and the sufferers after justice's sake. It taught men to turn the other cheek rather than band together in a revolutionary movement to correct the abuses of the world. It made men content to sit back and suffer the problems of the world rather than strike out to change it. For Marx it was a type of drug (or opiate) which dulled men's senses to what the world could become. Only the Marxists with their modern, scientific view of human experience could handle the future.

THE WORLD MOVEMENT

Once one country turned Communist, the leaders of the Communist movement in that country were to direct their attention to the rest of the world. Communism was to be a worldwide movement—for all men, or as Marx put it "workers of the world unite, you have nothing to lose but your chains." No one country could turn Communist until the world had been won over. Communism, by the self-definition of Communists, seeks world control.

Why? The logic is fairly simple. You see, the dictatorship of the proletariat was not to be the final stage of Communism. After the dictatorship had trained the people of an area to think as brothers, as comrades, to be more concerned about the betterment of the community than their own self-interest, there would be no need for the dictatorship any longer. Marx claimed that there would be no need for a large scale government, for a state, at all. After all, if all men were Communist brothers filled with a sense of sharing, what need would there be for armies, police, courts or judges? These agencies of the state exist to settle disputes among competing individuals. Men in this new brotherhood of workers would not be struggling *against* each other, they would be working *for* each other. The state simply "would wither away," to be replaced by local groups of Communist brothers who would run their community for the good of all. When, and only when, this final stage was reached could a country truly call itself Communist.

But there was a problem. If one country reaches this final stage—and phases out its armies and police—well, they'll get smeared. All the surrounding countries, the capitalist countries with their armies, and their selfish non-Communist ideas, would charge right in and conquer the gentle Communist brothers. So only when all the world was

Communist and willing to surrender their forces in arms could any one country reach the final stage.

Russian Communists have feuded intensely about *how* to carry out this plan for taking over the world in the name of Communism. Lenin, the leader of the Communist revolution in Russia and the first Communist dictator of that country, made a lengthy analysis of how colonies of the European countries longing for freedom from their European mother-countries could be won over to Communism. He studied how Communists could encourage "wars of national liberation" against the colonial rulers, and offered advice about how to turn the colonial revolt into a Communist movement. Modern Communist theoreticians have talked often of how Vietnam fits this pattern. The Communist revolutionaries there even go by the name National Liberation Front. The people of former colonies like Vietnam could be encouraged to fight for their "freedom" from foreign rule, while the Communists in control of the war made plans for setting up a Communist state at its end.

There was also a bitter feud between Leon Trotsky and Joseph Stalin over this issue. Trotsky and Stalin both were assistants to Lenin while he was alive. After his death in 1925 they struggled against each other for control of the Communist party, and Russia. One of the issues that divided them was this question of exactly how Communism was to be brought to other countries. Stalin insisted on building up a powerful Russian state, and then using its military might to "spread the revolution." Communism would come to other countries on the backs of Russian soldiers, or on the tips of their bayonets. Trotsky disagreed and argued that Stalin was becoming excessively concerned with *Russian* power, and was allowing his Russian nationalism to come before his allegiance to Communism. Trotsky insisted that the Communists in Russia should concentrate their time and Russia's resources to encourage Communist revolutionary groups in other countries. Trotsky accused Stalin of being "too Russian" in interest, of "nationalizing" the Russian Communist movement, thereby destroying its ideological purity. The issue was eventually settled in Stalin's favor. Trotsky was forced to flee for his life from Russia. While in exile in Mexico he was found one day with a mountain climber's axe buried in his skull.

But, again, the feud was not over *whether or not* to make the rest of the world Communist, but *how*.

There are some experts who insist that Stalin's view has won over in Russia so completely that Russia today is not interested in spreading Communism as much as they are in spreading Russian power. In the short run, that makes little difference to us. Being dominated by Russian nationalists would be just as much a loss of freedom for us as being dominated by Russian Communists. In the long run though, it could make a big difference. If the Russians give up their scheme for encouraging Communist revolutions and takeovers all over the world perhaps we can work with them in preserving peace through a balance of their power against ours. Perhaps we can work to keep them within the territorial limits they are entitled to as representatives of the Russian people (which is what they might become if they stopped insisting on trying to make everyone, including the Russians, Communists).

But just for the record, the Communists openly admit to their continuing desire to spread Communism in every Communist Party Congress they hold. Mikhail Suslov, the leading Soviet theoretician in 1974—the time in history when our liberal politicians tell us we can work with the Russians for the cause of world peace—has boasted of "the strengthening of the public forces that are destined by history to play a revolutionary role of transforming society on the basis of progress and socialism." Robert Morris, a syndicated columnist, reported an account of a conversation of Nikita Khrushchev printed in the Australian magazine *News Weekly*: "After his first meeting with Kennedy, Khrushchev said to the Czech Communist leader Novotny: 'After this meeting, the Americans will not be so anti Communist: and in this way I have opened the doors wider throughout the world for Communism to enter.

"'Kennedy proposed to me that we should not make trouble for each other.

"'I promised not to do this—in the name of the Prime Minister of the Soviet Union. But in my capacity as First Secretary of the Soviet Communist Party, my hands are free.

"'It is our duty to build up such strength that the whole world will tremble before it. All we need is that the Americans give us enough time.'"

We could take the time now to argue against these theories in detail, but our concern here is more with why the modern liberal does not. But let it be said: The whole package is a sorry mess. It is based on a mistaken view of human nature; calls for a plan which destroys human freedom; separates man from his God; calls for the end of national independence. Common sense tells most people that human nature will never allow for a government anything like the final stage of Communism. People just are not going to work their best for the entire community without the incentive of a salary which rewards them for their efforts. A man might be willing to break his back for his own family—but for the family down the road, or half-way across the country? The Judaeo-Christian tradition calls imperfections of this sort the result of original sin. Whether we accept that explanation or not, it is clear that people do not have an inborn sense of self-sacrifice, and that selfishness is the more observable character trait in this world.

The most obvious question that this brings up is why surrender our freedoms to a Communist dictatorship that promises us in the distant future a change in human nature which all of our religious belief, history, and common sense tell us cannot take place because of man's imperfect nature? Even if they could make the world the perfectly cooperative place they describe, and even if it would be pleasant to live like bees in a communist hive rather than as individuals (which most of us agree it would not), is it worth the brutal Russian- and Chinese-type dictatorships we would have to endure until that millenium arrives?

But what about the liberal? Well, take a look at the Communist promises in outline form:

a) end of social injustices; end of political and economic inequality

b) a world run without religious influences

c) a world run by scientific methods and reason

d) the end of nation-states in favor of a one-world workers' community

e) end of private property and capitalism

f) government control of the economy

g) government control of the schools and the media by the enlightened, "progressive," leaders of the society

Sound familiar? It should. It is near-to-identical to the kind of future world the modern liberal envisions for us. The only difference is that the liberal wants to get people to these "ideals" through education and magazine reading and movies with a message, while the Communists want to move more directly through a totalitarian dictatorship.

This is Bozell's "twilight struggle." For the liberal, the Communists are like impetuous and idealistic children. They must be taught to calm down, to work more slowly. They must be shown that their ideal world can be achieved without their military dictatorships.

They should be cajoled, and scolded occasionally, but never really treated like an enemy.

The late Whittaker Chambers knew this liberal weakness as well as anyone. He was a Communist himself during the 1930's. He first came to the attention of the American people in the early 1950's when he came forward and admitted his Communist background, and accused Alger Hiss, a high-placed State Department official at the time, of being a Communist as well. The story of Chambers' involvement with Hiss and the Communist party in America is told in Chambers' moving autobiographical book *Witness*. It is a story which rivals the slickest of modern spy stories for drama and surprise. Even if it is impossible for a busy reader to go through the whole book, any one who is serious about understanding the challenge presented to America by the Communist movement owes it to himself to read at least the introduction: Chambers called it "Letter to my Children." Chambers was a Communist. He knew how Communism can appeal to idealistic young people. He knew Communism's lure—especially for the liberal:

> It is, in fact, man's second oldest faith. Its promise was whispered in the first days of the Creation under the Tree of Knowledge of Good and Evil. "Ye shall be as gods." It is the great alternative faith of mankind. Like all great faiths, its force derives from a simple vision . . . the vision of man's mind displacing God as the creative intelligence of the world. It is a vision of man's liberated mind, by the sole force of its rational intelligence, redirecting man's destiny and reorganizing man's life and the world.

When looked at from this perspective, Communism is merely the wayward twin-sister of liberalism. The liberal-Communist struggle takes place on the level of a family squabble, a squabble between two great believers who share what Chambers calls the same "great alternative faith of mankind."

THE RECORD

Our country's history over the past twenty-five years is filled with examples of liberal-Communist cooperative ventures—and with the resulting loss of American power in the world arena, and the weakening of traditional American institutions at home.

The years just after World War II are as good a place as any to begin. For most Americans the Russian-American cooperation during that war was a necessary evil. Since the Nazis were the immediate threat, the idea of allying ourselves with a totalitarian atheistic dictatorship—which in normal times would have been an unacceptable association for the American people—seemed just "common sense." We chose to repress our understanding of what the Communist dictators of Russia stood for in order to defeat the "common enemy"—the Nazis.

Many American liberals, in contrast, were actually enthused about the American-Soviet cooperative effort. They were the Americans who—like Lincoln Steffens, the American writer who returned from Russia with the famous statement "I have seen the future, and it works"—actually admired much of the overall approach to life in the Soviet Union, and hoped to be able to continue the spirit of wartime cooperation indefinitely after the war. Eventually this became known as the politics of *detente*—the American and the Russian superpowers working together, America becoming more socialized like Russia, and Russia more concerned with individual liberty like America, in the process.

President Franklin Delano Roosevelt, for example, talked of Josef Stalin, perhaps the bloodiest and most oppressive dictator in history, as "Uncle Joe," a friendly Russian peasant-type who could be worked with in pursuit of justice in Europe at the end of the war. At Yalta, a city in the Crimea of Russia, a peninsula jutting down into the warm waters of the Black Sea, Roosevelt met with "Uncle Joe" and attempted to work out a satisfactory arrangement for Europe after Hitler was defeated. The big question was over what we now call the Russian satellites, the Eastern European countries taken by the Russian army on the march into Germany from the East, while American and English forces advanced from the West in the famous pincers movement that crushed the Nazi state.

What would happen to those countries? Poland? Czechoslovakia? Hungary? After all, the American soldiers had fought to prevent Nazi dictators from taking over those areas. Now they were in the hands of Russian dictators. Should not we insist that the Russians leave those areas and allow for free elections so that the Poles and Czechs could freely elect a government of their own? Thousands of Americans had died to prevent the Germans from ruling the smaller countries of Europe. Were not the Russians just as unacceptable interlopers? No, said the liberal. They were different.

They could be trusted. They were dictators like the Germans . . . but different. They believed in economic equality, and scientific reasoning. They were internationalists, not super-patriot types like the Germans. They were not racists. They did not persecute Jews like the Nazis. (They persecuted everybody, including the Jews—but the liberal ignored that.)

So Roosevelt trusted Uncle Joe at Yalta. No demands were placed on the Russians. The Poles, the Yugoslavs, the Czechs were left to the tender mercies of the Communist "humanists." Do not worry, said the liberal, you can work with the Communists. They are not like the Nazis. They will join with us in helping to create a better world. Their standards of decency are high, their aims noble. (Hungary, Poland, Czechoslovakia, and all the other Eastern European satellite countries to this day are paying the price for that liberal confidence. In spite of bloodly uprisings and heroic determination to drive out the Russians, they still live under the tender mercies of the Communists. And the American liberal still does not seem to mind at all, as he calls for more and more cooperation with the Russian Communists.)

The situation in China in 1949 is another good example. Ever since the late 1920's the Chinese people had been deeply involved in a war with Communist revolutionaries. In the early 1920's the Russians sent into China the legendary agent Mikhail Borodin. His job was to take advantage of the existing political and economic chaos in China to build a strong Communist movement. The Russian Communists thought that China could be turned into a Communist country just as Russia had been a few years earlier in 1917. Borodin worked to organize a fledgling Communist party, and discovered a young Chinese radical intellectual who might have some potential as a leader. His name was Mao Tse-tung.

Two great and bloody series of wars were fought—the Communists (Mao and Borodin) against the Nationalists under Chiang Kai-shek, a young military officer who had risen to power under the tutelage of Sun Yat-sen, the leader of China's revolution against the old Manchu dynasty of emperors. Chiang Kai-shek won a decisive victory. Mao and his followers fled in haste from Chiang's armies to the barren, desolate western boondocks of China in 1934. Three out of four of Mao's three hundred thousand supporters were lost on this "Long March." No one expected to hear from Mao and his supporters again. Chiang and the Nationalists seemed firmly in control.

World War II and the Japanese invasion of China changed this picture. The devastating sweep of the Japanese war machine weakened Chiang and finally forced him to retreat up the turbulent Yangtze river to the ancient city of Chungking.

125

After the war and the Japanese defeat, the Communists and Mao, with Russian-supplied weapons, took advantage of Chiang's weakness to launch an all-out drive against him from their western mountain enclaves. A bloody, boiling stew of a civil war followed. The U.S., for a while, pumped in money and military supplies. Then, in 1949, just a few months before the Communists launched an all-out offensive, and in spite of a personal plea to American President Harry Truman by Chiang's wife, the U.S. cut off all aid. Why?

There are many theories floating around, some very logical, some less. Some stress the fear of being drawn into a major confrontation with Russia. Others argue that we knew that Chiang was going to lose anyway and decided not to waste any more money.

The liberal during those years looked on things from a different angle. All during the late 1940's groups of American scholars pushed a pro-Mao point of view, and a corresponding anti-Chiang point of view, in books, newspapers and magazines most popular with the liberals. Some of these individual authors later were charged by Whittaker Chambers and another ex-Communist, Louis Budenz, of being Communists, and with much evidence. But even if everyone who wrote a pro-Mao book was a Communist (and all were *not*), it would not have made much difference except for the fact that the American liberals proved to be so damnably predisposed to believe anything good they heard about the Communists. Once the American liberal began to push successfully the idea that Mao was the good guy and Chiang the villain, the arms cut-off became inevitable.

The liberals read and agreed with books such as *Human Endeavor* by Haldore Hanson which called Mao "a social dreamer, living fifty years ahead of his time"; Hanson insisted that "the Chinese Communist leaders are not anti-Christian." The view became acceptable in liberal circles that Mao and his Communist henchmen were just "agrarian reformers" and idealists eager to relieve the burden of poverty from their people. This was, of course, the same view pushed by the liberals about Fidel Castro.

And even now that both these leaders have turned out to be tyrants who do not even grant their people the right to leave their countries, and who execute and imprison "enemies of the people" by the thousands, the liberal praise continues. We are told that you cannot make an omelet without breaking the egg, that violence always accompanies periods of social turmoil in a country. Mao can kill hundreds of thousands, millions, "for the good of mankind" and be viewed by the liberal as a gentle grandfather figure who works for the poor of his country, but if someone like Premier Thieu in South Vietnam, or Franco in Spain, or Ian Smith in Rhodesia jails a Communist revolutionary without a lengthy trial there are protest letters from left-wing "humanists" in the *New York Times* and the *Washington Post*, and indignant, self-righteous speeches by liberal politicians and celebrities on television talk shows. Sir Arnold Lunn used to call it "selective indignation."

When liberal politicians, government officials, and school authorities try to handle left-wing revolutionary groups inside America, the same one-sided permissiveness is seen. Just as the liberals tell us to treat Russia with kid gloves, they suggest that our police and school authorities let left-wing student revolutionaries operate without restriction. Where Mao was just an "agrarian reformer," the Weathermen, the Yippies, the Black Panthers, or any one of dozens of other disruptive campus groups, are just "idealistic" young people forced to turn to anger in protest over society's injustices. We are told that it is idealism which leads the Black Panthers to urge readers of their paper to "kill racist pig cops" or an SDS leader to explain that "we are working to build a guerrilla force in an urban environment. We are actively organizing sedition."

The black and youthful revolutionaries pose a severe problem for the liberal. True, the liberal would admit, you cannot allow people to bomb buildings and ambush the police. Someone might get hurt you know. But the goals of the radical left are so similar to those of the liberals, that the liberal gets a case of schizophrenia. The liberal cannot act with the force of law to suppress the "kids." All the liberal can do is warn the young revolutionaries that they are moving too fast, and that they might invite a right-wing backlash—that the liberal wants what the revolutionaries wants, and that he has a better—slower, but better—way of getting it.

When the left-wing radical blows up a laboratory on a college campus because it is doing research for the military, he is trying to eliminate in a direct way the same "militaristic evils" that the liberal teacher has always been telling him about. "If militarism is as evil as you taught us, professor, then we cannot wait for the future to bring it to an end!" When the black revolutionary shoots a policeman in the back, the liberal is shocked—but he understands why the killing took place. He had been teaching about the racist nature of American institutions for years. He probably has used in his classes the same phrases that the killer will use in his statement to the press. Maybe that is even where the killer first heard those terms—"white suppression," "racist laws," "police brutality."

The radical is just an impatient liberal.

The result? Society becomes defenseless against its avowed enemies. The schools are as good an example as any. Try to imagine what would happen if a group of students in black shirts and swastika armbands began marching around the campus one spring afternoon demanding an Adolf Hitler study club to be moderated by America's leading Nazi theorist, and a separate Storm Trooper Memorial wing of the dormitory. Or what about a group of white-robed students demanding that the local high school set up a branch of the Ku Klux Klan to be headed by the local Kleagle. They would be marched off the school grounds as quickly as possible by as many police as necessary. And they should be. But demonstrating black groups arguing that whites are "racist pigs," naming themselves after admitted black Communist W. E. Dubois, are brought into the principal or dean's office as if they were emissaries from a foreign country, and are given conferences in which their demands are met—separate dormitories, special courses, special teachers. Left-wing demonstrators at college after college across America in the late 1960's met with the same lack of resistance as they quoted Mao and Che Guevara and Marx in pressing their demands. They burned buildings, vandalized deans' offices, and attacked dissenting teachers and students—and ended up being treated as heroic idealists by television newscasts and Hollywood directors.

Policemen sent to control these riots and demonstrations met with the full wrath of the liberals. The force of arms was to be used against "evil doers," the liberal told us, not against the finest of America's young people out there on the streets protesting social injustice. When a policeman used his club to control a riot, or fired his gun after being bombarded with a shower of bricks, he was treated as a bloodthirsty maniac—"fascist pig" was the word used.

THE CRISIS

We are in grave trouble if we cannot free ourselves from the death grip of the liberals. A country cannot last for very long without some noble sense of purpose—*especially when it concedes to the nobleness of its enemies' sense of purpose*. Famed English economist Walter Bagehot put it well: "History is strewn with the wrecks of nations

128

which have gained a little progressiveness at the cost of a great deal of manliness, and have thus prepared themselves for destruction as soon as the movements of the world gave a chance for it." Liberalism has done this to us. It has pictured America's religions as medieval superstitions, our economic system as "exploitation," our patriotic longing as obsolete nationalism—while at the same time applauding the ultimate aims of the Communists. James Burnham calls liberalism the cause of the "suicide of the West." It is not too strong a statement, for the weakness and indecisiveness that liberalism promotes can only lead to disaster. As Whittaker Chambers warned:

> . . . that gentleness which is not prepared to kill or be killed to destroy the evil that assails life, is not gentleness. It is weakness. It is the weakness of the merely well-meaning. It is the suspended goodness of the men of good will whose passivity in the face of evil first of all raises the question of whether they are men.

Unless America can rediscover the ideals upon which our country was founded—liberty, national independence, and especially the commitment to a Christian way of life—we will have no faith to match that of the Communists. We will not be men—not free men anyway.

9

Conservatives Are Not "Racist Pigs"

Why are there so few black conservatives? Are conservatives anti-black? Racists? Race hatred is anti-Christian. Are conservatives anti-Christian?

It is true that liberals have managed to paint a picture very much like that. They have succeeded in picturing as anti-black those who are opposed to the current methods and demands of the civil rights movement in America. They have made it appear as if opposition to these demands is rooted in a hatred for the blacks making the demands, rather than in the conviction that the demands are unsound and unlikely to help either blacks or whites. (Which is very much like arguing that American opposition to Hitler's policies was rooted in anti-German attitudes.) They refuse to accept the argument, in this case anyway, that you can oppose what a man says without hating the man.

So while it is true that conservatives usually oppose busing, excessive welfare payments, easily obtained welfare payments, quotas for blacks and other minorities in schools and jobs, it is not true that

130

conservatism contains any built-in racism. On the contrary, the religious foundations of society so dear to most conservatives provides the only really workable reason for being opposed to racism. The secular liberal tells us to treat our fellow man as a brother, but cannot tell us why. If all religious conviction is a medieval superstition, or just another opinion in our society, why should we love our brother? If all opinions are of equal value, as the liberal insists—relative to the man holding the opinion—then the opinions of those hating blacks must be equal to the opinions of those who encourage brotherhood. If not, why not? Who says? The liberal has no answer. Only the Christian emphasis on the brotherhood of Christ, and the creation of all men in the image of God, can give an effective reason for racial justice.

That does not mean, of course, that there are no racists who call themselves conservatives. They exist. They use conservative rhetoric to cover their hate. But that, in itself, does not invalidate the conservative arguments they use, any more than the fact that a Communist might pose as a liberal invalidates liberalism.

The fact that so few blacks call themselves conservatives is a historical phenomenon, a result of the social forces at work at this time and in this place in history. Since the leaders of various civil rights groups across America have chosen to seek justice for their people through the centralized, big-government social and economic programs most favored by the liberals, opposing those liberal programs can appear to be opposing the black people's struggle. An American black speaking out against welfare cheats or busing, for example, cannot help but get the feeling that he is speaking out against his people. Even if he feels that the programs and the laws are doing more harm than good, it would be difficult to make the break. A not-entirely-unadmirable sense of loyalty holds him back.

In all likelihood, however, this solidity of blacks will not last much longer. There already are signs of it breaking down. The modern black, in fact, has more reason to be "conservative" on many issues than does the typical white. If he is a working man, without the benefit of inherited wealth and influence, the tax burden that accompanies all the liberal schemes hurts him as much as anyone. The lack of law and order makes his neighborhood as victimized by muggers and dope pushers and pimps as any white's—probably more so. The liberal "permissiveness" in the schools makes it impossible for his children to get a sound education—and they will need that education even more than whites. Polls taken among black Americans indicate a far greater conservative leaning on these issues than the press

131

releases of civil rights leaders would indicate. It is not likely that you will find blacks calling themselves "conservatives." That word has been used by the liberals to mean "racist" for too long now. But their voting pattern will be a clue. These days even Governor George Wallace has the support of a substantial majority of the blacks in his state.

DISCRIMINATION

Is all discrimination bad? An understanding of this word is essential to an understanding of why conservatives oppose much of what is demanded under the rubric of "civil rights." In general, conservatives would disagree with the idea that all discrimination is "bad," and subject to correction by law. Now that does sound like a controversial—and anti-black—idea, but only because the word "discrimination" has become so associated in our minds with the Ku Klux Klan and lynchings. But there are hundreds of examples of discrimination in our life that we accept as normal, and good. For example:

You are driving through town looking for a restaurant. You see a Chinese restaurant and an Italian restaurant facing each other across the street. You "hate" tomato sauce and Italian food: you pick the Chinese restaurant.

You are thumbing through the papers looking for a concert of some kind to take your friend from Philadelphia to when she visits next week. Tito Puente and his band of Latin musicians are in one place. The Clancy Brothers, Irish folk singers, are in another. Your friend's name is Finnegan; you choose the Clancy Brothers.

You are riding through the Catskills looking for a good resort hotel for a week's vacation. Your name is Goldberg and you have heard about the famous Borscht Belt, the resorts so popular with East Coast Jews. You drive into one place, near Cairo, and you see twenty men or so on the front lawn playing bocci and shouting "Mama mia!." You leave. You find another place over in East Durham called "Shamrock Inn." You are signing up at the register, while looking nervously over your shoulder at the bagpipers and stiff-armed girls dancing reels. The woman at the desk notices your apprehension, turns the book and sees your name, and whispers to you about how to find "Grossingers." You thank her and leave.

You are looking for a band for the school dance and put an ad in the paper. You get a call from "Pinky Shaw and His RagTime Boys," specialists in fox trots, polkas, and barbershop harmony. You turn him down.

You want your car fixed. There are two mechanics in town. One is always drunk, never finishes on time, and dropped your rotor into the crankcase the last time he worked on your car. The other is a perfectionist. You pick the perfectionist.

In each of these cases there was an act of discrimination based on the nationality, tastes, age, or ability of the person you "discriminated against." In the strictest sense you acted *against* the person, and hurt him financially because of nationality, age or ability.

Common sense and your emotions, however, tell you that there was nothing wrong with these actions. But how do they differ from what Southerners did when they segregated restaurants and swimming pools, or established "white only" country clubs? And what Northerners do when they flee neighborhoods where the black population has become substantial, or remove their children from schools with a large percentage of black students, or hire whites before blacks? It is different—but how?

Other "groups" within America seem to welcome the experience of living and working and playing and having their children go to school with people "like them." There are hundreds of German-American, Irish-American, Italo-American, etc., clubs across the country. In some parts of the country people thinking of buying a home in a certain area ride slowly down the road checking the names on the mailboxes to see "what kind" of people live in the area. Ethnic groups have always searched for neighborhoods with their favorite bars, bakeries and delicatessens—to say nothing of churches and synagogues.

This is the same experience blacks—at least if you listen to their leaders—seem to reject. They resent being told they are not in the "right place." They applauded the Supreme Court decision in 1954 which called separate schools for blacks "inherently unequal"—at least they did at the time. (Now more and more blacks are realizing that that statement is truly racist, an overt slap in the face, implying as it does that only whites can build a successful school system.) They seem to dislike the idea of living in an all-black community, or going to an all-black section of the beach—again, if one were to judge from their leaders' statements. Why the difference?

For one thing, the blacks' demand for access to homes in certain neighborhoods, restaurants and other public facilities, in many ways, is made just to "make a point." The blacks were the only people in America to have had large-scale *legal* restrictions placed on their movement within the country. Discrimination against other groups

133

existed, but almost always on a personal and private level. There were country clubs which would not admit Jews, or factories with "No Irish Need Apply" signs on the wall, or men's clubs which would go out of their way to keep out Italians. As offensive as these restrictions might have appeared to people who were limited by them, they are not comparable to the entire legal structure of a state openly forbidding access to public and private facilities—which is what blacks faced in much of America.

First-class citizenship for blacks depended upon the erasure of these *official* prohibitions. It was a scar that had to be removed. Consequently, blacks demanded the right of access to restaurants they never intended to frequent just to make the point that the wide range of prohibitions against them was illegal and invalid, and something that first-class citizens would not live with in patience.

Another difference is the fact that discrimination against blacks "hurt more" than the discrimination faced by the other minorities in America. Ethnic whites could move freely in society *as a whole* even if certain restaurants or country clubs excluded them. Blacks were not kept out of certain, small restricted areas; they were *restricted to* certain small areas. All of society—every ethnic group imaginable—was set up as an opposite and superior group by segregation laws.

Discrimination, in other words, in order to be a "problem" has to do appreciable damage to the person discriminated against. The polka-playing band was hurt financially when you refused to hire them for your school dance, but they could find work elsewhere, and in places more to their liking. The same was true, in a different way, for the person who was "nudged" into leaving one country club for another.

But, in addition—and this is a most important point—if discrimination is to be attacked by legal authorities, conservatives insist that the discrimination must be irrational, *without good reason*. The drunken mechanic with the slippery fingers might have been a Pakistani, but your refusal to do business with him cannot be interpreted as an anti-Pakistani action. It is an anti-lousy-mechanic action, nothing more.

It is over this question that most of the civil rights controversy of today rages. Is the white who demands that students from a black neighborhood across town not be bused into his children's school displaying race hatred? Is the employer who hires five whites after interviewing six whites and six blacks showing racism? Has a college behaved shamefully if there are only two blacks out of a total student body of two thousand? Is a community racist if it fights to prevent a federal housing project for low-income families being built in its area?

DISCRIMINATION OR COMMON SENSE?

I can remember hearing a discussion on a radio show about five years ago. The late Louis Lomax, a black civil rights activist, was being interviewed on the subject of white racism. Part of the show consisted of telephone calls from listeners. Most of the callers were sympathetic to Lomax's views that white Americans displayed a high degree of anti-black sentiment, in many cases without even knowing it. There were comments about businessmen who will call a sixty-year-old black porter "boy," homeowners who try to squirm out of selling their homes to blacks on the excuse that the black family "won't be happy here," factory workers who make disparaging remarks about the ability of black co-workers; and also about people who are "too polite," who go so far out of their way to be nice to blacks that it can only be interpreted as a patronizing attitude—trying to make the "poor dumb" black feel good by allowing him to feel what it is like to be treated kindly by a "superior" white.

Then, late into the show, there was a phone call from a man who complained that an incomplete picture was being painted; that whites were being pictured as "bad guys" who hated blacks for no good reason. The caller made the point that the crime rates in city areas indicate a much higher percentage of blacks than whites involved in violent crimes. He argued that if blacks were a more law-abiding people they would be accepted more readily by whites.

The heretofore calm discussion ended. Lomax exploded; the show's host started shouting about this "example of what we have been talking about." Finally, Lomax settled down and began to lecture the caller about his racism—about how he was branding all blacks as criminals because of the action of a few, how there were millions of decent, law-abiding black citizens for every criminal. But the caller insisted that he was not bigoted, that he was just talking about "statistics." Finally, Lomax, in despair, offered to show the man how bigoted he was.

"Suppose," said Lomax, "that you were coming home late one night, and that as you stepped into your elevator, two blacks turned a corner and followed you in. Would you be any more frightened of the idea of riding up that elevator with them than with two whites?"

"Damn right!" said the caller.

135

"See, my friend," shot back Lomax, "you are a bigot. You are what is wrong with America. You assume that black men are going to act like criminals. You expect the worst. You don't give a man a chance."

The caller protested. But the host of the show agreed with Lomax that it would not be worth any more discussion. They, apparently, were dealing with a hopeless case.

Were they? Maybe. But not because of anything he said during that brief phone call. For the fact of the matter is that blacks, in a much higher percentage, are involved more often in violent crime than whites. There are many good reasons for that fact. Slum-dwellers all down through American history have been more likely to turn to a life of crime than those fortunate to live in comfortable middle-class neighborhoods. Machine-gun Kelly, Bugsy Siegel, and Lucky Luciano are examples of members of other American ethnic groups succumbing to the lure of crime during the times of their worst poverty.

The caller's fears about entering that elevator were not racist—at least on the surface. They were common sense. Look: if you were on patrol in a Pacific island jungle during World War II and you met an Oriental coming through the bush, you would not be anti-Oriental if you raised your rifle to your shoulder. You would be foolish if you did not. He might not be the enemy. He might be a Chinese soldier parachuted onto the island to help the American war effort. Perhaps. But you still had better get him in your rifle sights. If solid mathematical odds are that the enemy looks a certain way you would be insane not to protect yourself. Only someone who has not experienced the fear of being assaulted in the streets of an American city high-crime area could have the temerity to call that fear racist. (It is amazing what a shot of fear can do to someone's love for his fellow man. I can remember hearing a woman who had always prided herself on her liberal, open-minded concern for the problems blacks in America face because of discrimination and poverty, tell the story of her ride on a New York subway one evening. Four blacks started making obscene remarks, then jostled her a bit with their shoulders. She smiled and stepped down the aisle. They laughed at her. The train stopped and the woman decided she had better get off. As she left, they laughed uproariously at her, and two of the boys who had been drinking orange soda took large mouthsful and spit it over her hair and white cotton coat. That brought forth an even greater wave of laughter from the group as the doors closed and the train pulled away. "If I had a gun I would have shot them," she told me. "Not really," she added. She was an understanding liberal. But I wonder.)

What is the point? Well, simply that as long as crime rates for

136

black youths continue to climb like a rocket, whites have good reason to fear blacks, and to try to organize their lives so as to avoid being faced with threats to their own or their children's safety. Even if blacks have been severely disadvantaged in their early lives, and even if you were to buy the liberal argument that blacks are like houseplants and not to blame for their behavior, it is still very logical and understandable for whites not to want to subject themselves to violence. Why the liberal who always asks us to "understand" the problems of the blacks—the fatherless homes, the poverty, crime-ridden neighborhoods, legacy of slavery, etc.—cannot show any sympathy for this white fear is hard to comprehend. Blacks who resent being identified with the criminals of their race are reacting as they should. Sober, hard-working Irishmen do not like being considered drunks, law-abiding Italians do not like being thought of as people "in with the mob" when they make a little money for themselves in business or the professions, Germans do not like being associated with Hitler and the Nazis. In this world, however, people are going to generalize—especially when they feel that their safety is at stake. If blacks feel comfortable sharing in the undeniable glory of black athletes in America, and are willing to call Duke Ellington's and Count Basie's music "our music," they have to accept the other images associated with their people as well. It is the same process.

But again—what is the point? No one is asking Americans to make subway rides every so often through the ghettoes to give black criminals an equal shot at them. No one is asking people not to avoid groups of young men roaming the city streets at night—black or white. No one wants you to leave your door unlocked at night if you live in black neighborhoods. Correct.

But there is a concerted effort by liberals in America to deny the right to people to find for themselves neighborhoods and schools which will minimize their family's chances of experiencing violence. When people in mostly white neighborhoods protest the building of apartment complexes for low-income families, they are usually treated by newspapers and magazines and news reporters as spiteful anti-black bigots who do not want to give poor families a chance to get out of the slums. When families protest the busing into their schools of children from neighborhoods heavily populated by blacks, they are pictured as cruel, hateful adults who would deny poor black children the opportunity to get ahead in life. The photographers always seem to be able to find some screaming heavy-set woman with her mouth wide open for the evening news.

But it really is not the fear of blacks *as blacks* that motivates this

137

opposition. (Not all of it, anyway. There is racism in America, as much as in any other society. There are whites who hate blacks. Just as Idi Amin, the black dictator of Uganda and his followers, hate and persecute whites and Asians). It is a fear of black neighborhoods and black schools based on a factual knowledge of what those neighborhoods and schools are like. The crime rates are higher; there is more drug addiction, violence, and sex-related crimes. People living in white neighborhoods *know* that. It is not a prejudice, or an irrational fear. It is a common-sense fear.

To ask people to accept a large apartment house complex for low-income blacks simply is to ask them to accept the presence of hundreds of muggers, dope addicts, pimps, and prostitutes on their neighborhood streets. The liberal will protest—"How horrible! You assume that because they are black they will be criminal types. How prejudiced!" Well prejudice means a pre-judgement. In this case the pre-judgment is one which any betting man would "give book on." The facts and figures are there. It cannot be escaped. A high concentration of low-income blacks means a high concentration of crime—whether those blacks are victims of society or not.

Blacks know that. That is why they want to get themselves and their children out of those neighborhoods.

The same can be said of large numbers of blacks bused into an area. Coming from crime-ridden neighborhoods, these children will bring crime and vice with them. It is true that these children can be seen as victims of their environment. You could write moving and saddening stories of how their youthful experiences have scarred their characters, of the gangsters and prostitutes and dope-pushers who have been part of their lives since infancy, of the fatherless homes, of beatings and desertions—a modern version of James T. Farrell's book *Studs Lonigan*, the story of an Irish boy growing up into a punk on Chicago's South side—that is all true. But nevertheless, by the time these children reach the age of twelve or fifteen many of them have become violently anti-social—dope pushers, rapists, murderers themselves. To demand that people who have struggled to escape that kind of environment for themselves and their children, perhaps by working two jobs for years on end, now welcome it is to demand that they inflict not only pain, but degradation upon themselves. It is a demand for a truly unnatural act, and any liberal who lives safely tucked away in an upper-middle-class neighborhood or doorman-guarded inner-city high rise who makes it should be ignored, treated with scorn, or given the biggest horselaugh we can work up, until he subjects himself and his family to the same kind of social conditions.

"Everything is moving too fast. Now <u>they're</u> middle class."

If this world were run "properly," a large percentage of low-income blacks might not be a menace to the rest of society. If lions were given fresh steak five times a day in the jungle, it would be safe to sunbathe in lion country. In this world of ours we have to deal with the realities that surround us. We have to do the good that we can, but we also have an obligation to avoid the evil that we can avoid. It is not enough for a group of urban planners to "mean well," when they set up a low-income housing project in a middle-class neighborhood so as to give the poor an opportunity to enjoy the better surroundings, or for a group of school administrators to mean well when they bus in ghetto youths to middle-class schools with higher academic standards. All over America in city after city, plans like these have resulted in the white city population "fleeing" to the suburbs, and the subsequent growth of city slum areas, and race wars in the racially mixed high schools. The saddest paradox is that the liberal claim that the races would learn to get along "once they got to know each other" has proven completely wrong. All the experts who have studied race relations in America agree now that race hatred is strongest among the lower-class black and whites who do live together and go to school together in the urban areas. They have become opposing armies in many schools, splitting up certain areas, school activities and sports as their "turfs"—and occasionally going to bloody war to defend them. There are high schools now where a white boy with the basketball skills of a Jerry West would not even dream of trying out for the all-black basketball team, and where a black boy with a fastball like Vida Blue's would not think of trying out for the all-white baseball team. High-minded idealism about loving your brother is found, more and more, to exist only in comfortable suburban areas where whites see blacks about as frequently as they see Tahitians, or on television.

"But how will blacks escape those neighborhoods and those crime-ridden schools? What hope can they be offered if they are not allowed into the better schools and better neighborhoods?"

Well on one level you can answer that question by another simple question. If blacks do not feel that it is right for them to have to live or go to school in areas with too many blacks, why should whites have to either? It is an illegitimate goal by any sensible standard to make everyone equal by making everyone equally badly off. And that is the only sure result of all these government-programmed integration schemes. It can hardly be called a step in the right direction to equalize things by making sure every neighborhood has an equal share of violence and drug-addiction.

Blacks will overcome their environment. They are doing it every day. The number of black college graduates, successful businessmen, and members of professions is growing rapidly. They are making these advances in the same way other immigrant groups have advanced in America—by building secure and solid home-lives for their children, by studying hard, working hard, saving money. There is no question that the blacks have more going against them than other groups who climbed up through poverty. The difference in skin color they carry with them is an identifying characteristic that all the education and training in the world cannot erase. It will take the blacks longer to achieve the level of acceptance enjoyed by the descendants of German, Italian, Irish, Polish, and other similar immigrants. But we have to remember that this is one of history's greatest stories— the struggle of the black American ex-slaves for equality with the slave-master society. There are no short cuts to the end of a saga like that. False solutions like busing and quotas only lengthen the journey by diverting attention from the road to success.

The fact that many blacks leaders have turned their backs on busing as an answer and have begun to stress "community control" of their schools in their own neighborhoods is a sign that blacks are becoming aware of that. The road to self-respect and self-sufficiency is one which a man, or a race, must travel alone, in the final analysis. Society can remove many of the obstacles which deny opportunity, but society cannot make the journey for anyone. Blacks who have made a success of their lives know that there is no substitute for hard work and self-discipline. Unfortunately a society can enslave a race, break up families, and destroy their sense of dignity. America is guilty of that. But a society cannot put the broken man together again. Black workingmen, raising strong and virtuous families know that white society is not responsible for their happy homes, and that, if anything, the decadent, permissive liberal society in which we live is making their struggle more difficult.

Of course, it must be remembered that total "acceptance" for blacks—if that means having everybody like you and want to be with you—can never be achieved, not on this earth anyway. That kind of all-encompassing social compatibility is just simply beyond the scope of correction by law. I can remember hearing William Buckley interview the black actor Godfrey Cambridge a few years back. Cambridge told the story of how he took some white friends of his out on his expensive yacht. When they pulled into a docking space to refuel, the attendant assumed that Cambridge was a deck boy working for the white folks on board, and called him "boy" when he asked for the key to the gas tank. It must have been an angering and humiliating experience for Cambridge.

But as Buckley correctly pointed out that kind of "misunderstanding" cannot be corrected by any government program or law. I can remember working as a waiter in a country club where a wealthy Italian owner of a construction company was treating a doctor friend of his and his family to a dinner and an evening cruise on his sailboat. The Italian host was rough hewn, with large and scarred hands and a rough style of talking; the doctor genteel to a fault. A few of the other waiters in the club, who did not know the real "host," assumed the doctor was giving one of his employees, maybe the gardener, a treat of a night on the town.

Blacks will never be accepted as a white group. They will have to find their sense of belonging *as blacks*, and come to enjoy that sense of identity, as do other ethnic groups. A man can only be free when he is proud of what he is. He will never be free if that means pretending to be something else, as if you are ashamed of your own people. The modern black's pride in his Afro heritage, and his talk of being a "soul brother," are social phenomena our society should welcome—recog-

141

nizing at the same time the danger that they can be carried to an extreme. There is a difference between a German-American Social Club and a wing of the Nazi Bund.

WELFARE

Welfare is hardly worth arguing about as a point of great differences of opinion. There isn't anyone of any intelligence, black or white, who does not agree that it is a disgraceful situation at the present time. The "defenders" of welfare are those who think that it is an unbelievable mess, but can't think of any other way to handle the problem. Women with seven or eight illegitimate children receiving as much money as other women out scrubbing halls all night long; welfare mothers demanding finer clothes for their children so that they will look as well-dressed as the kids from homes where the parents support themselves; drug addicts on welfare because their addiction prevents them from working; six-foot-six muscular blacks in floppy hats and purple pants waiting for their checks; people on welfare as a way of life—illegitimate children having more illegitimate children having more illegitimate children, financed by the American taxpayers.

It has made the cities a time bomb. Hundreds of thousands of welfare babies growing to their teens without the guidance of stern and loving fathers—growing into drug addicts and violent muggers. What to do? Some "conservative" answers could better be described as radical: forced sterilization of welfare mothers for example. Ordinarily that would be a grant of power to the government that conservatives would not even consider. But this issue drives people to extremes. Christian conservatives are rightly repelled by the idea of the government interfering with the right of human beings to have children. But what then?

Clearly there has to be some way for society to provide for people in need—keeping them healthy, warm, and clothed—without making it so attractive that the welfare recipients prefer to accept the handout rather than go to work.

Henry Hazlitt has recommended that welfare recipients be denied the vote until they get back to work. His logic is that a person who is not contributing to society should not have a say in determining public policy—especially the right to cast votes for those politicians who seek their votes by promising higher payments. William Buckley has suggested that surplus food such as soybeans (healthy, but not to a gourmet's standards and inexpensive for the taxpayers to provide) be used to feed welfare recipients. The food would be chosen by government nutritionists to keep people healthy, but would be dull enough for people to get the point that life would be better if they were back at work.

There is, obviously, much room for creative conservative thinking here. Some way must be found for us to help those truly in need, without encouraging those who can work to sit back and wait for the welfare payment—and while never forgetting that the biggest help we can give to a man is the determination to help himself.

QUOTAS

The latest liberal attempt at putting together a government "program" to bring racial justice is the so-called quota system in schools and employment. The argument for quotas runs something like this: since blacks and other minorities in our country have been discriminated against by schools and businesses for so long now, the only way to insure that some significant remedial steps will be taken is for the government to insist that schools and employers include a percentage of blacks comparable to the percentage in the population as a whole. (Similar quotas are being demanded by women's lib groups.) A school, then, or a business, with few blacks must go out and "recruit" blacks to get the quota up to where it "should be."

Problems develop over the question of quality, as you would guess. If the employer is a company which runs ice cream stands along the boardwalk at resort areas, there should be no great difficulty in getting their quota of countermen—if they can get enough blacks willing to do the job. Or if it is a school for hairdressers with room for an unlimited number of students.

But what if it is an engineering company working on precision instruments? Or a school of engineering with a curriculum designed to graduate engineers capable of working on precision instruments? What if aptitude testing indicates that the fifty highest-scoring applicants for the fifty openings are all white? What if the engineering school wants to pick the three hundred applicants with the three hundred highest scores on the College Board examinations, and they are all white?

As hard to believe as it sounds on first hearing, the federal government, through the Department of Labor and the Department of Health, Education, and Welfare, has issued guidelines, and sends out

143

investigators, demanding that quotas be met regardless of scores on tests. Blacks and other minorities are to be given "preferential treatment." Some people have called these "Crow Jim" laws, a play on words on the old "Jim Crow" segregation laws in the South.

The result of these quotas will be felt mostly by young people. High school students looking for places in the more prestigious American colleges will find black students with lower grades and entrance test scores being admitted before them. High school graduates and college graduates will find blacks being hired before them even though superior training would seem to give them the edge.

Not only conservatives have voiced opposition to this practice. Many liberals have argued for years for equality of opportunity and advancement on the basis of training and merit. They have long opposed the idea of preferential treatment when it was done by white groups in positions of influence and power. Now that blacks are getting the preference many feel divided loyalties. It seems an unacceptable threat to those liberals who have assumed for so long that a good education was the key to success in America. For them, it was acceptable to demand that the trade unions admit blacks over more-qualified whites, but now that blacks are being admitted before their children in medical school and law school, something seems unfair.

Those who favor the quotas argue that minorities have to be helped to overcome the disadvantages they faced in their youths—poor family life, schools, and neighborhoods. They argue that someone from a ghetto environment cannot help but score much lower on a standardized test in comparison to a white from a white middle-class home, and that the quota just gives the minority youth another chance.

Probably the best argument against quotas is the one which stresses the damage they do to the minority youths they are supposed to help. Think of the implications. If blacks without the proper qualifications are going to be admitted to schools of professional training, for example, and helped through school with "gift" grades, then the only way for anyone to be sure that he is hiring a qualified dentist, doctor, lawyer, or engineer will be to employ a white. All blacks who earn legitimate grades and earn their degrees by meeting the same standards as whites will have doubt cast on their abilities. They too will be seen as the "quota people."

In addition, the quality of goods and services in the country as a whole will deteriorate. Our phones will be "fixed" by people who do not know what they are doing, manufactured products will get inspected by people who are inspectors because of their color instead of their abilities, school classes will be taught by people who do not have the skills of the profession. The society as a whole will be forced to pay the price of poorer goods at higher prices. And all because of the assumption that blacks will not be able to make a place for themselves in America in the same way as other groups. It is a slap at the dignity of blacks and a threat to the career aspirations of young whites —paid for by the American people.

Instead of striving for excellence our country will be pushing mediocrity. (And that is only an anti-black statement if you assume blacks cannot make it on their own, and are by definition mediocre.)

It would not be surprising if the greatest opposition to these quotas will come eventually from the blacks and other minorities.

The blacks in America have faced severe hardships—there is no doubt about that. But there are other things we must consider in trying to do them justice—the health of our local communities, the safety of our people, and the entire social and economic structure of the country. What a shame it would be for the black to achieve total integration in a country not worthy of his presence, a country about to collapse at least partially because of the unnatural demands placed upon it in the name of integration.

10

The New Left Does Not Have all the Answers

Revisionism is as old as history itself. With the passing of time and the discovery of new information, historians have always tried to clarify and correct the explanations, when necessary, of past events. In times as distant from us as ancient Greece, Thucydides was revising some of the fanciful exaggerations and one-sided interpretations of great battles recorded by the earlier historian, Herodotus. There are at least six different, widely accepted theories for the fall of Rome. Historians to this day argue whether the French Revolution was a glorious milestone in man's search for freedom or a bloodthirsty disgrace.

Revisionist interpretations reflect both the historical and social forces at work at the time they were written and the political, psychological, and religious attitudes of the historian doing the reinterpreting. A French historian's coverage of the Franco-Prussian war is likely to be different from a Prussian's; a Catholic's coverage of the career of Martin Luther different from a Protestant's; a retired military man's view of the Battle of the Bulge different from a pacifist university teacher's.

In American history there have been many waves of revisionism. The Civil War is a good example. Immediately after the war there was the usual one-sided victor's interpretation, a spate of books picturing the Southerners pretty much the way Harriet Beecher Stowe did in her famous *Uncle Tom's Cabin*—as cruel, heartless, fiends who treated the black slaves worse than they did their dogs. Near the end of the nineteenth century and in the early years of the twentieth, a tone of reconciliation became evident as Americans sensed a need to pull together for the good of the growing and prosperous American nation. The feeling seemed to be that we could not afford to be divided against ourselves in the modern world of advanced communication and weaponry. The history books of that period stressed the evils of Reconstruction and the cruel carpetbaggers and scallawags who came South after the war to take advantage of the beaten Confederates, more than any of the evils of the slave-holding South. *Gone With the Wind*, the phenomenally successful book and movie, although fiction, is a reflection of this revisionism of the first third of the twentieth century. Then, the war against the Nazis generated a new wave of Civil War revisionism. In the late 1940's and 50's, historians convinced of the nobility of America's war against the Nazis looked back on the Civil War as an earlier American military campaign against racism. The North became the hero again.

The revisionists getting the most attention at present in America are called "New Left revisionists." New Left? Old Left? Right? These terms are difficult to define in a precise way. They originated in the days of the French Revolution, when the radical supporters of an all-out war against the entire social and political order in France sat on the left side in the National Assembly, while those in favor of working, perhaps even with the king, in pursuit of more moderate reforms sat on the right. The "left wing" won in France in those years as Robespierre and his Jacobin supporters launched the Reign of Terror, a dictatorship pledged to the goal of executing on the guillotine all the supporters of the king and the old order in France. Charles Dickens' *A Tale of Two Cities* paints an unforgettable picture of life in France in those bloody days of revolutionary excess. It was a short-run victory for the left, though, since by 1800 Napoleon Bonaparte had come to power to restore order as a military dictator. Eventually he declared himself Emperor.

Since then, "left" or "left-wing" has been used sloppily. It seems at times to mean nothing more than "those in favor of change." For example, Communist student groups in America will be called "leftist" by newspapers which call supporters of Communists in Russia "right wing." But generally, when the term "left" has been used in America over the last fifty years or so, it implies someone with a pro-socialist or pro-Marxist, if not pro-Communist, point of view.

The "new" left then are those Americans who have decided that the American Marxists are old hat—not radical enough. They are usually young academics and intellectuals, and would-be intellectuals (they might never have read a book but consider themselves intellectuals because they have the "enlightened" attitude on things) who feel that the older Marxists, even the Communist party, have become too much like old fuddy-duddies and compromisers and not interested enough in all-out revolutionary change. They usually are attracted more to the Communism taught by Chairman Mao Tse-tung in China than in what is going on in Russia.

Unquestionably, the Vietnam war was the seedbed of these New Leftists. They were often members or leaders of the mobs which roamed American colleges during the 1960's, protesting our Southeast Asian war effort. It would not be an exaggeration to say that they came to view America as the "bad guy" in that conflict. One of their favorite demonstration-cheers was "Ho! Ho! Ho Chi Minh! The NLF is gonna win!"

They ended up in some cases describing America as a "fascist" state, ruled by "new mandarins" of power (Noam Chomsky's term—one of the most quoted New Left historians); and picturing our military campaign as an attempt to prevent the people of South Vietnam from running their own country, because that might prevent American capitalist domination of the economy there.

From here, the more scholarly new leftists took a look back at the rest of our history, and rediscovered some of the old Marxist analyses, such as those by Herbert Aptheker. If America was the villain in Vietnam maybe it was not just an exception to an otherwise admirable national record. And, of course, the New Left "discovered" just that, that American capitalism has built into its operation the need for America to be "imperialist"—to seek to dominate other countries around the world. Socialism, in one form or another, became their recommended answer for our future.

Who exactly are the New Left revisionist historians? Some of the more famous names are William Appleman Williams, Noam Chomsky, Gabriel Kolko, D. F. Fleming, Robert Van Alystne, Staughton Lynd, Barrington Moore, David Horowitz. You might not have heard of any of them. If that is the case, it will soon be changed if you go to college. I have been told by a New Left professor who is aware of campus trends that 90% of all college history teachers have come to accept the New Left interpretation of American-Russian relationships in the last twenty years—which is that America, not Russia, was the aggressor and initiator of the Cold War. Perhaps he was overestimating in a fit of wishful thinking, but he was right to the extent that New Left thinking is becoming a most influential voice in college and high school history departments all over the country. New textbooks and films made for school use reflect their views with remarkable regularity. Young secondary school teachers seem to have studied nothing but the New Left point of view and seem genuinely surprised that there is still some disagreement over the issue. School programs in American history seem to have become nothing more than a primer on the evils of America.

William Appleman Williams just might be the best source for an understanding of what the New Left is all about. Williams is definitely of the New Left, but his scholarly and research techniques are thorough and well developed. He seems less interested in attacking America than in genuine scholarship. (Although there was a great controversy about his work early in 1974. Professor Robert James Maddox did a study of New Left writings, including Williams', and discovered numerous and deliberate misinterpretations, even altered quotations. And in fact, Williams admitted to Maddox's charges, but insisted that he only changed quotes to "make sense" of them for his readers and accused Maddox of being too "literal minded." Maddox's evidence, however, certainly does give credence to the charge levelled against the New Left that they deliberately "use" history by misinterpreting it to make America look bad. Serious students of these issues owe it to themselves to read Maddox's book— *The New Left and the Origins of the Cold War.* Anti-leftists should demand that it be placed on library shelves—especially school library shelves—to give some balance to the downpour of New Left books inundating us at the present time.)

Even if Williams is wrong overall, he deserves a serious hearing. His analysis of America's behavior in history poses a real challenge to those who have traditionally viewed America's past with pride and admiration. The anti-capitalist, pro-socialist sympathies so evident among today's college students has been developed largely as a result of Williams' work. Not that many have actually read Williams themselves. But they are surrounded by a Williams atmosphere on the campus. Their professors have studied Williams and the other New Leftists. So have the brighter and more dedicated leftist students. At

149

student lounges, coffee shops, beerhalls, and pot parties, whenever the discussion gets serious anyway, the Williams analysis, perhaps in a grossly simplified version, comes to center stage—which is more damaging since all that means is that America gets sledge-hammered, instead of pin-pricked, to death. Without an understanding of Williams' work, it is difficult to understand why so many apparently normal young people seem to have actually learned to dislike and be ashamed of the American national experience.

His basic claim? It could be said that it is fundamentally an exten-sion and a pressing, through the advantages of modern research thoroughness, of a kind of combination Charles Beard-Frederick Jackson Turner reading of American history.

Charles Beard became famous for his *Economic History of the United States*. In that book and many others Beard attempted to show that the American past can be explained more by the actions of selfish politicians and greedy businessmen seeking personal profit than by the striving of courageous and idealistic statesmen for justice and high-minded democratic principles. According to Beard, the Constitution was designed by wealthy landowners and lawyers as a way of keeping the poorer classes in place, rather than as a way of building a nation dedicated to the well-being of its citizens. Wars were fought so that wealthy businessmen in cahoots with the politicians could get control of foreign markets. The slaves were freed so that Northern industrialists rather than Southern plantation owners could get control of the developing American West. Reformers in industry and commerce were motivated more by the desire to protect the wealthy employers rather than the average man. In Beard's world all the words of men like Washington, Jefferson, Jackson, and Lincoln about justice, freedom, and equality before the law, were just a smokescreen behind which the powerful and the wealthy could line their pockets.

It has been said that this analysis tells us more about Beard than about American statesmen of the past, and there is much truth to that idea. Either Beard imagined himself to be the only person in American history capable of acting for the purpose of defending truth and justice (in which case we have to suspect his mental balance) or he was writing his books for the same reason as all the Americans he writes about, just to line his pockets (in which case we have to be suspicious of what he wrote).

Frederick Jackson Turner should not be considered a leftist. He probably would be surprised to see how his work is being used by the New

Left. Turner was most famous for his so-called "frontier thesis." For Turner, the American frontier, waiting to be explored and settled, was the most important factor in the development of American history. It provided what he thought was a healthy "safety valve." The waves of immigrants pushing in on the East Coast had a land of opportunity in the truest sense of the word. Instead of clustering together in the American cities and becoming a sullen mob of poor and unemployed and potentially revolutionary illiterates—Marx's proletariat— they took Horace Greely's famous advice "Go west, young man, go west" and became solid citizens, land owners, businessmen. America, unlike Europe, as a result, was not forced to face up to great working class revolutionary movements and to organize massive government programs of social reform in response. In America, anyone willing to work could find it and the chance for success in the massive, open, nineteenth-century American continent.

Williams carries Beard's and Turner's thesis another step to the left:

> Men had talked specifically about what they called the safety valve provided by the Western lands very early in the eighteenth century, and the discussion was revived during the depression of the 1870's. As a result the famous frontier thesis began to be formulated at the grass roots level by various agricultural spokesmen almost twenty years before it was stated by such intellectuals as Turner and Brooks Adams. Implicitly, if not overtly, that explanation of democracy and prosperity pointed toward the necessity of finding a new frontier.

I will try to put it simply. Picture America as a big blueberry or apple pie. In the early nineteenth century just a small slice of the pie had been taken—the eastern seaboard. But the population is growing. Immigrants are pouring in through the Golden Door. Sooner or later that little sliver of pie would have too many hands making a grab for it. The waves of immigrants were not going to starve to death in shanty houses in the slums while a wealthy few held all the money and property. Two choices develop. Either take the wealth from the few and split it up among the many in an early version of socialism. Or expand and find new territory where the growing population could secure land, wealth, and opportunity for themselves. Of course with the open frontier waiting to be taken there was not much brooding about the choice. The West was opened, the railroads were built, the cavalry moved in to take care of the more troublesome Indians who got in the way. For Williams, this was our first deliberate decision to turn to imperialism.

151

The American free-enterprise outlook developed. Unless a man could enter freely into the competition to get a piece of the economic pie for himself he could not be a freeman, with private property of his own. But what happens when you get down to the last slice? Well, then take a little from everybody's plate and give it to the new-comers. Or get a new pie. Williams' point is that it became American public policy, unofficially anyway, to always get a new pie—Arkansas, Texas, Missouri, Nevada, Utah, California.

And when the American frontier ran out? The Philippines, Hawaii, Cuba, Panama. Imperialist America.

Running through Williams' writings, especially *The Contours of American History* and *The Roots of the Modern American Empire* are examples of and quotes from government and business leaders making this case. New markets, new economic frontiers had to be found as the only alternative to a radicalization of the poor, calling for a wealth redistribution, socialism. The poor would only be willing to live with the very rich in their midst if they and their children had a chance to get rich through Indian land, Asian trade or South American mines.

When Williams examines our history in a grand sweep he becomes quite convincing (Professor Maddox's findings notwithstanding). Why did the Indians have to be moved westward and placed on reservations? Why the Louisiana purchase? The Texan annexation? The Mexican War? The annexation of Hawaii? Panama? Why our fear of Communism? Why our war in Vietnam?

Each of these events, when taken and viewed as a separate entity, can be discussed in terms other than those suggested by Williams. Self-defense, benevolent concern for oppressed native populations, fear of imperialistic monarchies or aggressive dictators, making the world safe for democracy, the Four Freedoms, the domino theory, are just some of the explanations that come to mind. Williams insists, in contrast, that a clear "contour" is evident. The "marketplace" mentality demanded that opportunities for the creation of new wealth be ever present, whether west of the Mississippi, Hawaii, Imperial China, or Southeast Asia. Unless these new sources of wealth could be tapped, America would have to face up to the radical alternative—a redistribution of wealth at home, socialism.

America's great twentieth-century military crusades against total-itariansim—Wilhelm II's Reich, Nazism, Japanese militarism, Russian and Chinese Communism—Williams argues, can also be seen in this light. Because the totalitarian, managed economy in strong and centralized governments like these would not cooperate fully with American-style capitalism, these systems threatened to cut off American investments and markets, and close the frontier. The marketplace value of our products could be undercut by state-owned or controlled industries. The Russian Communists, or German Nazis, could make the sale of, say, American shoes illegal in their country or subsidize their own shoe industry so that American manufacturers operating on a profit margin could not compete profitably. They might even outlaw American trade altogether. American business genius would not be able to dominate the market in totalitarian countries, and would be unable to open up the profit-making potential. No new wealth—no new pie. What, then, would America do to satisfy the demands of the ever-growing population? Williams argues that since we were unwilling to turn socialist and split up the wealth within our borders we decided to go to war, to use the American military machine to protect the interests of an American capitalist elite. Kaiser Wilhelm's Germany was fought not to make the world safe for democracy, but to protect English-American control of world trade routes; Nazism and Fascism were bombed into a total collapse to guarantee American capitalist investments, not for the Four Freedoms Franklin Delano Roosevelt told Americans about; Russia was treated as an enemy after World War II to stop her from spreading her system of socialism throughout Europe and Asia, thereby destroying the interlocking capitalist ventures American business had in mind for the world, not because we cared a dog biscuit's worth about the East European nations the Russian dictators were putting within their Communist orbit; South Vietnam was "defended" to stop North Vietnamese Communists from ending our investment potential in the oil and manganese of Southeast Asia.

You can see why some college students refused to serve in Vietnam after taking a couple of history courses. Some of them might have been cowards, but most simply believed that they were acting nobly, that there was no reason for them to fight, kill and maybe die to protect the fat-cat businessmen's interests that their history teachers told them all about. They became unable to find anything noble in anti-Communism since they accepted what they were taught, that America started all the trouble with Russia and China just to serve the Almighty Dollar. They came to agree with Walter LaFeber, another New Leftist: "Stalin's thrusts after 1944 were rooted more in the Soviets' desire to secure certain strategic bases, raw materials, and above all to break up what Stalin considered to be

153

the growing Western encirclement of Russia." And with I. F. Stone, one of the grand old men of the American left, who argued that the Cold War was started by President Harry Truman in order to get through his political program, the Fair Deal, at home: "The Fair Deal, like the New Deal, was denounced as 'communistic.' How better disprove the charge than by active hostility to Moscow? On the other hand, how fight off the Red-scare bogey at home, if one was also open to attack for making an agreement with Moscow?"

Is the New Left right? Should we agree with Williams that "in Eugene Debs, America produced a man who understood that expansion was a running away, the kind of escape that was destructive of the dignity of man . . . [who] believed and committed his life to the proposition that Americans would one day prove mature and courageous enough to give it up as a child's game, that they would one day 'put away childish things' and undertake the creation of a socialist commonwealth."

What of their conclusion that we were the aggressors in our dealings with Russia after World War II? Did America start the Cold War? Was Russia just a frolicsome giant under Uncle Joe Stalin, forced to turn to anger by American capitalist, imperialist ambitions? Well, we have already discussed the open Communist admission that they desire world domination in an earlier chapter. It should be sufficient here to say that if the Russians did not intend to dominate Europe after World War II they were going against every public pronouncement they have ever made as leaders of the world Communist movement at every one of the World Party Congresses ever held in Moscow. If they are not intent upon spreading their revolution, it does not seem unreasonable, at the very least, that we Americans should insist that they stop saying that they want to, and stop supplying and training Communist groups, like the Viet Cong, who are working for a Communist takeover in their countries—and that if they do not, that we should go on supplying and arming groups fighting this Communist expansion. Remember that after all is said and done, after you list every American "atrocity" that you can come up with, that it is the Communist countries that build Berlin walls, and put barbed wire along their borders to imprison their people, not us.

But what of the historical analysis he makes? Did not much of what Williams insists took place, take place? Does he not make the kind of analysis of wars and the need for military action short of war, that statesmen, scholars, and informed citizens make among themselves, but hesitate to make in public statements where high-sounding rhetoric and noble slogans seem to be the accepted mode of speech. It is not true that there was more to the Spanish-American war than rescuing the Cubans from the tyranny of the Spanish, more to World War I than rescuing the gentle Belgians and French from the "rape of the Hun," and more to the Vietnam war than sending our young men to die in order to save the purity of the electoral process in Southeast Asia?

Certainly. There is a difference between a slogan and a geo-political analysis of why a country must go to war. Slogans serve a purpose, as do war songs and posters. Many uneducated people (and many people were uneducated when these slogans were used in our country) need a simplified explanation for why they are being asked to take up arms. And so do young children whose fathers are being sent to battle. Slogans, songs, and war movies are made to fill this need.

The great modern irony is that educated young people who seem so proud that they are able to see through our simplistic war slogans fail to also recognize the slogan for what it is or was—just a slogan. It is as if a nineteen-year-old insisted on going around shouting at the top of his voice that there is no Santa Claus. The New Leftists are creating and exploiting this curious paradox. Working with young students, they have no difficulty in pointing out the inconsistencies and short-comings of the slogans. They show their students that we could not have been fighting in Vietnam to stop the spread of dictatorship and the loss of freedom since we are on friendly terms with many dicta-torships in the world—Spain, Haiti, South Korea, for example. They show their students, too, how South Vietnamese authorities deny many freedoms Americans see as natural rights, and that we, there-fore, could not have been defending democracy in South Vietnam. And the naive students sit back like sponges—which might be under-standable in a situation where a teenager is faced by a PhD—and shake their heads and say sadly: "Yes, yes, America does not always behave the way the John Wayne movies would have us believe. Our only goal is not making the world safe for democracy. America must be the villain in the world."

The New Left deserves harsh criticism for the way that they are playing with young minds. Perhaps justice will come when some of their ex-students look back and realize how they were used as can-non fodder in anti-war demonstrations by professors who never left their faculty lounges; how they were taught to see through slogans without being told as well that there are reasons for our military his-tory that can be understood by anyone bright enough to see through a slogan, and that these reasons were never kept secret by the slogan makers.

155

The complex, intricately intertwined reasons for using military force—the need for markets, buffer zones, free sea routes, military outposts, naval stations, raw materials, balance of power—have always been openly discussed in America in books and military analyses. Serious students of politics, geography, and military needs have written as many articles and reports and position papers as anyone. It is just that you do not find them in war songs designed for the teeny boppers of the time—or on the book lists of New Left teachers. The full fraud of the New Left lies in this pretense of their's that Americans were called to war with nothing other than the explanation of an Uncle Sam poster designed by a sinister cabal of capitalists. And that just is not true.

What Williams and other leftists call American "imperialism" is nothing more than an assertive and determined foreign policy in defense of our military and economic needs. Countries since the beginning of time have acted to insure these interests. If they did not they did not survive as a free people. They were conquered or reduced to abject poverty by the more bold countries around them. Thumbing through any world history book, chapter after chapter, this process can be seen taking place—Rome rising and falling, Charlemagne, Louis XIV, Napoleon, Germany, U.S. A country which does not enter into this world arena does nothing more noble than make life easier for neighboring countries who do.

Can anyone seriously believe that if the U.S. had not pushed across the Mississippi that the Apache would still hold Arizona? All that would have done would have been to encourage Spanish expansion up through Mexico. Or that if we were not an active world military power that Europe would not be under Russian domination? Much of Europe is under their sway even through we are active and strong. Or that China would not control all of Asia up to and maybe even including Australia?

And yes, it does follow, that America would probably interfere a great deal in Russia if it were not for their military might.

That is the way the world turns. Countries have a tendency to push their own standards of justice and righteousness on as much of the world as they have the power to control. And it is true that economic self-interest motivates much of this expansionist thrust. It may be an unattractive side of man's nature, but the fact remains that if America does not defend its interests energetically, we will, in short order, be swept aside by other countries seeking economic and military security for their people.

For their people? Yes. It cannot be denied. It is no accident that a country's standard of living always seems to rise and fall in direct relationship to its military strength. Perhaps certain citizens profit more from their country's military capabilities, but their fortunes are the other side of the coin which brings the workingman a home in the suburbs and two cars. The oil crisis of the winter of 1974 is a good example. Certainly American oil companies had more to gain from continued access to Arab oil than the average American motorist, but if you asked any one of the men and women waiting in line for gasoline if the Arabs were hurting the average American there is no doubt that their answer would be a resounding "yes." We all share in America's economic and military success and failure, just some more than others. But a man with a $30,000 home would not feel any less conquered than a man with a $300,000 estate if a foreign army were to march down our streets.

It just might be true that certain of our wars were not worth it: that, for example, Communist expansion into Vietnam would not have hurt us enough militarily or economically to warrant the lives lost there. Maybe. But the danger is that the New Left mentality will weaken our will to take up arms in defense of other, more important, interests by picturing all of our military actions, by the very nature of our capitalist economy, as mere defenses of corporations and their owners—And all that would do is make it easier for the Russians and the Chinese to move into the resulting power vacuum—which would be an attractive proposition only for a Communist or a traitor of some other sort.

Without access to foreign trade America could survive, but as a much poorer nation. The food we eat, the clothes we wear, our cars, and homes all depend upon access to the world's raw materials. If we were unable to buy oil, coal, rubber, copper, etc., from the rest of the world, it would make life less pleasant for us (which might be desirable if the poorer nations of the world would be helped demonstrably in the process. But that is hardly the case. The poorer countries would just lose their best customer—or have to sell to the Russians instead. And who but the Russians would profit from that? Do the Russians give green stamps?)

SOCIALISM AS MAGIC

The New Left's claim that if we had turned socialist in our past, we would not have had to turn "imperialist" is equally suspect. Once again let us remember the pie analogy. Socialists, instead of seeking a new pie—new markets, a new frontier—would take the existent pie and redistribute it, give everyone a smaller slice, take from the rich and give to the poor. That is, as we know, what socialists do. They declare all property to be public property, which can be redistributed by the state along lines it thinks best for the common good.

It should be noted that at this point the New Left historians stop being historians and become out and out political propagandists. There is no historically accepted way of demonstrating what America's behavior *would have been* if we had turned socialist any more than there is of demonstrating what *would have* happened if Babe Ruth had not liked good liquor so much. It is pure speculation, an educated guess at best. "For of all sad words of tongue or pen, The saddest are these: 'It might have been'"—to quote John Greenleaf Whittier.

If you grant that no one can tell accurately how history would have turned out if some event or other had been changed, then you have to marvel at the New Left's air of certainty on this issue. If we had turned socialist, they tell us, we would have taken the Rockefellers' and the Duponts' money and given it to the poor instead of opening up Asian trade or Middle East oil wells. We would have learned to live with the wealth within our borders, and split it up fairly. We would have learned to live like socialists.

Like who? Like socialists! Talk about a snow job.

Think about the history of the last fifty years. Name the most aggressive countries that you can think of, the countries most determined to dominate other areas of the globe, the countries most determined to build war machines capable of maintaining a dominant world power position. Nazi Germany and Soviet Russia, right? No contest. Who else? What other countries have tried to openly dominate other weaker and smaller nations. And what do these two European superpowers have in common? Socialism. Nazism—the National *Socialist* Workers Party. Soviet Russia—Union of Soviet *Socialist* Republics. Now certainly Nazi Germany is not the New Left's idea of a healthy socialist society, but the Nazi dictatorship did feature the kind of state control over private industry that the New Left tells us makes imperialist conquests unlikely.

The New Left claims that socialism leads to less aggression and conquests. But the record reads otherwise. The Russians now, and the Germans before World War II, far outdid the capitalist powers in trying to dominate world sea routes, Ukrainian wheat, Middle East oil, and so on. Not that capitalists were not interested in those kinds

158

of things. Great Britain at the height of her power controlled almost one-third of the earth's surface. But defenders of capitalism do not make the claim that their system somehow makes imperialism and war unlikely. It is the New Left that makes that claim for socialism. And, the point is that the record proves them wrong. The Greeks and Romans were not capitalists, neither was Genghis Khan or Napoleon Bonaparte. Countries with widely varying economic orders have expanded their spheres of influence and control all down through history. Certainly when a capitalist country expands, those who control the seats of power in the economy show the greatest increase in prosperity from the increased and profitable trade which results—just as leading Communists ride the nicer cars and wear the better clothes which come from Russia's increased prosperity, and Attila the Hun's chieftains got the most loot and the best women after one of his raids. The economic system will determine to a very large extent how and where a country reaches out beyond its borders—but not whether or not it will. Confident, healthy and growing countries accept the responsibilities that fall upon them as major powers—especially the responsibility to defend their interests against rivals. If that is imperialism it has been practiced by strong and free countries since antiquity. Only crumbling and dying nations retract from that arena. And only those interested in encouraging a national decline would want their own country to pull back into a shell by abdicating that role.

America can be criticized for the way in which we have treated other smaller countries around the world. Trading and opening plants and mills and mines in other countries does not give American corporations the right to pay slave wages, or to drain the natural resources of a country, or to dominate the governments of the countries where we do business. (Although we do have a right to protect our investments.) That is not up for question. There have been cases where American corporations have overstepped the line, and where they are deserving of severe criticism. Again, being conservative does not mean defending everything done by American business. What the New Left suggests, however, is that the very process of opening up trade, mills, mines, and plantations, is somehow sinister, and an example of an American wish to dominate the world.

How exactly would the world be better if Americans had not invested heavily in the past in things like Bolivian mines or Venezuelan oil? Well, for one thing, there would probably be no mines or oil wells in these places. Unless the Russians went in there and built them instead. It is no slur on the Bolivians or the Venezuelans to say that. History moves in strange, ineluctable ways. Some countries are better than some others at certain things at certain times. Englishmen were living in caves when the Egyptians and the South American Mayas were building majestic pyramids and temples and exploring astronomical charts. That does not make the English an inferior race. A twentieth-century fact of life is that modern science and technology has been an almost exclusively European and North American development. The Bolivians or the Venezuelans just were not going to develop industrial skills on their own. The minerals would have sat underground, doing no one any good, if it had not been for the American involvement.

You can argue that American industries should have paid higher wages (although they were higher than what were being received before the Americans came south.)

Should American corporations be allowed to control forever the mines or whatever, that they have developed in foreign countries? Even the leaders of American corporations have come to agree that there does come a time when a country has a right to demand that foreign control of its natural resources must end. It is an inevitable development. Americans would become resentful if some foreign country owned all the oil in Texas and was selling it at a high price, and then using the profit for the good of its citizens back home. All that American businesses have come to demand is a fair price for the mills or mines when the country in which they are located takes them over—nationalizes them. Of course there is always squabbling over the price. And American businesses, rightly, do oppose Communist groups which plan to take over their property in outright confiscation without pay.

When you look back at the whole history of American business expansion without any ideological axe to grind, it simply does not display any inordinate degree of greed or desire to dominate others. Ask the Hungarians or the Czechs if they would rather have IBM controlling the computer market in their country rather than the gentle ministrations of the Russian Communists.

11

You Don't Have To Be a "Gun Nut" to Oppose Gun Control Laws

At first glance the question of gun control does not seem to be one which can be discussed in conservative vs. liberal terms. Many tough, law-and-order-type police chiefs and federal law enforcement officials, for example, have been very vocal in their support of strong gun control laws. (The National Police Officers of America, on the other hand, has joined with the National Shooting Sports Foundation in a joint resolution in favor of the continued American right to bear arms.) And, undoubtedly, many of the hundreds of thousands of American hunters most opposed to gun control would not be willing to call themselves conservative.

But there is a strange and deep emotional undercurrent to the debate over gun control, sometimes difficult to locate, but unmistakably there. And in its swirling waters can be found perhaps as good an indication of how the modern liberal mind works as any. It remains beneath the surface when the debate centers on whether or not to have this or that kind of gun outlawed, or this or that kind of registration filled out by every hunter in the country. These issues are usually

161

debated rationally and in scientific terms, with charts and studies and diagrams to measure the cost and effectiveness of the proposed version of gun control. The real struggle, in contrast, goes on far deeper than these charts and facts and figures—all the way down to that undercurrent. For in a very real sense, the facts mean near-to-nothing to those in favor of strong gun control laws. They do not want gun control. They want gun confiscation. They do not want guns out of the hands of criminals; they want guns out of the hands of hunters. Let me be blunt: They do not like hunters.

Why? Well, I suggest that hunters are a symbol to them of a breed of American man who stands in the way of the creation of the kind of Godless, internationalist, big-government, pseudo-sophisticated, and computer-managed world they want. To the liberal, the hunter is the patriot, the independent-thinking, American family man; he is a symbol of our traditional ways—and he is armed. For the big-city "intellectual" liberal, who sees his way of life and his values as the American ethic of the future, who sits around his faculty lounges and student centers deriding patriotism, calling for defense budget cuts and American disarmament, diminished religious influence, big-government control of education, gay rights, open pornography, and the end of the family, the knowledge that there are strong and healthy American men, loyal to the ways of their fathers and the rhythms of nature, apparently beyond the reach of all the trendy liberal opinion-makers and their magazines, roaming the nation's countryside, using and refining their skills with firearms, is a nightmare. They know, perhaps only subconsciously, that their brave new world can only be created once American boys have stopped looking to the rigorous, loyal, brave and pious male image of a Daniel Boone and a Davy Crockett, and have turned instead to that of a peace protestor or a gaudy rock musician. How else do you explain the cruel and distorted image of the hunter as a gross, bloodthirsty, beer-swilling slob which the liberals push so enthusiastically in movies like *Bless the Beasts and the Children*, Stanley Kramer's savage attack on the American hunter.

But even if the facts are not going to convince the anti-hunter types, it is necessary to get them straight, since the facts clearly favor those who reject the claim that rigid gun control is the way to stop crime.

First of all, let us define what we mean by "gun control." There is no one in the country, certainly not responsible hunter groups, who opposes all gun control. Control over the sale of machine guns and heavy artillery and silencers, for example, has aroused no opposition worth mentioning. And if a law were passed requiring all gun owners to file the serial numbers of their firearms with the police, few hunters would object—although they would keep their eyes open to see if this was just the beginning of the road toward eventual confiscation. There are some gun owners who would warn, for example, that having a list of every gun and gunowner on file with the government would make life very easy for an invading foreign power or a revolutionary dictatorship. This kind of thinking, of course, always elicits a barrage of snickers, sneers and catcalls from those in favor of gun control. They accuse gun owners who talk this way of being "insane," and "paranoid," and being obsessed with an "anti-Communist mania." Why? That is the question. Invasion and revolution are experiences most countries on this planet have gone through. Only a mindless pollyanna who has never looked at history at all can be confident that America will *never* have to worry about these things. Maybe we won't. I pray that is true. But is it "paranoid" to be prepared just in case we have to live through the rest of the world's experience? Certainly the victims of Russian Communist aggression in Eastern Europe—Czechoslovakia, Poland, Hungary—just a few years back must have been sorry that they had registered and surrendered their right to bear firearms.

What good would hand guns and hunting rifles have done against Russian tanks and artillery? Maybe not much. But it would have allowed Czech and Hungarian men to die honorably in combat against the invader rather than have to stand back defenselessly, throwing a stone or two, while their country was ravaged. One of the most precious of all human rights, even though it is too mysterious to define in a constitutional legal form, is the right to fight, or die like a man, in defense of home and family. American men—all those who have not succumbed to the liberal attacks on bravery, courage, and honor, anyway—know that it is far better to die in armed defense of home and family than to watch them being despoiled and used by an invader.

Far out? No, deep within—difficult to put into words, but there are things worth dying for, and free men must be willing to die. Ask any victim of aggression who has survived an assault on his people—Hungarian freedom fighter, Jewish survivor of a Nazi concentration camp —whether he would have preferred to die in a hail of gunfire rather than live to remember seeing his family being brutalized by the enemy. No, these are not everyday experiences, but to ask a man to take that right to die in combat from his total living experience is to ask him to surrender an essential part of his manhood. The liberals make fun of this idea, of course. They talk of the gun as a "phallic" symbol, as a substitute for manhood, as something only weak and troubled men, obsessed with their masculinity, would need. Everyone has seen the anti-hunter ads where some out-of-work movie star sex-goddess ridicules the manhood of hunters with exactly this kind of inference, or come across books, movies, and television shows which make the same point. It is sad, but apparently a liberal outlook on life does that to a person, makes living comfortably more important than honor, pleasure more important than sacrifice, and compromise and surrender more intelligent than valor; makes the ancient and holy image of man as warrior, knight, and defender of his loved ones something worthy only of ridicule. There just might be no better indictment of liberalism imaginable.

Certainly the case against gun ownership is not always pushed in such an outrageous manner. The attack most often centers on a) how gun control would cut down substantially on the number of murders in the country, and b) how hunting is cruel to animals and threatens the survival of many species of wildlife.

The liberal claim that outlawing guns would somehow prevent murderers from murdering is another indication of their view of human nature—of man as a houseplant. Just as crime for the liberal is a result of poverty, and bad students the result of bad teachers, and Communist aggression the result of American threats, and our lives the result of our environment, murders are the result of guns—not murderers. They use a logic here similar to that which they use on the question of capital punishment. The liberal cannot understand evil. He denies man's capacity to plan and plot a crime, including murder. It is only uncontrollable anger, or temporary insanity which leads a man to strike out against another, they tell us. And, obviously, when the poor houseplant man reacts to these forces beyond his control, if there is a gun floating around, he will use it. If you get rid of the gun, the logic goes, then he will not have an instrument of death available and will therefore not be able to kill.

Well, that kind of nonsense might be so obviously wrong that it does not have to be refuted very thoroughly, but just to set the record straight, the facts go against the liberals. Even when they come up with the facts themselves. Let me give you an example. The late Senator Thomas Dodd of Connecticut was one of the leaders in the United States Senate pushing for a strict federal gun control law. Most of the research facts and figures and charts used by Senate committees pushing for gun control in the 1960's were compiled under

164

his name. One study which Dodd pushed enthusiastically examined the "gun murder" rates in states with gun control law and compared them to states with few or no controls. Dodd's supporters thought that they had the cat in the bag on this one. Two of the states compared in the study were New York and Nebraska. New York has the strictest gun control laws in the nation, Nebraska a comparatively minimal set of regulations. The comparison focused on the percentage of murders in the state committed by guns. In New York 32% of all murders were from gunfire, in Nebraska 70%. See, said the gun control advocates, if you get rid of guns the gun murder rate goes down!

Pretty impressive? No! It is like a magician's sleight of hand. Whether it was deliberately misleading is another question.

Remember, the gun control advocate's claim is that gun control would substantially decrease the murder rate, since people murder because they had guns at their disposal. Guns, not people, they told us, are the cause of the murders.

All Dodd's comparison proves, however, was that limiting guns makes it less likely that a gun would be used as the weapon—the "gun murder" rate. The liberals would really have the statistics going in their favor if the *actual* murder rate, the number of people killed, by whatever means, went down in the state with rigid gun control laws. But the "gun murder" rate says nothing about that at all.

A far better figure to work with, then, would be the total number of murders committed per 100,000 residents—figures which are compiled and made available regularly by the FBI. The National Sports Shooting Foundation, a group which has done some of the most thorough research on this whole question, did just that, by comparing Sen. Dodd's "gun murder" rate examples to the *actual* murder rate. And Dodd got pie in the face.

In the very state chosen by Dodd as example of the benefits of gun control, New York, the murder rate was 4.6 per 100,000 residents, while in Nebraska it was 2.4. True a lesser percentage of murders occurred from gunfire in New York—they used knives, can openers, clubs. But they used them twice as much as the people in Nebraska. The point? Murderers murder, with guns if guns are available, if not with whatever they can get their hands on. In Vermont in 1965 every murder was committed with a gun. All five of them. Does that make Vermont a dangerous place and New York an exemplar of domestic tranquility? Hardly. The murders take place when murderers, for all the varied and complex motivations that drive them on, decide to murder—not when a gun is somewhere in the vicinity.

Another revealing statistic along these lines can be seen by studying the growth in the number of murders in New York City—an area where gun ownership is strictly regulated and where private ownership of a pistol or a revolver is forbidden except for those with very special needs. Mark K. Benenson, an attorney, prepared these figures in an article entitled "A Controlled Look at Gun Controls," which he wrote for the Winter 1968 edition of the *New York Law Forum.**

	1963	1964	1965	1966	1967
Total homicides	549	637	634	654	746
Knives, sharp instruments	225	266	268	263	277
Physical force	109	131	110	110	165
Blunt instrument, or other	77	68	82	73	68
Pistol or revolver	101	130	150	184	205
Rifle or shotgun	37	42	24	24	31

As you can see, the one method of murder which has increased substantially is the method which was most controlled and regulated. It appears that murderers just do not pay much attention to whether or not there is a law against the possession of the kind of weapon they intend to use in breaking the other law—the one which forbids one man to kill another.

One of the most detailed studies ever done on this overall topic is that of Professor Marvin E. Wolfgang, the Graduate Chairman of the Department of Sociology at the University of Pennsylvania. After months of extensive research and numerous case studies one of his conclusions was:

> It is probably safe to contend that many homicides occur because there is sufficient motivation or provocation, and that the type of method used to kill is merely an accident of availability; that a gun is used because it is in the offender's possession at the time of incitement, but that if it were not present, he would use a knife to stab, or fists to beat his victim to death.

Certainly if you want to use some statistics to make a really interesting case on gun control, how about this one: there have been studies which indicate that a widespread pattern of independent gun ownership might actually lessen the rate of violent crime. One such study by Allan S. Krug actually shows that the violent crimes and robbery rate tends to be lower in states where the most hunting li-

*Reprinted with permission; ©The *New York Law Forum*, New York Law School, winter 1968 edition.

censes are sold. Conclusive proof? No—but as valid as any of the charts the anti-gun people come up with. Think about it. If you were planning a robbery or a riot would you rather strike at a neighborhood where hunters take pride in their weapons, or a Greenwich Village or Sunset Strip flower-power den? One of the most impressive examples of what Krug's research points out developed in Texas in the Summer of 1974. Three convicts escaped and went on a week-long murder and rape spree there, touching off a fifty-mile-radius manhunt. Towns and villages within that orbit were put on alert. The news cameras visited one such town to see how the residents were holding up under the threat. The women were in a town hall knitting and playing cards. The men had formed a cordon around the town, pickup trucks manned by men with rifles. One young man looked down at his rifle, and smiled faintly at the reporter while he said calmly: "No sir, I don't expect them to come along this way." And they didn't.

"If Guns Are Outlawed, Only Outlaws Will Have Guns." Just about everybody in the country has seen the bumper sticker. It is usually treated by the liberals as an example of "gun nut" philosophy, as sheer kookiness. Movies and television shows abound in which some dumb, bloodthirsty brute drives around in a four-wheel-drive jeep with it emblazoned across the back. And, most importantly, with an American flag decal in his window.

In early mystery movies more often than not, you could assume that "the butler did it." He was a favorite villain, sneaking along on dark staircases in his nightgown with a lighted candle in one hand and a butcher's cleaver in the other, until Sherlock Holmes or someone like him uncovered the fatal clue. Nowadays—and you can bet your last bag of popcorn on this—if there is a hunter in a movie, especially if his truck carries that bumper sticker, he is the villain.

But, more seriously, what answer is there to the basic thrust of the argument: "If Guns Are Outlawed, Only Outlaws Will Have Guns." Ever since the National Firearms Act of 1934, most of the weapons we have learned to associate with criminal activity have in fact been strictly controlled: machine guns, sawed-off rifles, sawed-off shotguns, silencers, have had to be registered. The only problem has been that gangsters did not comply too enthusiastically. Why would they start to abide by the restrictions on a more inclusive list? Especially since our liberal courts have assured them that they do not have to!

I am not exaggerating. In 1968, in a typical fit of liberal fuzzy-headedness, the United States Supreme Court (*Haynes* v. *United States*) decided that an individual could not be prosecuted for failing to register an illegally held firearm as demanded by the law since that would violate the Fifth Amendment's protection against self-incrimination (a person not having to give evidence against himself).

You have to take a step back, take a deep breath, and look again, and again, but that is what it says. You have to register an illegally held gun, but if you are a criminal that would mean giving the authorities information about the weapons you use in the commission of crime, and that would be giving evidence against yourself; therefore you cannot have charges brought against you for having failed to do so.

It is as obvious as the stripes on a zebra. Only law-abiding citizens would register or admit to their ownership of guns, or surrender the illegal weapons which they would not have in the first place. Criminals would not, since they are criminals precisely because they do not obey laws—and would not be penalized for not doing so anyway! It boggles the mind.

Would gun control make it more difficult to buy a gun? Sure, for the average guy who does not have contacts with the underworld. But for criminals it would be no more difficult than it is now to get their machine guns and silencers, or for radicals like the Symbionese Liberation Army to get automatic rifles for Patricia Hearst, or for a group of teenagers to get a bag of marijuana or goofballs. Every two-bit punk in the country knows how to get a "piece"—an unregistered handgun, perhaps most easily in New York City where they have been outlawed since 1911.

Would the registered serial numbers of all firearms in the country make it easier for law enforcement officials to track down law breakers? In theory it sounds likely—if criminals would be so kind as to file their serial numbers for the police. In 1968, a questionnaire was mailed to law enforcement officials in every state in the union, asking them to report on any cases of murder, robbery, or assault which they were able to solve as a result of tracing a firearm through the serial number during the years from 1959 to 1968. Every state except Alabama, Rhode Island, and Massachusetts replied. The reporting states reported a *total* of six homicides and six robberies over the entire ten-year period. Typical comments were from Maryland: "We have no record of a major crime being solved by tracing a firearm serial number." Georgia: " . . . none of our involved personnel can recall any case that was solved through the tracing of a firearm." Missouri: "To my knowledge, no criminal cases have been solved by means of tracing a firearm by serial number."

It must be remembered as well that even if gun control could greatly reduce crime (which the figures indicate is not true) and if criminals would obey the law and register and hand over their weapons (which is absurd), it just might not be possible to launch an accurate registration procedure, and that even a program that was a dismal failure of an attempt might blow the roof off the barn in tax-dollar cost.

First of all, rough estimates of the numbers of guns in America come in somewhere between 100 and 200 million. Guns are not built to fall apart in five years; there is no planned obsolescence in the manufacture of quality firearms. Old muzzle-loaders, blunderbusses, riverboat-gambler derringers, muskets, as well as the latest magnums, are in homes all over the country. They change hands frequently as collectors and gun enthusiasts buy and sell, trade and collect. Could any government program really get an accurate record of all of them? Even those not held by mobsters and criminal types? Not likely.

But if they could, consider the cost. To be meaningful, gun control would require investigative teams as well as computers and a secretarial staff. In New York City, in 1968, the average cost of their gun registration and control program was about $72.87 per gunowner. It sounds like a lot, but by the time an office is set up, computers installed, investigators hired, forms processed, and records filed it is easy to see why it is so high. Estimates make the case that it would be second in Washington only to the Social Security operation. Now, with inflation going the way it is, especially the salary of government officials, let us estimate the cost now to be about $100 dollars per gun owner. With about 40 to 50 million gunowners in the U.S. that would mean four to five billion dollars for the operation to be put into motion. That is four to five *billion*, not million. The figure is so high that it would appear to confirm the suspicion that those eager to get guns registered really want guns outlawed since no one in his right mind would want to saddle our economy with that kind of expense year after year, or even the lower price which would come once the initial setup was completed.

The argument that hunters are responsible for wiping out valuable and cherished species of wildlife is so lacking in any sound foundation that you have to marvel at the ignorance of those anti-hunter types who keep repeating it over and over. Either their ignorance or their willingness to do anything to end hunting in America. For the facts are solidly on the side of the hunter. There is no group in America that

169

has done more for conservation than the hunter. Let me quote directly from *The Hunter and Conservation*, a genuinely informative booklet available from the National Shooting Sports Foundation (1075 Post Road, Riverside, Connecticut 06868): "Hunters today spend more than $105 million a year on licenses and permits to hunt. Together with fishermen, they provide more than $200 million a year to support the 50 state fish and game departments." Ever since the Pittman-Robertson Act of 1937 an 11% excise tax on the sale of all sporting arms and ammunition has been given to state wildlife projects. The bill was passed mostly because of the organized pressure of hunter groups. In addition responsible hunter organizations and gun clubs have managed to convince the private owners of the roughly 70 million acres of woodlands in America to keep their forests open to the public—hikers and birdwatchers, as well as hunters.

But don't hunters kill animals? Won't they wipe them out eventually? First of all, not everyone who shoots an animal should be called a hunter. Poachers or butchers is a better name for those who kill animals without respect for the rules of wildlife preservation—rules set up as a result of experimentation and wildlife study financed and supported by hunters.

Ecological balance, it must be remembered, depends in large measure on the presence of predators. Our streets are not overrun with mice because snakes and birds eat them. Our streams are not packed full of dying fish because larger fish eat the smaller fish.

Ever since man has been on this earth, certainly within the memory of history and archaeological speculation, man has been one of these predators. Our ancestors never doubted that in the natural scheme of things men were to kill game for the family table. The earliest carvings on the walls of caves, medieval tapestries, colonial woodcuts, all bear witness to the revered image of man as the hunter, the provider. Men killing pheasants were no more likely, in their eyes, to end the existence of pheasants than hungry trout were going to wipe out mayflies.

There have been instances when certain species were hunted in excess and pushed near the brink of extinction, such as the buffalo, but that occurred as the result of indiscriminate poaching—the kind of activity hunter groups have been responsible for discouraging and outlawing.

Wildlife research has demonstrated that certain species can be hunted in almost limitless numbers. Quail and dove, for example, experience a 75 to 80% mortality rate each year whether they are

170

hunted or not. Despite an annual harvest by hunters of millions of doves, their numbers have increased in the last two decades. It is no more likely that hunting them is going to make them an endangered species than digging for nightcrawlers in your backyard for a day's fishing is going to exterminate worms.

Other species, such as deer and bear, cannot be hunted without limits. That is why hunting groups fully subscribe to the findings of the wildlife research they financed in the first place, and accept willingly the legally enforceable limits and specified seasons on species such as these. No one receives more scorn from responsible hunters than the greedy poachers who violate these sportsmen's rules.

As a result of these hunter-financed wildlife programs there has been, in fact, a veritable wildlife explosion. In 1900, for example, the total white-tailed deer population in North America was about 500,000. The deer population in America today is over 16 million, more than when the Indians were the only people on the North American continent. The pronghorn antelope only forty-five years ago was considered an endangered species—on the verge of extinction. With the restoration of its habitat—once again paid for by hunters—the number has grown to the point where it can be hunted again.

What about those alligators and baby seals we have all heard about? Aren't unscrupulous hunters killing them in unprincipled abandon? No. They are not. This is the work of what have to be called poachers. And they use clubs to kill these animals, not guns. Gun control has nothing to do with this issue—and hunting groups have not defended this kind of commercial hunting in the least.

If hunters stopped hunting at the rate prescribed by all available research, if man rejected the role of predator he has played all through history, and stopped playing his role in the natural cycle of life and death on the planet, the same thing would happen to bear and deer that would happen to field mice if you outlawed cats and snakes and hawks. They would multiply at an *unnaturally* high rate. There would be more deer and bear or whatever than food and water to feed them and land to sustain them. They would die of old age and sickness rather than from a hunter's fire. People who are willing to allow horses to be put out of their misery—and who in many cases favor abortion, and mercy-killing of old men and women—somehow find it merciful to allow deer to starve to death. Why?

What can you make of it all? There is no other answer: The anti-gun, anti-hunting people just do not care about these facts; *they just do not like hunters.* Gun control does not stop murder; it does not help to preserve and promote wildlife—it would worsen the situation dramatically. But they still want guns outlawed. They still want hunting stopped. People who stuff down steak with the best of them, even though they have to know that the cow was butchered in a way nowhere near as painless as a well-placed hunter's bullet, show shock and anger at the sport of hunting—maybe while burping after that steak dinner.

Why do they dislike hunters? Earlier I hinted that much of the dislike springs from the symbol of the hunter as a man of traditional values, as a man apparently immune to the lure of the new permissive lifestyle being advocated by prominent parts of the communications media in and around certain large cities and universities. I stand on that. The image of the hunter is the exact opposite of the one being pushed by the liberals. Where the liberal is an internationalist one-worlder, the hunter is an unashamed American patriot; where the liberal is for new experiences, the hunter uses the disciplined, ancient rhythms of the hunt to introduce his sons to the pieties of our forefathers; where the liberal is an advocate of "do your own thing," the hunter knows that guns do not leave room for too many experimental mistakes; while the liberal going from his air-conditioned faculty room to his electronically regulated high-rise apartment is likely to be too convinced of man's capacity to control this world to accept the existence of God, the hunter is likely to believe in the Creator as he watches nature spring to life from his deer stand or duck blind on cold autumn mornings, as the blue ocean of stars gives way to the triumphant streaked reds of sunrise, as he waits for the appearance of the creatures whose hide and flesh so miraculously provide man with the means to survival. He knows that life comes from blood—as did Christ. Hunters are not likely to sit cross-legged on the floor and gesticulate wildly and sentimentally—like a hippy telling of his last LSD trip—when they speak of the majesty of their outdoor experience, but it is this total immersion in the Divine Order of life that they are talking about when they use the term "spiritual"— as they often do—to describe the magic of the hunt. It is a side of life that those who get their nourishment from TV dinners and their thrills from dope, will never know—to their great loss. Plastic-packaged, chrome-bordered modern city life has taken much of man's mind and heart away from the full experience of life—the magic part. It is no coincidence that nature and natural are almost identical words. Those who know nature know the natural in life and feel intuitively how unnatural are so many of the so-called liberal social-betterment schemes.

172

Not that hunters are angels. They have vices just like the rest of us. But their vices are the ones that our society has learned to live with. A little too much wine, women, and song in some cases. In general, though, the experience of hunting seems to bring decency, stability and a spirit of discipline and self-sacrifice to those who experience its rigors. Or maybe it's the other way around—maybe the most upstanding of our citizenry is attracted to hunting. Take your choice. Both make hunting look pretty good. Go to any rod and reel club, shooting range, gun club; read any of the popular sportsmen's magazines, and you cannot help but be impressed by the willing acceptance by hunters of the self-image of husbands, fathers, and family men. They just might be the last bastion of those American men who actually seem to like to be with their children. They are not the middle-aged dreamers trying to make it as playboys and foppish swingers. They know themselves and their place in the world. They know God's will for man. You do not find muggers, pimps, gays, and welfare cheats at a shooting range. Hunting brings fathers closer to their children. The generation gap does not exist on the hunt. In a hunter's family, the boy is likely to be eager to learn the ways of his father and to prove himself worthy to enter the long line of American men who have earned the right to handle their own guns—unlike the liberal home where the father seems to be more intent to adopt the hairstyles, latest dance steps, ways of dress, attitudes, and manner of speech of the "in with it" son.

The hunter is derided and scorned by the liberals for the same reason that West Point cadets are ridiculed when they get off busses in New York City, and policemen trying to take a stronghold of some revolutionary group are called "trigger-happy." There is no room for these men in liberalism's America.

12
Joseph McCarthy: He Was Not America's "Great Threat"

"McCarthyite". . ."McCarthyism." The verdict seems to be in on his career. He was a villain we are told. Dictionaries even list the words right there in the *M* section—"one who accuses another of wrongdoing without sufficient evidence; an irresponsible attack on the character of another." I once heard a woman who called herself a "conservative" say, while complaining about the teachers in American schools, that "We are not engaging in McCarthyite tactics here. We have proof of our charges." Samuel Eliot Morison in his otherwise calm and reasoned *History of the American People*, the kind of much-praised book that parents buy for unopinionated coverage of American history, calls McCarthy "cruel, greedy" and "one of the most colossal liars in history," someone who "injected poison into the body politic." And Morison was one of the temperate, middle-of-the-road-type liberals when it comes to McCarthy. Richard Rovere, one of the first authors to do a book on McCarthy, calls him "a crook," a "foul-mouthed bum," a "rattlesnake." The late Bertrand Russell, the left-wing English philosopher and historian, charged that

174

McCarthy was making it unsafe for Americans to read Thomas Jefferson. Recent New Left revisionist books, as you might expect, such as *The Nightmare Decade* and *The Truman Doctrine and the Origins of McCarthyism*, try to paint an even bleaker picture, implying that earlier writers were too intimidated by McCarthy to write honestly about his actions. School textbooks usually treat his career as an example of a threat to democracy (that might even be the chapter heading they use) and some go so far as to imply, by noting McCarthy's partial German heritage and his critical statements against the trial of German World War II criminals at Nuremberg, that he was a potential American version of Hitler or Mussolini.

Why raise the issue again, then? If such an overwhelming majority seems to agree that he was a villain, if even his supporters agree that he could be imprecise and boorish in his accusations (as do his most noted defenders L. Brent Bozell and William F. Buckley in *McCarthy and His Enemies*, their meticulously researched and brilliantly argued book in overall support of McCarthy), what good can be served by reviewing his career and its implications? Certainly the liberals are not going to change their minds about him, and conservatives can go on being conservative without having respect for the memory of a dead and disgraced Senator from Wisconsin. Or can they?

I think not. McCarthy, his boorishness and sloppy accusations notwithstanding, has become the symbol of an issue much larger than himself. Just as G. K. Chesterton once noted that Dreyfus' innocence could not be used to excuse the things said against France by his defenders, neither can McCarthy's errors excuse the fundamental premise which motivated the vicious attack against him. There was much more at stake in the clash over this man's career than his individual behavior. For in defending McCarthy one defends as well the American people's right to act energetically in defense of their way of life against the revolutionary assaults of secular, international liberalism. But let us proceed slowly and carefully.

BACKGROUND

McCarthy first hit the limelight in February 1950, when in a radio-broadcasted speech to the Ohio County Women's Club of Wheeling, West Virginia, he asserted that he had knowledge of a substantial number of Communists working in the United States State Department, the arm of our government which helps make and administer our foreign policy. He demanded that the State Department "clean house" since this Communist infiltration, he alleged, was responsible for setting policy which went against America's national interest; and he demanded that the United States Senate, with its investigative powers find out why no such internal supervision had yet taken place.

Within two days of this speech, it was proposed that the Senate Committee on Foreign Relations investigate McCarthy's charges—but more with an eye to proving the charges wrong than to see if there was substance to them. The feeling had already grown in certain Senate circles that McCarthy was a troublemaker and that if he were correct, or if a substantial number of Americans came to believe that he was correct, there would be hell to pay for elected officials as they went around the country trying to explain to potential voters how they managed to allow this subversion to go on right under their noses in Washington. And McCarthy was attracting much support. The American people seemed ready for his charges.

Why? It is not hard to figure out when you remember the era. For the average American, the ex-World War II foot soldier, the late 1940's and the early 1950's were becoming most distressing and perplexing years. You can imagine easily the latent anger of these working men as they read their evening papers, remembering the months spent in foxholes and on lonely Pacific atolls and their countless dead comrades in arms; you can imagine the sorrow of American widows and mothers of the dead while they listened to their radios. Americans had been killed by the hundreds of thousands, billions of dollars had been spent in history's greatest war effort, to stop totalitarian dictatorships from dominating Europe and Asia. But now the news told them of Communist dictatorships dominating those same areas. We had won the war, but the Russian and Chinese Communists seemed to have profited most by the victory. Seven-hundred million Chinese under Communist control; Hungary, Czechoslovakia, Poland, East Germany and the other "satellites" under Russian control. Winston Churchill spoke of an "iron curtain" descending upon the ancient capitals of Eastern Europe. A familiar wisecrack could be heard making the rounds in bars and factories and on front porches. "We won the war, but lost the peace."

But the big question was "Why?" America had a degree of military supremacy unparalleled in history. We had the atom bomb; no one else did. How could we have allowed those Communists to get so strong, especially just after—only five years after—we had proved our willingness to bomb to the point of near-annihilation the German and Japanese fascist dictatorships in order to secure our demanded "unconditional surrender"?

Then, a series of incidents provided clues to an answer. Ex-Communists Whittaker Chambers and Louis Budenz came forward and accused high-ranking government policymakers of being Communists. Alger Hiss, a chief advisor to both Franklin Delano Roosevelt and his successor Harry S. Truman during the crucial negotiations with Russia over the fate of Europe and Asia after the German defeat, was one of those accused by Chambers; Klaus Fuchs in England was convicted of passing atomic secrets to the Russians; a Russian defector, Igor Gouzenko revealed the existence of a spy ring in Canada so mammoth and extensive that liberal Canadian prime minister MacKenzie King "could not believe" that Stalin "countenanced it"; ten top American Communists were convicted of conspiracy to overthrow the government, including the Rosenbergs who eventually were executed for their roles in delivering information about our atomic weaponry to the Russians. It all seemed to fall into place. American foreign policy "seemed" to be designed to further Communist rather than American national goals, and now McCarthy told us why. He had "evidence" of Communist infiltration.

When McCarthy appeared before the Senate investigating committee, the so called Tydings Committee, he became in short order a household word. Here, and in later Senate hearings he organized and led himself, he launched a campaign to expose Communists in government. In the early 1950's there wasn't a bar, social tea, or card game, where the talk did not turn, sooner or later, to McCarthy and the question of Communists in our government. One of the popular TV shows of the time was "I Led Three Lives," the adventures of Herb Philbrick, the FBI agent who posed as a Communist. America became divided into McCarthyites and anti-McCarthyites and ugly charges of "Communist" and "Fascist" were thrown back and forth with reckless abandon.

Certainly, it must be noted, defending McCarthy does not mean defending every hare-brained idiot who went around during that time accusing everyone who disagreed with him of being a Communist. McCarthy might have been responsible for stirring up that hornets' nest, but as dangerous as some of the McCarthyites might have been, that in itself does not mean that McCarthy should not have launched his campaign. Our World War II effort unintentionally created a great deal of irrational anti-German and anti-Japanese sentiment—"the only good German is a dead German" kind of thing.

People did fail to distinguish between the people of those countries and the leadership. But that does not mean that the war effort should not have been expended. Likewise, if McCarthy was right, if there was a Communist or a pro-Communist infiltration in our government, it would have been criminally wrong for him to hold back and ignore that threat to our security just because some irrational zealot would begin to see Communists under every bed.

THE EVIDENCE

Those opposed to McCarthy usually make their case against him in a nutshell by saying something like "He accused all those people of being Communist without enough evidence to prove a thing. He dragged people's good names through the mud, smeared reputations, ruined careers, and *never* came forward with enough information to get a single conviction."

Well, it is true that McCarthy never did get a conviction, and that certainly would be important criticism if that had been his goal. However, McCarthy was after something far different. It is truly fascinating to watch how all the anti-McCarthy books manage to avoid coming to grips with this issue.

McCarthy's oft-stated goal was, in contrast, not so much getting those he accused of pro-Communist activity sent to jail (not that he would not have liked to see that happen), as it was simply in getting them *fired* from their government jobs. His main interest was in the "security risk" involved in allowing people with pro-Communist backgrounds, associations, and even leanings, to stay in government positions where they might have access to secret military information, or be able to influence policy decisions to favor Communist goals.

This is, as is obvious, a crucial distinction. American jurisprudence—our legal traditions—insists, and wisely, that a man cannot be convicted and punished for a crime until he has been proved "guilty beyond a reasonable doubt." The scales are deliberately tipped in favor of the accused in order to avoid the possibility of convicting an innocent man. McCarthy would have admitted himself that in most of the cases he presented to the Senate committees he did not have evidence sufficient to convict those he accused—if he were accusing them of a criminal offense. He did not have enough to send them to jail for espionage.

But he did insist that he had enough to have them fired from their government jobs! And that is a big difference.

Americans have a *right* not to be sent to jail for a crime without evidence beyond a shadow of a doubt. But a government job is not a right; it is a privilege. And McCarthy insisted that in the case of government employment, especially in the instance of jobs involving security matters, the scale should be tipped not in favor of the accused, but in favor of the government—that if there was a *reasonable* doubt about a man's loyalty, that in itself was enough to have him fired. In the atomic age, when the Soviet Union and world Communism have the capacity to destroy our major cities, McCarthy's sense of logic told him that we just could not take a chance with people whose past behavior and associations indicated a "chumminess" with Communist groups or world-goals. He insisted that we just could not tolerate "security risks" like these. Too much was at stake.

The heart of the argument, then, over McCarthy's "proof"—or lack of it—is another liberal straw man. The main thrust of his accusations was not that he had enough evidence to have people sent to jail—and he should not be condemned for failing to produce that kind of evicence.

At this point, however, anti-McCarthyites bring up a criticism that deserves careful treatment. "Do not you supporters of McCarthy" they argue, "realize that when you fire a person from a government job because of the fact that he seems to be too close to Communist groups, you are ruining his reputation, perhaps for life. Don't you realize that if someone is fired for being a 'security risk' he might be branded as a traitor and be unable to find work again. You just cannot do that to a man or a woman on flimsy, circumstantial evidence of the McCarthy type."

Two issues are involved here: a) was it McCarthy's decision to make the names public in the first place, and b) can it be said that McCarthy's evidence was "without substance" even if it would be inadmissable in a court of law? Tape recordings are almost always unacceptable in court since they can be doctored-up too easily, but that does not mean that the Watergate accusations against Richard Nixon were "without substance."

Since one of the main charges against McCarthy was that he was a publicity hound using the "Red-scare" tactic to make a name for himself that he would later use in a campaign for the Presidency, it probably will do little good to tell his enemies that, in fact, it was McCarthy's original intention—stated intention, admitted to by the members of the Tydings Committee—to make known the names of those he suspected of being either Communists or under Communist influence only behind the closed doors of the Senate committee room. The anti-McCarthyites would argue that even if his original charges were made in private, he later would have sought headlines with open name-calling. The fact remains, however, despite this kind of liberal assumption without proof (a "McCarthyite" tactic?), that McCarthy kept the names to himself until the Tydings Committee in effect told him to put up or shut up. They were the ones who insisted that things be made public. Remember, the people who would bear the brunt of McCarthy's charges were the elected officials who allowed the alleged Communist infiltration to take place. Only by discrediting McCarthy could these politicians save face before the voters. They had to prove that they had been doing their job as well as could be expected and that McCarthy had not been more diligent than they, just more irresponsible, in coming up with his "evidence."

McCarthy's intention, in contrast, was to get the Senate committee to look at his evidence and launch a Senate investigation based on it. He did not want to make his suspects' names public because he admitted that some of them would be likely to receive a "clean bill of health" and that *he* was afraid of ruining their reputations needlessly. McCarthy's accusers, the Tydings' Committee leadership, were the ones who insisted that the names be made public.

THE ACCUSED

Who were the people accused by McCarthy? What kind of records did they have? How irresponsible was he in asserting that they should not have been allowed to continue to work on the public payroll? Bozell and Buckley's book has an appendix which lists all those charged by McCarthy, with a summary of the statements McCarthy made in public about them—statements, then, for which he could have been sued for libel if they contained lies. Anyone wishing to get a full grasp of these tumultuous years in American history should read and re-read this section of the book. For our purposes here it should be sufficient to take a few of the cases for which McCarthy was most criticized by the liberals—cases where he was supposed to have behaved most shamefully.

Before taking that step, however, it is necessary to remember what is meant by a Communist "front group," since much of McCarthy's evidence consisted of membership in such an organization.

Ever since the 1920's there have been organizations in America openly calling themselves "Communist." An official Communist

Party, under Russian control, was even established. But Americans, especially the working class which is supposed to be the backbone of a Communist movement, proved to be relatively immune to the appeals of Communism. The membership of the Communist party grew, but never to the point where they posed a serious challenge to "take over" America at the ballot box, or in any mass political movement. Communist leaders in Russia, recognizing that, decided to try another attack—to appeal to the many Americans who would not openly join a Communist Party but who might be reached by appeals for causes which furthered Communist aims without direct affiliation with the world Communist movement. Their hope was to get well-intentioned Americans to push for Communist objectives while working under other banners, for "social justice" or "racial harmony" or "mankind." For example, during the Civil War in Spain in the 1930's, Russian Communist leaders decided to work for the victory of the side known as the "Republicans" against the side known as the "Nationalists." A Republican victory was seen by them as likely to lead to a situation in Spain chaotic enough for them to be able to try a Communist takeover. Consequently, the Communists sponsored in America rallies, letter-writing campaigns, committees, and even encouraged young men to join the famous Lincoln Brigade, volunteers from outside Spain who came to fight for the Republican side. The Communists played up the help that Franco was receiving from Hitler and Mussolini, the anti-democratic theories of Franco and his Falangist supporters, and put much stress upon wartime atrocities committed by Franco's men. Many idealistic Americans responded, and wrote their letters, contributed their money, and even joined the Lincoln Brigade. Ernest Hemingway's *For Whom the Bell Tolls* tells the story of one such recruit in what he thought was a noble crusade for democracy against dictatorship. They might have had no knowledge whatsoever that the group behind the scenes all the while was the Communist Party—just as John Lindsay while Mayor of New York might never have known that one of the groups which sponsored the anti-Vietnam War rallies at which he spoke was a Communist Trotskyite group and he may never have expected a Viet Cong flag to be unfurled in the wind as he spoke of the evils of America's involvement.

There were other front groups formed in the 1930's to protest racial injustice in America and the persecution of Jews in Hitler's Germany. In addition, the problems of the Depression were used as the reason for front groups set up to protest the failures of the capitalist

181

system, and many Americans, keenly aware of the depression dislocation of our economy, responded. Eugene Lyons painted a memorable picture of the proliferation of Communist-sponsored organizations in colleges, intellectual circles and labor unions during these years in his best-selling book *The Red Decade.*

This ambiguity about the reasons why someone would join a Communist front group has to be kept in mind, for it is the key to the dispute between McCarthy and his enemies. What does it mean to have been a member of a Communist-led group? Or to have been close friends with Communists? Subversive intent? A high-minded youthful idealism?

The adult liberals of the late 1940's who attended the colleges and frequented the intellectual gatherings of the Red Decade knew, first hand, the youthful radicalism of the time and their generation. Perhaps they shared in it. And they, simply, refused—in a coverup that makes Watergate look like peanuts—to allow McCarthy and his supporters to punish 1930's radicals, now that they were adult and now that Russia had become an enemy of America, thereby making a youthful and idealistic fling with Communism a flirtation with the enemy.

They insisted, too, that McCarthy failed to take into account the psychological effects of the American-Russian military alliance of World War II. Many liberals in political and academic circles became convinced that their internationalist, one-world dream just might really become possible if only the American-Russian wartime cooperation could be continued after the Germans and the Japanese were beaten. Taking literally the one-worlder's dream which liberals had been pushing since John Dewey's days anyway, they decided that what was best for the world in the late 1940's was not a period of American military dominance but a sharing of power between Russia and America. Their goal was not to stop Communism, but to work with it in pursuit of a new world order—perhaps an actual world government under UN auspices. Why should America be the only country with the atom bomb? they argued. Why should America make Russia uneasy by encouraging the growth of anti-Communist governments on the Russian border in places like Poland, Hungary, and Czechoslovakia? In the liberal internationalist scheme, success for America was not a defeat of Communism. Far from it. Communist internationalism was the spark to be encouraged in the name of one-world peace. America's real interest, to these liberals, called for at least a partial surrender of American dominance, a strengthening of the UN, not an American-led anti-Communist cordon of states around the world. That kind of American strategic supremacy, they feared, would take the world further down the path of nationalism. Internationalism was the goal. And the Communists, even if through a distorting prism of Marxism and dictatorial rule, could see that. They could be worked with.

The anti-McCarthyites, to be blunt, sympathized with those in our government who were working against our interests. They knew and admired those afflicted with the one-world temptation, and believed that even those well-educated intellectuals who were actually working to help Russia were more interested in an enforceable world peace than in Russian domination of the world. To be sure, they might agree, some of their old classmates and colleagues went overboard in helping the Russians, but the liberals knew how idealism could boil over into Communist sympathies. They remembered their own academic days when the temptation had been such a common experience for an entire generation of Ivy League and big-city students.

The McCarthyites, who by and large were working-class and businessmen types, and who just did not understand the one-world temptation, did not see that a man can think that he is serving his country's best long range interests more by helping the enemy than his own country. McCarthy and the McCarthyites had to be put in place, to be cooled off until they or their university-bound children could learn to think internationally and see beyond "narrow" American patriotism. And most importantly, those intellectuals who went too far too soon in pushing Russian interests had to be protected from the old-fashioned patriots and religiously motivated anti-Communists who just could not grasp why men and women do the kinds of things that shocked a McCarthy. They had to be taught a lesson. And they were. Look in your dictionaries under *M* and you will see that they "learned" us right well.

Most of the people accused by McCarthy were of this "front group" type—intellectuals and do-gooders, "bleeding hearts" who had supported the "noble" causes in the 30's and 40's. Just a few examples of McCarthy's charges should make the point. (The quotes are McCarthy's as listed in Bozell and Buckley's book).

Esther Brunauer—"belonged to a sizeable number of organizations named as fronts for the Communist Party. . .she was chairman of a meeting of the American Friends of the Soviet Union at which the principal speaker was a well-known Communist and frequent writer for the official Communist Daily Worker . . . she admitted that her husband had Communist connections and had been a member of the Young Communist League."

Stephen Brunauer—"an admitted former member of the Young Communist league, (and who) was suspended from his job as head of the Navy's high explosives section."

Lauchlin Currie—"named under oath by Elizabeth Bentley as the man who tipped off her Russian espionage agents that we were about to break the Japanese code. . ."

John Paton Davies—"accused by General Hurley of operating behind his back to support the Communists (in China)."

Theodore Geiger—"There are witnesses who will testify that he was a member of the same Communist Party unit as they were."

Haldore Hanson—"a man who worked on the Communist edition of a magazine, who praised the Communists, who was co-editor of a Communist paper in China; who was named by a government witness under oath as a member of the Communist Party."

Dorothy Kenyon—"the case consisted of photostatic documents showing membership in and sponsorship of 28 Communist front organizations, named as such by the Attorney General or Congressional Committees. I erred. Kenyon's files show membership in exactly 52 organizations of this type—not 28."

Owen Lattimore—"Ex-Communist Louis Budenz testified he attended Communist Politburo meetings of the Communist Party and that at one of those meetings a Party line was transmitted from Moscow to the Politburo from Owen Lattimore via Frederick Vanderbilt Field.

"Budenz testified unequivocally that his official information was that Lattimore was a member of the Party and that one of the tasks assigned to Lattimore was to recruit Communists and fellow-traveler writers to sell to the American people and to the State Department the Communist Party line on China.

"Budenz further testified that Lattimore was a member of a Red cell in the Institute of Pacific Relations—the job of which was to sell the Communist line on China.

"Budenz testified that top secret information which went out to Communist leaders throughout the country were seen by him and that they bore Lattimore's Party identification symbol XL."

John Stewart Service—"Service was named by our Ambassador to China as one of the men who was serving the cause of Communism in China. He asked the President to remove Service. He said that this man's actions are not good for the United States, they are good for Russia . . . Among other things, the FBI produced microphone record-ints from a hotel room which showed that Service had turned over to a known Communist, not only State Department documents, but also secret military information."

Whatever room for discussion there is over these people's back-grounds, even after you grant that much of evidence has to be called circumstantial and hearsay, it has to be admitted that these are peo-ple with backgrounds worthy of a great deal of suspicion—to say the least!

These are just a few examples, but they are not extraordinary in any way. As mentioned earlier, in fact, these are the cases which most infuriated the anti-McCarthyites. And the facts are not con-tested. The anti-McCarthyites response is "so what?" These were the career deplomats, the respected writers and scholars who were being persecuted unfairly by the uneducated "rattlesnake" from Wisconsin.

It is difficult, it is true, to come down on all fours in McCarthy's favor. The evidence he presented was not as conclusive as it should have been in many cases. The testimony of an ex-Communist is, of itself, not enough to send a man to jail for treason. Membership in front groups does not necessarily imply knowledge of the Communist sponsorship. Although membership in 52 such organizations does say something about a person's political disposition—where there is smoke there is fire and all that. And if your husband admits that he is a Communist that does not mean that you will *have* to tell him what you know about your country's military secrets. You might be willing to stand against his mission in life. You might . . . but . . . well, what can you say? The situation could not be ignored.

McCarthy's argument was that our country could not afford the "risk" of keeping people like these in positions where they could be-tray America's national interests. His opponents argued that you could not ruin their names because of youthful associations, or coinci-dental agreement with the Communists on specific issues. You could have been opposed to continued aid to Chiang Kai-shek, for example, and not be a Communist, even though an arms cut-off would help the Communist world. But in times of great international tension can we afford to keep men and women in positions of influence who have shown sympathies for the enemy? McCarthy said no. Certainly someone with a Nazi background would not have been allowed to lead our war effort against the Germans.

185

Looking back on those tumultuous years we have to agree that probably many of the people accused by McCarthy were not actually working for the Soviet Union. Maybe not even Owen Lattimore. I guess we will never know for sure. Probably most of the accused were more what we would now call "radical chic"—well-educated, upper-middle-class, liberal do-gooders who are attracted out of a sense of guilt over their own very comfortable lives to causes which claim to be aiding the poor, the oppressed, the minorities. Communist rhetoric about equality and world-wide economic cooperation appeals to their sense of righteousness. It happens in our own time so often that it is part of most modern Americans' own ring of acquaintances. Think, for example, of the thousands upon thousands of well-meaning American college students who marched and listened enthusiastically to Communist speakers and applauded statements by Angela Davis in favor of Communism and cheered during flag burnings in protest against the Vietnamese War during the last ten years. Many of them are now selling real estate and commercial insurance, fully part of the American "establishment," having grown out of their youthful excesses. What would you think, for example, if an employer twenty years from now refused a man a promotion in an electronics industry operation because he was spotted in a picture of a campus crowd watching a flag-burning? Or what if a future candidate for elected office is shown as a teenager in a picture of the crowd scene listening to John Lindsay speak against the war in Vietnam while Viet Cong flags blow in the breeze? Should that be reason enough to suspect his loyalty? Involvement in the Vietnam protests of the 1960's does not make someone a Communist any more than did radicalism in the 1930's

But certainly any fair-minded person should agree that McCarthy's list contained information more specific and suggestive of guilt than being in a crowd organized by a Communist group.

Why then the liberal *hatred* (there is no gentler word) of McCarthy? Self-defense. Their reaction was based on their fear that his sledge-hammer attacks would fail to make the distinction between one-worlder idealist and an actual Russian agent. Which is a reasonable fear. What is disturbing, however, is their willingness to overlook those with enough evidence against them to suggest that they were working for Russia, in order to keep the protective cover over their liberal internationalist intelligentsia buddies—and themselves. No, McCarthy did not have enough proof for conviction. But it is clear that the kind of thorough media-supported investigation that drove Richard Nixon from office in the Watergate scandal could have gone a long way toward coming up with it for him. An error in the direction of Communism, however, can be excused by the liberal. That temptation is close enough to the liberal's own heart to be understood, and forgiven. It is only anti-Communist zealotry that gets the media guns out in a full frontal assault.

ANTI-McCARTHYITES—HOW MUCH BLAME?

How much does well-meaning idealism excuse? Well certainly not as much as the anti-McCarthyites suggest. As William S. Schlamm says in the Prologue to *McCarthy and His Enemies*: "What is one to say of an intellectual who, having advocated in the past a tragic interference with innumerable lives, now thinks himself entitled to claim for his immense act the irrelevancy of a meaningless infatuation? To a man who leaves an indefensible position, society owes understanding and confidence, provided his motives in taking the indefensible position had in themselves been defensible, and provided he himself tries to understand the impact of his error and to atone for it. But to a college professor, who, on leaving organizations which are demonstrably engaged in a total upheaval of human existence says "Oops, so sorry, and let's not ever mention it again!"—to such a man society owes nothing but contempt!"

And we may add, certainly not a right to a job in our State Department when we are engaged in a struggle with the main supporters of his old infatuation.

The liberal nonchalance in dealing with Communism, perhaps generated in part by the World War II alliance with Russia, just could not be allowed to go on during the Cold War struggle. It is that simple. The liberal blinders which allowed a man like Paul Appleby of the Bureau of the Budget to say that "A man in the employ of the government has just as much right to be a member of the Communist Party as he has to be a member of the Democratic or Republican Party" had to be stripped off. At times, McCarthy went after the problems with a broad-sword when a fine surgeon's scalpel would have been the right instrument. He was not the best man for the job. He did not have the information-gathering apparatus to research his cases with proper thoroughness. But all that tells us is that the official intelligence-gathering operations of our government, under liberal control, which are supported by our tax dollars to protect us from subversion, were not doing their job, and that McCarthy had to slog through clumsily in his attempt to expose the Communist presence in our government without their full support and assistance.

There can be no doubt on this point. There was a Communist presence in our country in those years worthy of our apprehension. It makes little difference that it was inspired in large by a dream of Soviet-American cooperation in pursuit of a world order designed to promote peace, and that the years of Soviet-American cooperation during World War II had led many one-worlders to see a strong and influential Russia as essential to that dream's realization. Once Russia had become our enemy and China had turned Communist we could no longer afford that kind of pro-Communist leaning. They were no longer helping our ally.

The liberals know how many of their ultimate goals come close to those of the Communists. They know that their hope to convert America to the idea of a one-world government and a more socialized economy could be dashed to pieces if Americans joined with McCarthy in condemning those things in a strong wave of anti-Communism. They foresaw the danger that the American people would define the tenets of Communism as enemy ideas, not admissible in America's public debate, and that that condemnation would subsume—make part of it—many of the central tenets of liberalism as well.

The liberals were arguing beyond McCarthy, in defense of the idea of an "open" society, a society in which there would be no limitations on the free exchange of ideas. They were defending themselves and their right to continue to push for the kind of America they want. A rigid and knowledgeable American anti-Communism would end their hope for a conversion of America to secular international liberalism.

Liberals know that a society with a sense of purpose, a society committed to the "self-evident" truths of our Founding Fathers cannot be manipulated in a "progressive" direction.

Conversely, those Americans not interested in having their national sovereignty and Christian way of life withered away with each successive year should learn the lesson of the McCarthy years.

Perhaps it is too late to rescue McCarthy's memory, but it is not too late to raise to respectability the idea that we have a right and a duty to define Communism as an enemy political philosophy, opposed to the ideals we hold as our precious heritage—Christianity, private property (even if limited in some ways), national independence, and political liberty—and therefore a philosophy we will not allow to be held by men and women entrusted with running our government or our schools. Those liberals whose ideas are so close to those of the Communists that they are made uncomfortable by such a demand, have to be made aware of the fact that they are treading on thin ice, and that we certainly are not going to subsidize their attempts to move our thinking and our government policy away from our traditional ways and wishes. It is our country.

The McCarthy years raised this issue into our direct line of vision, but it has long been there beneath the surface. No society can tolerate the existence of movements opposed to its fundamental truths, except when these groups are so small and uninfluential as to cause little danger. America up until the twentieth-century growth of Marxism had no need to face up to this issue, no need to describe precisely what kind of political groups would be treated as beyond the pale—illegitimate contestants for power in the public arena. Almost all Americans in the past accepted the fundamental truths of our social order. With the growth of Marxist influence in our schools and colleges, we are going to have to shake loose from that kind of confidence, start to define what kind of a nation we intend to be, state those things which are not going to be allowed to appear in the guise of legitimate alternatives to our way of life. We are going to have to become modern McCarthys. Or else watch those radical ideas and movements grow and spread until either they take over our society, or violent and frightening anti-revolutionaries like Hitler and Mussolini come to power to stop them when things reach the crisis stage. But it is our responsibility to not let things reach that extreme, to act legally and determinedly to preserve our way of life by keeping our enemies in place.

It is ironic that Joseph McCarthy's reputation is likely to be rescued only if the Marxist threat to America someday reaches the point where our whole society becomes menaced enough for everybody to see what kind of dangers he was shouting about. I would bet that, wherever Joe McCarthy is now, he would rather have us keep those enemies to a minimal size and position and pay the price of having his name live on in history as a synonym for ruthlessness.

13

God Is Not Dead

"God is dead"—the epigram received much attention in America during the mid-1960's. Even *Time* magazine ran a cover story on the increasing number of theologians who were attempting to construct a religion for man now that he has outgrown the need for belief in a Creator.

Originally the quote was the brainchild of Friedrich Nietzsche, the famous and eccentric nineteenth-century German philosopher. The legend goes that the quote appeared all over Europe at the height of his fame—"God is dead," signed "Nietzsche"; but that upon his death someone scrawled "Nietzsche is dead," signed "God" across his tombstone.

Surveys and opinion polls of the American people indicate that a substantial majority in our country still believe in the existence of some kind of Supreme Being. But that makes little difference to the average student since that portion of America that does not believe in God is, by and large, the same portion that calls itself liberal—and teachers tend to be liberal, especially social studies teachers. The term that could best be used to describe the tone of educational programs in America though would be "agnostic"—a thoughtful, deliberate and proud "doubting" of the existence of God. There is very little open hostility toward the idea of God and our responsibilities to God, on the surface anyway. It would be more accurate to say that the whole idea is treated as an irrelevancy, an idea unworthy of scholarly opposition, which is of course worse than hostility in many ways.

So while it is true that court decisions have made courses or activities which promote or preserve belief in God illegal, since that would violate the "religious freedom" of those without any religious beliefs (yes, it is illogical; no, it was not at all what the Founding Fathers had in mind for our country), that was hardly necessary since the overwhelming majority of young college graduates, the last ten-year batch of new teachers, seem to have proudly "grown up" out of their belief in God, and consequently think of the whole idea as beneath academic consideration. Even if the courts had never dealt with the issue of separation of Church and State in the schools, there would be scarcely any attention paid to the idea that there is a God and that man's duty lies in service to Him. "Open-minded," "progressive"-thinking, "modern," "enlightened," liberals did not need the Supreme Court to tell *them* that God is dead.

The attitude toward God which a young person from a religious family is likely to meet in a modern school, then, is more amused and pseudo-sophisticated condescension than scorn. Wisecracks and sly innuendo will greet the notion of God and His laws: "The candy man In the sky" . . . "when we get to our happy hunting ground . . . "maybe if you say a prayer God will help you pass that exam." Or fake piety—folded hands, raised eyes, a hasty sign of the cross—when something goes wrong. It is the same air of scorn a student will see used to deride patriotism and respect for tradition. The impression projected is that educated, thinking people go to school to rise above old-fashioned religious superstitions, that modern men should learn to live without these antiquated "crutches." (And use drugs, rap sessions and psychiatrists instead? That might be a wisecrack, but there is an amazing correlation between the rejection of God and the need for psychological counseling. More than once I have been told by people paying a fortune in psychiatrists' bills that they envy those with religious convictions. However, they say it with an air of superiority—the way they would remember how easier and simpler a belief in Santa Claus made life, as if psychiatric disturbances were something to be proud of, a sign that one is brooding over the existential nothingness of life. But the fact that those who live lives in search of knowing and serving God seem happy and at peace with themselves, and that those who have rejected God seem always depressed and "not whole" says much about the old catechism idea that man was made by God to know Him, love Him and serve Him, and that a life lived with some other objective, such as self-service, is never what it should be.)

THE AGE OF FAITH

From the perspective of our Godless age, it is hard to believe that there was time in history when the great majority of men accepted the existence of God, and that the greatest minds of history, up until very recently, spent much of their lives writing and teaching about the way men could live closest to His law, and how to construct a society and a government in a way most likely to achieve that goal. And we are not just speaking of medieval monks. The modern intellectual's mutiny against this tradition would be understandable if some scientific discovery had made belief in God illogical. But the explanation lies elsewhere.

There is no scientific fact that any modern intellectual has to deal with that makes it any more difficult for him to accept the existence of God than those St. Thomas Aquinas faced in the fourteenth century. The advances of science and technology have given us more knowledge about how things work on this planet, but they tell us nothing about the spiritual world that man has always pictured as God's. If anything, the scientific discoveries about the wonders of nature and the intricate and dazzling exactness of life patterns in the universe, the awe-inspiring pictures of the vastness of space brought back to us by our astronauts, should make us more convinced of the necessity of a Creator with at least as much personal intelligence as the scientists who figure out relatively microscopic portions of His universe after years of multi-million-dollar research. If no one would believe a story of how a Cadillac Eldorado came about accidentally in an auto-parts shop after a violent hurricane threw things off the shelves, how could anyone believe that our intricately orderly universe was created in a strange ancient accidental gas explosion? Everything around us lives and grows in an obviously designed pattern: the human heart pumping life through the body, the planets in motion, the yearly rhythms of the season, the precise and balanced framework of the human skeleton, the capillary action on a leaf, photosynthesis. In fact, the more someone looks at the wonders of life, the more he should feel compelled to fall down on his knees in awe and devotion to the Creator of it all. And some of the most brilliant of modern scientists—Einstein for example—although often not religious in the usual sense of the word, have admitted to experiencing just that kind of awe when they view the magnificence of the universe around us.

ST. THOMAS AQUINAS AND THE EXISTENCE OF GOD

For clarity's sake perhaps we should make the above case in a more precise and orderly manner. The Christian thinker most associated with the use of reason as an argument in support of God's existence was St. Thomas Aquinas. Often referred to as the Angelic Doctor, St. Thomas spent much of his lifetime formulating a defense of the Christian Faith which could be organized in the terms of reasonable thinking about life suggested by the giant intellect of ancient Greece, Aristotle. In St. Thomas' times, translations of Aristotle became available for the first time in Europe and swept through the scholarly world of the European universities like wildfire. Like most works of complex genius, Aristotle's ideas were in short order misinterpreted and distorted by the scholars of the time. In certain circles the claim developed that Aristotle's rigorous use of human reason had made the Christian revelation unnecessary and unacceptable to a clear-thinking human mind. It became St. Thomas' mission, as a result, to answer these charges, to Christianize Aristotle, so to speak, by indicating that where Aristotle was truly rational and orderly in his thought he agreed with Church teachings, and that reason and orderly thinking in no way challenged the Faith. On the contrary, argued St. Thomas, a rigorous and precise application of human reason would actually make the Christian Faith all that more acceptable to the human mind.

The very existence of God was one of the elements of the Faith which St. Thomas undertook to test against Aristotle's standard of human reason. And by and large, these "Thomistic" proofs he developed are still the most commonly used ways of explaining why there must be a God. The late French philosopher Jacques Maritain, the great defender and explainer of St. Thomas to the modern world, goes so far as to say that Thomas's arguments "are part and parcel of what has been called the natural philosophy of the human intelligence . . . They are grasped by common sense before being the object of philosophical consideration." In other words, St. Thomas explains to us how God exists in a way which we all can know and perhaps do know without having to be able to put it into words. The proofs are: I—By Motion: II—By Efficient Cause; III—By the Contingent and the Necessary; IV—By the Degrees Which Are in Things; V—By the Governance of Things.

Does St. Thomas "prove" that God exists with these arguments? Well, I'll go through them in a surface way for you, using quotes from Maritain to avoid error, and you can make your own judgement. But before I begin I feel obliged to note that these proofs of St. Thomas meet all the tests of the modern, scientific mind. Those that hear the argument, and still reject the idea of a God, can only do so by an act of faith *against* the existence of God far more difficult to justify than any religious belief. St. Thomas' proofs can only be rejected by those who are willing to say that "Yes, by all the tests of reasonableness I live by on this planet there must be a God—but I still don't *believe* it." Remember they have to use that word *"believe."* That says much in agreement about the theory that modern man does not accept the existence of God because he does not want to limit—out of pride and selfishness—his personal pleasures and independence. A Supreme Being would cramp modern man's style and that is why modern man will not *believe in* God but will *believe against* God. It is the sin of Adam—the desire to be as God.

I—FROM MOTION

"Everything that moves is moved by another . . . how could a thing give to itself what it does not have?" . . . In the first year of high school every student learns from his science teacher the law of inertia: Bodies at rest tend to stay at rest; bodies in motion tend to stay in motion. Or as Maritain puts it: "Every body which undergoes a change in regard to its state of rest or of motion changes under the action of another thing." If you get hit in the back of the neck in the cafeteria with a half-eaten tomato sandwich you are not likely to buy the argument that it flew off the table by itself. If you come back to class after a fire drill and find your books gone you are not likely to accept the idea that they just went away. True, apples and leaves fall from trees—but not by themselves. The astronauts floating across the surface of the moon showed us how gravity works, if we doubted the theory. And although no one else makes us move when we walk or makes a goldfish move when he swims, these actions are the result of a will and an intelligence, even if a very limited one as in the case of the goldfish. Our mind has to move our body. A corpse no longer has motion.

Our earth is filled with motion. The planets, plants, the tides, bees, aardvarks, yeasty dough, the wind, and humans combine in an intricate, complex, but purposeful, whirl of motion. What is the source of all that motion? Who was the first mover? The obvious answer is God. The Unmoved Mover—moved by no one or nothing else—who always was and always will be.

II—EFFICIENT CAUSES

We have all heard the atheist's explanation of the creation of the world: Evolution. Gas did it. Way back when, even before Fred Flintstone's days, some gases came together somehow and turned into water and earth and plants and toads and trout and, eventually, man. While some Christians buy this evolutionary process, they do insist, against the atheists, that even if this slow process of creation was the method used by God, that there was a Being, God, who originated the process and who controlled its development, at least up until man and his machines and bombs came along (some Christians would argue that God's control continues even into this modern age) Logic, again, tells us that this must be so. If someone asks you why you are healthy you could say because you eat spinach. But then they would ask, Why is there spinach? The seed, the earth, the rain, the air, and on and on back. But this process must stop somewhere. There must be a First Cause—the Uncaused Cause. Why does your car stall? You check the sparkplugs. Why are they dirty? Burnt oil. From where? Around the cylinders? Why? Which ring is defective? But again you come to the first cause of your troubles—the answer, the explanation.

We live our entire life by this rule. If we are too warm in our room on a winter day, we check the thermostat. We do not content ourselves to say that it is warm just because it is warm. We demand an explanation. When we look at a finely carved leather belt we will not accept the explanation that it got that way after someone ran over it with a lawnmower. Beauty, order, design, rhythm, all require an intelligent cause—an intelligent Creator. And surely a sunset on the Gulf of Mexico matches a leather belt in these respects—as does Mount Everest or the Midnight Sun.

195

III—CONTINGENCY AND THE NECESSARY

This proof requires a bit more of a philosophical disposition, but not so much that it cannot be grasped by the average reader.

Remember, what we are trying to prove is the existence of a Creator who by all logic must exist—must *be*. From all our experience, *nothing* is not capable of producing *something*. Magicians talk of pulling rabbits out of the thin air (and even air is not nothing—it is air) but as clever as they might be, they don't really do that. A trick is involved. That is what amazes us about them—how they do it. If you go back though in time, through the evolutionary process explaining how man came from apes, which came from hyenas, which came from salamanders, etc., you must eventually come to a cause which had to exist, and forever. For if it did not always exist, then it must have been made, and by something or someone. But then who created that someone or something? And it? and on, and on. The First Cause, God who always was, by necessity.

If at one instant in time there ever was nothing, then there never could have been something. Nothing cannot make something. And we know that there is something. We know that we exist, if nothing else. A First Cause, a Necessary Cause must exist. Or as Martain puts it: ". . . you can imagine all the causes you wish, each of which, in turn, is itself caused, and it will nevertheless be necessary to stop at a First Cause which accounts for all the necessary there is in things, and whose necessity is not caused, that is to say a First Cause which is necessary through itself and in essence in the infinite transcendance of the very act of existence, subsisting by itself." On first reading that passage might seem difficult. But read it a second and a third time if you have to. A careful reading will make it crystal clear—and formidable in logic.

IV—DEGREES WHICH ARE IN THINGS

Maritain states that "It is a fact that there is a qualitative 'more or less,' that there are degrees of value of perfection in things." And that "wherever there exists degrees (wherever there is a *more* or a *less*) it is necessary that there exist somewhere a supreme degree of a maximum (a most)." We see this approximation of perfection clearly in many areas of life, perhaps most noticeably in art. We see a child's fingerpainting, a grade school student's drawing of a schoolbus, self-portraits from a high school art class, comic book drawings, covers of quality magazines, expensive family portraits, Rembrandt.

Even an unlettered hillbilly could, without difficulty, arrange them in order of excellence for us. We could use music, or human relations to make the same point—music as it comes close to the standards of Mozart, Wagner, or Beethoven (or your choice); family love as it approaches the perfection of the little carpenter's house in Nazareth. But what is it that the masters in the field of the arts resemble? Something to do with Nazareth too? Is it not logical that all our earthly standards be judged by that same paragon? Maritain: "Since goodness, beauty, life, knowledge, love and ultimately Being are in things in diverse degrees, it is necessary that there exist somewhere a maximum or a supreme degree of these values." In other words, it is necessary that there exist somewhere a maximum, a supreme degree of goodness (and the other values of which we spoke). The All Good, All Just, All Beautiful—God.

V—GOVERNANCE OF THINGS

In many ways this proof resembles greatly the arguments based on causality and motion. Order requires an orderer. Purpose requires a plan. We might think it an unbelievable sight if we saw apples falling up from a tree or squirrels sprouting from a pumpkin plant, or dogs with birch bark skin. But really what is more fascinating is that these things don't happen, that night after night, year after year, season after season, the sun rises and sets and trees grow and animals and humans are born in the same incredibly identical pattern. The same thing over and over. That is the miracle. If the whole planetary panorama were started by an accidental explosion as the evolutionists tell us (where did that gas come from again?), why are not there more such accidents? A freak show can make a bundle with a man a head higher than the rest of us or a cow with a runty fifth leg. Imagine if they had a human who gave birth to a platypus. Or a squid. But no, the same darn pattern. As constant as the north star—and the north star is pretty amazing too when you think of it. All our experience tells us that a system requires a governing intelligence—from a working mousetrap to a computer. But what of the marvels of human life? The veins, the corpuscles, a baby gasping for the first breath as it enters the world. Talk about the difficulties of Faith! Those who don't believe in God believe in the second most incredible fairy tale of all—the accident of creation. The most incredible is not that a Creator, God, made the world, (that is quite logical) but that that Creator loved us enough to have sent His only begotten Son, Jesus Christ, to

197

help us share eternal life with Him. But we have Christ's word that this most incredible fairy tale of all—and the one with the happy ending—is true.

WHAT EVER HAPPENED TO C. S. LEWIS?

The English Protestant literary great C. S. Lewis made a name for himself in the first half of this century by attempting to put this logic of St. Thomas, and the quite different approach of St. Augustine, to use to explain the attractiveness of the Christian Faith in terms understandable to those who did not have formal training and advanced degrees in theology and philosophy. In book after book, article after article, whether a study of medieval literature, a fable, a book of contemporary criticism, or his famous science fiction novellas, Lewis worked on the theme that the Christian Faith makes sense and brings happiness and sanity to an otherwise incomprehensible life on this planet. A collection of speeches he delivered over English radio, called *Mere Christianity*, is the most direct of his explanations of the Faith, and the most easily understood. Unfortunately it is not available in the average local library and might even be hard to come by in most college libraries where the "God is dead" religious teachers seem to make the bookshelves these days to the exclusion of men like Lewis.

Lewis uses most effectively an argument which is very much like St. Thomas' argument based on degrees of excellence, but includes in it an Augustinian notion that God has planted deep in our minds some kind of knowledge of Himself, perhaps even a memory of Him which we hold from before birth (although that idea gets into murky theological waters). He takes note of the fact that all men, whether they live on remote jungle plateaus, or in bustling modern cities, share a basic understanding of justice, fairness, decency, and charity. Even Nazis, mass-murderers, rapists, and child-beaters, if asked to explain their behavior, would construct a line of reasoning to make their actions seem acceptable or at least not as condemnable as they appear at first look. They share the *universal* human need to define and excuse their actions by placing them as close as possible to a standard of justice and truth.

As Lewis notes, and correctly, however: "The minute that you say that one set of moral ideas can be better than another, you are, in fact, measuring them both by a standard, saying that one of them conforms to that standard more nearly than the other."

Pinocchio, because he was a puppet, had Jiminy Cricket. We humans have an intuitive knowledge which we call "conscience." Even gangsters have a code of honor of sorts. There is, as the saying goes, honor among thieves. What or who, then, asks Lewis, is it that is "directing the universe, and which appears in me as a law urging me to do right, and making me feel responsible and uncomfortable when I do wrong?" Who is the author of conscience? Well, Lewis goes on, "We have two bits of evidence about the Somebody. One is the Universe He has made. If we used that as our only clue, then I think we should have to conclude that He was a great artist (for the Universe is a very beautiful place), but also that He is quite merciless and no friend to man (for the Universe is a very dangerous and terrifying place). The other bit of evidence is that Moral Law which He has put into our minds. And this is a better bit of information than the other, because it is inside information. You find out more about God from the Moral Law than from the Universe in general just as you find out more about a man by listening to his conversation than by looking at a house he has built. Now, from this second bit of evidence we conclude that the Being behind the universe is intensely interested in right conduct—in fair play, selflessness, courage, good faith, honesty and truthfulness. In that sense we should agree with the account given by Christianity and some other religions that God is good."

The modern liberal, in contrast, because he denies the existence of God and man's capacity to discover His will and live in accordance with it, is left with the empty, despairing, relativist alternative. The school of psychology called determinist, especially the works of the modern behaviorist B. F. Skinner, has become the most popular explanation of this alternative way of viewing human behavior and moral standards. High school courses with titles like "Behavioral Science," "Modern Psychology," "Life Studies," and even "Health" more often than not center on this outlook. For the liberal relativist, Skinner's views corroborate his own views about right and wrong, purity and impurity, the brutal and the gentle, the ugly and the fair— that all these codes of conduct we live by are the result of our social environment, and that man consequently—like a houseplant—is more a result of his surroundings than a free moral agent. Instead of being involved in the Christian struggle with evil to save our souls, men, in this relativist view, are walking sensate sponges who soak up all the impressions they receive in life and act accordingly. There is no guilt, of course, since we cannot control what our sponge-minds will soak up as we go along. Our job in life then, by this relativist standard, is to come to grips with all the environmental forces at work in our life, and adjust, adjust, adjust. We are to find the most "meaningful" way of life for us, the most comfortable self-image, and eliminate those influences in our moral environment that trouble us. We are to get rid of our hangups. Bend and adapt are the keynotes. "No hangups, man! That's what it's all about!" How many times has the average modern student had to listen to that idiocy as the key to living life?

All of this, obviously, is completely opposed to the Christian teaching that life is a struggle to do good and overcome temptations to evil, and not just a search for as much carefree pleasure and comfort as is possible. Teachers conducting courses with this kind of relativistic and amoral "self-knowledge" and "learning for living" as goals would be horrified if they were charged with being anti-Christian. But they are, even if they tell us that all they are doing is introducing young people to the findings of modern psychology and psychiatry. They fail to see, perhaps in excusable ignorance, that their emphasis on truth, values, and virtues as mere opinions developed by man in society goes against the entire Judaeo-Christian ethic from the Ten Commandments to the Sermon on the Mount. And that when they tell us that if those "opinions" of Moses and Christ make someone feel guilty and uncomfortable, he should shuck them off as another "hangup," they are advocating an irresponsible and immoral life, and going against the wishes of Christian parents.

They fail to see that for Christians the term "hangup" expresses an idea pretty close to that which we call "learned virtue," and that a moral man or woman is *supposed* to feel guilty when he or she violates God's law, not try to escape it through rap sessions and encounter groups. We should be proud of our "hangups" about illicit sex, cowardice, dishonesty, selfishness, and sloth—not try to deaden our God-given sense of shame about these violations of His natural law.

It is the great irony of the modern world that the liberal who has worked diligently to separate man from the duties to follow God's law as taught by the Christian religion—in the name of "individual liberty" and "self expression"—now has to try to control the resulting social chaos. The disorganized, purposeless, drug-ridden, vandalized modern school is an example of what happens when men behave as if they had no obligations to discipline themselves and conform to a code of behavior separate and above their personal whims. The liberal teacher working in those schools is caught in a dilemma of poignant appropriateness. He knows he does not want to work on a teacher's desk with four-letter words carved on its surface, or dodge spit in the hall, or have his tires slashed every week, but does not know how to define any of this behavior as *wrong*. Society says it is wrong, but as he has told his classes, society has no right to enforce its standards—"opinions"—on the free thinkers of the world. Even though drug use, pre-marital sex, and open pornography have become a regular part of many teenagers' school day experience, school authorities, under the influence of liberal-teacher demands in many cases, do not quite know how to go about bringing a return to decency. They have no way of acting authoritatively against actions which should be impermissable—except by referring to any traces of conviction about the Ten Commandments that might remain in their own hearts and minds; and that of course, they have learned from the liberals and the Supreme Court, cannot be done in our society—since, well, who knows whether the Ten Commandments are valid any more, or any nobler that what the kids think is right. As a result they have to live in the mode of those who live without the learned wisdom of their people—as barbarians. And I do not use the word "barbarian" loosely. A "civilized" way of life, one which is not barbarian, comes as a result of one generation passing down to the next the visions of truth, justice, beauty and decency which they, in turn, have learned from their own elders. The uncivil, primitive and dangerous impulses of the young in this process are supposed to be controlled, harnessed, and refined. The young are to be disciplined, to learn how much freer they can become, when they learn the skills, attitudes, and capacities developed by their people over the course of time. Just as the young do not have to discover the wheel all over again, they do not have to puzzle over whether man should be gentle, brave and true. Neither do they have to be deprived of the right to enjoy beautiful music, inspiring books and the company of good people, just because an appreciation of these things does not come to a child as instinctively as the ability to sneeze. And most important of all, a Christian people should not have to send their children to schools which are run as if Christ never walked this earth and never told men how to live.

But this is exactly what American Christians are faced with today. The civilizing process has broken down in the schools. Instead of educational authorities running the schools as if they had values to teach and standards to preserve, they have copped out under the banner of "student freedom." (Again, not necessarily the individual school authorities, who often are as angry as anyone else that top-level educational authorities and the courts make it impossible for them to tell girls not to dress like hookers and boys not to parade around with degradingly impure slogans emblazoned across their tee-shirts).

Schools used to be places where gentle, kind, well-mannered students felt more at home than the local hoods and sluts. The reverse is true now. Without adult aid to assist the students who wish to follow the ways of their forefathers, there is no way to prevent the school from becoming a reflection of the street and the beer hall, where other values reign. Just as a group of artists, philosophers, poets, ministers, and saints would not be likely to get to watch the TV shows of their choice if they were imprisoned in the same cell block with a chapter of the Hell's Angels, schools will never be a place where the finer things in life are appreciated and preserved without adult help—the civilizing process. Without structure and authority, the law of the jungle prevails. Civilization is a result of an ongoing and determined fight against the jungle. The violence and obscene halls and classrooms of many modern American schools is the jungle triumphant.

School authorities have betrayed an entire generation of young Americans. They have abdicated their responsibility to work with well-intentioned and decent young people to build an atmosphere of learning and culture, and surrendered the directive powers to the worst elements in a school population. The same kids who control the street corner have been given the schools too.

It is an instructive moment for Americans. The one institution within our society which we have allowed to be completely dominated by the liberal ideologues has degenerated in a single generation. Unless we want our streets, hospitals, libraries, government, armies, and businesses to end up in as much disarray, we must learn the lesson of what liberal relativism does to a society—and not let the liberals do to the rest of American life what they have done to our schools. If we learn that lesson, maybe we can even begin to consider the next one—getting our schools back from the nihilists.

14

Sex Education: Doing Your Thing Is Not the Right Thing

The question of sex education has raised more parental hackles than any other issue in recent years; and not inappropriately. For in the dispute over the teaching of "healthy" attitudes toward sex, the wide difference between the moral standards of "free-thinking," secular-liberal teachers and those of the average parent is raised to full view, without the confusion of contorted intellectual explanations to cloud over the dispute. Parents *know* intuitively when their religious convictions are being challenged in front of their children, and will react in opposition—even those who might not be able to formulate their opposition to teacher behavior over issues like politics, literature, or religion. The least educated of people have a strong moral sense about what constitutes indecency, purity, faithfulness, and normalcy when the question is sex. And that goes for the large number of adult Americans who might see an off-color movie now and then, read a pornographic book, or even cheat on their husbands or wives. Hypocrisy? Maybe. But hypocrisy, as they say, is the homage vice pays to virtue. Most men, even those with a near-to-consump-

203

tive taste for "dirty books" and movies, know that they do not want their children exposed to this seamy side of their life, and often go to great pains to make sure that none of their off-color material is found around the house. They display the quite understandable wish of a father for his children to rise above his vices. Responsible adults simply do not have a desire to perpetuate their vices in their children, and most certainly do not want to pay for a school program which does. And, of course, if those who give in to their temptations toward illicit sex feel this way, those who struggle successfully to live disciplined lives are even more determined to prevent the schools from working against their home- and Church-taught approach to love and marriage. Thus the sex-education flak of today.

Once again, teachers and school administrators will protest: "But we are not working against religious standards! Our only concern is with health and factual knowledge. We do not push our views! Our classes are free! All opinions are respected! Etc., etc."

To be as accurate and as fair as possible, then, the only way to proceed is with an examination of the actual "pat-myself-on-the-back" statements made by sex educators. We seek to condemn not an interpretation of their intentions, but their actual words. The most distressing thing about the brouhaha over this issue is that the Christian view of life has been rejected so completely by so many of our "professional educators" that they really cannot see how menacing and offensive they are when they push their vision of a "free" and "healthy" attitude toward sex in the classroom.

The group which has worked most determinedly for widespread programs of sex education in America is SIECUS—the Sex Information and Education Council of the United States—a group dedicated, as it says on the cover of their book *Sexuality and Man*, "to the establishment and exchange of information and education about the human sexual behavior." Based in New York City, it is perhaps the most important force in sparking awareness of the need for sex education in schools and colleges. Most American sex-education teachers are either members of SIECUS or were trained by members of SIECUS or studied with the books and pamphlets and magazines prepared by SIECUS.

The reader should remember that a book like *Sexuality and Man* is basically a public relations release, an attempt to explain SIECUS' goals and to win support from as many Americans as possible. It is not the place for controversial statements or for proposals which will anger the average citizen. Words are chosen precisely and sentences constructed carefully to avoid the danger of saying more than is wise or diplomatic. Consequently, it is safe to say that the following quotes are as mild and as uncontroversial as the SIECUS leaders could get them to be. They are not the views of the most radical members of SIECUS. But, nevertheless, they are a declaration of war on those Christians who practice their religion as did their forefathers. Even if the average liberal sex-education teacher-enthusiast wanted only what SIECUS proposed in this book it would be unacceptable. As a symbol of the sex educator's larger dream of a permissive, pleasure-as-an-end-in-itself world, it is truly worthy of all the anger and up-roar that sex education has generated, and then some.

DIFFERENT STROKES FOR DIFFERENT FOLKS

As usual, liberal relativism is the villain. The liberal sex-educator truly believes that he is being fair if he gives an equal hearing to all the different points of view about sex. He thinks he is being ob-jective and neutral when he presents the views of a prostitute, an abortionist, a homosexual, a sadist, a masochist, and a Christian priest or minister as equal participants in the debate over sexual propriety. "See I didn't choose sides!" he tells us. It bothers him not at all that it is a malicious assault on the beliefs of the Christian peo-ple of the country to allow the revelation of the Bible and of Christ, refined and corroborated through the nearly two thousand years of Western civilization's experience to appear as having only an equal claim with perversion and degradation for the minds of America's young people in schools built and supported by the hard-earned dol-lars of their parents. ("But who is to say what is perverted!" shouts the relativist in opposition—thereby proving my case—although the relativists cannot see why.) They see nothing wrong in the de-liberate demotion of Christian values from the center of our life to the rank of mere competitor. This is of course consistent with the liberal denial of the legitimacy of the educational goal of preserving our heritage. Just as a comic book is equal to Shakespeare, perversion is equal to moral virtue—openmindedness, they tell us. There is no other term for this state of affairs, of course, but absolute *moral bankruptcy*—the lack of any moral standards whatsoever. They used to put people with ideas like these in asylums instead of in charge of schools. It is liberalism's curse that it has made sane people say such insane things, depriving us of that remedy for their social dis-ruptiveness.

The Christian heritage of the American people is not just another proposition out there for the students of America to look at, weigh, and then accept or reject. It is our way of life, the values we hold "self-evident." Our Founding Fathers made it very clear that there were to be certain truths beyond attack in the country they established. That is what they meant when they accepted Jefferson's memorable phrase "We hold these truths to be self evident." "Hold" means take as our own, accept—not "think about," "consider for a while," "propose for debate." "Self-evident" means obvious to all, acknowledged to be true—not "possible," "probable," "tentative." Those who were willing to be members of the American society—upon their expression of a desire to join us as a people—were to agree to accept the Christian foundations of America as well. Not to bring with them to our shores, and then spread energetically, some alien atheistic, Marxist, nihilistic creed from revolutionary quagmires of nineteenth-century Europe, and demand that it receive equal hearing in our schools, and then act shocked at the close-mindedness of Americans when they get infuriated about how their schools are being used to convert their children to the undisciplined and profane way of life that follows. America as a new country defined herself through early laws, both federal and local; as a mature country we have a right to act without embarrassment to continue to define our way of life, to promote the values we hold dearest. A country cannot be open to its enemies' advances—if it wants to survive. A country cannot be neutral about itself, just as a man cannot be open-minded, open to all opinions, about whether to allow his family to be assaulted or not.

But getting back to SIECUS . . . First of all we must be fair. The SIECUS quotes that follow are not the words of raving maniacs. The leaders of that organization and its supporters are likely to be leaders in their community—open-minded, unprejudiced, unbiased advocates of freedom of choice. Their villainy is unintentional—but nevertheless real. It is their demotion of Christianity to the level of a contestant which is the root of the problem—but that is what our liberal spirit of the times insists is a healthy state of affairs. SIECUS types often don't look the parts of enemies of civilization. It is more likely that you could mistake them for librarians or morticians. Which is worse of course because, then, tearing down our Christian way of life seems somehow a gentle activity. At least Attila the Hun looked like the scourge of the world. It was easy to arouse opposition to him as he growled out his determination to crush Rome. It is not easy to get Americans to see in the same light the grandmotherly matron handing out instructions to the local abortion clinic; or the custom-tailored MD passing out birth-control devices to young girls without parents' consent; or the gentle, bespectacled health teacher telling his students that a healthy attitude toward sex can be summarized in "Do your own thing." And they should be seen in the same light.

GOD AND LOVE AND LIFE

Without God's law, the SIECUS folks, like all liberals, are left trying to explain the "should nots" of sexual behavior in terms of whether or not they make you feel good. Consequently, they end up saying, for example, that masturbation should not be condemned or even discouraged: "Students of human sexuality and of mental health seem increasingly to be taking the position that masturbation may be regarded as a part of the normal process of sexual maturation." So "As a general rule, parents and adults concerned with youth are best advised to disregard evidence of private masturbation in juveniles, not to look for it nor try to prevent it directly or even indirectly." Why bother the kid with all those moral problems and guilt-feelings, when "In adulthood as well as in childhood, masturbation by individuals in private is coming more and more to be regarded as an acceptable means of releasing sexual tension."

Now if they were trying to help young people to realize that masturbation is a most common problem in adolescence and that a young person should not consider himself weird or sick because he has trouble overcoming his temptations, that would be fine. Even if they comforted young people with the idea that some people find it very difficult to overcome the temptation at all, and that God knows that, and is not as likely to condemn a young person who cannot control himself as he is to condemn, say, an adult who cooly and calmly and maybe even in return for profit, tries to weaken a young person's resolve to serve God's will by struggling to overcome sin, that too would be fine. But SIECUS message is—forget the moral struggle. If it makes you feel good, do it.

Neutral about religion? Hogwash! This is a deliberate attempt to deny the Christian notion that there is a God and that our sex life must conform to His laws, not our maximum-pleasure principle. "Because of the traditional emphasis upon this practice as not only a sin, but a childish form of behavior that becomes abnormal when engaged in beyond adolescence," SIECUS complains, "many older persons are disturbed by their need to masturbate and require the assurance of counselors to accept it as valid practice."

Try a few more on for size:

"By the time the individual reaches adolescence, he has formed a whole series of strongly rooted emotional attitudes about sex. These attitudes cannot be changed by a casual, superficial kind of instruction but only by a process of serious instruction that recognizes the importance of emotional re-education and reconstruction." Tsk, tsk. All those Christian kids with those silly ideas they learned at home about illicit sex have to be converted, you see, shook loose from their "deeply rooted emotional attitudes" and taught to see that "it is essential for people to be aware of differential sex patterns and to be able to accept and interact harmoniously with those whose sexual norms differ from their own." Come on kiddies, grow up, shake loose your prejudices that your mother is any more virtuous than the Happy Hooker—like, I mean, whose opinion is right? Right? Trash.

But they get even more specific. The goal of sex education is to encourage sexual open-mindedness since "Attempting to indoctrinate young people with a set of rigid rules and ready-made formulas is doomed to failure in a period of transition and conflict such as ours." The Christian rules are going out—so let us help them on their way a bit. Neutral, eh? Let enlightened educators free American school-children from the condemnatory attitudes of their parents because "Today the significance of such sexual expression as youthful erotic play, masturbation, homosexuality between consenting adults . . . and other variations from heterosexuality is being re-examined in the light of new knowledge. The enhanced capacity among educated people to look at sexuality with objectivity suggests that some things formerly considered to be of social concern might now be re-classified as private and personal or having social concern for different reasons than formerly." Get the drift—"Educated people" (not those backward Christian folk) now "look at sexuality with objectivity" (no Christian hangups about sex for these educated people) and therefore old-fashioned ideas can be "reclassified" (described as normal and acceptable no matter what the parents think). High school teachers two years away from living off daddy's paycheck on a college campus filled with drugs and kinky sex, while in between sessions with their psychiatrists and divorce lawyers, are going to come to local communities and be paid by parents to straighten out the young people so that they won't have to live out their lives with their parents' hangups about sex. Talk about the inmates running the asylum!

America is ready to be enlightened now, SIECUS tells us, unlike "fifty years ago" when "sex education scarcely recognized the possibility of choosing among alternative patterns of sexual behavior." That's right, back in those days Christians had not been corrupted by liberal ideologues and would have tarred and feathered—which does not seem too harsh a penalty—any villain who came around telling their children that perversion and promiscuity were an "alternative pattern of sexual behavior." But none of that zealotry nowadays, SIECUS tells us with a sigh of relief. In those dark days of yore "the thought of consciously choosing a course of sexual behavior occurred only to the brash or highly emancipated. The flouting of conventional standards did occur surreptitiously, but it was regarded as a violation rather than as a matter of choice." Yessir, that's progress for you. Now you don't have to be "emancipated" to be a homosexual or a lecher. No more surreptitiousness about our immorality. SIECUS has set us free. Whether Christian parents like it or not.

And that is no exaggeration. In defining the role of the sex-education teacher in relationship to the parents, SIECUS pulls no punches. They know how their new morality is likely to be greeted by parents with even a trace of the Christian tradition. They warn sex-educators that "Parents bring all of their personal life experiences to the bearing and rearing of children. They transmit values mostly in terms of these experiences and in terms of the situations confronting the family. Little of this transmission is cool, rational, objective, scientific. A parent is too emotionally involved with his child to take a calm, detached attitude toward that child's values and behavior to be an objective educator." The parent might have ideas about immorality and self-discipline and guilt, you see, and will try to transmit them. The teacher's job is to save the student from this one-sided presentation. SIECUS, in its generosity, agrees that the parent has a right to try to push his values, but not with much chance of success. That would not be fair to the student. It would deprive him of the wide variety of opinions to which he is entitled and from which he has a right to make his choice of lifestyles, like picking apples in a supermarket—"teachers have been urged to provide reliable data and help their students reach their own decisions in as objective and unbiased a manner as they possibly can." Let the parents tell them about God, marriage, birth and fidelity. That's one opinion. Now the teacher is to give them the other equal opinions floating around America so that the student can make a fair choice—his parents and his pastor? or the Happy Hooker, Mick Jagger, and the gay-lib boys? Who cares what the parents want? It is only their money which supports the schools. And their children. The teachers job is to let the student know that it is the "right of the individual to engage in any form of sex behavior within the limits of social obligation and welfare." (Whatever that means.) If it feels good do it—no matter what you hear at home and in church. Who knows what is right and wrong anyway? "No possibility of consensus exists in a country as large and diverse as we are, and it does not seem fruitful to attain it." And students must come to that, learn to free themselves from their parents "prejudices" about sex. The teacher "to the best of his ability . . . must provide knowledge and insight so that adolescents may learn the negative and positive consequences of alternative courses of action and choose for themselves with some measure of rationality among competing codes of conduct." Competing codes of conduct—their parents' and rock groupies.' Take your choice, man.

It is a new world they tell us. The great and thoughtful scholars of our time, the wise and thoughtful men of the modern age, offer serious criticisms of the Wisdom of the West, of Christendom, you see. "The wisdom of chastity has been seriously questioned on a regular basis in mass circulation magazines such as Playboy and Cosmopolitan." Heavy, heavy—make your choice, Christ or *Playboy*. And if the sex-educator does not reflect this new wisdom of *Playboy* and *Cosmopolitan* he is only giving in to the backward-looking people out there trying to keep the kids fooled with the idea that sexual responsibility and self-discipline are not just the last of the great superstitions that modern man is about to dispel on the way to total happiness. "For the sex-educator to rule out premarital intercourse as a debatable subject in the classroom does not rule out the subject as a debatable one. It merely means that the subject is handed over by default to many of the less responsible agencies of society." That's true. In the old days a kid would hear from his parents and minister and priest that sex belonged in marriage, and from the neighborhood bums that you should get whatever sex you can whenever you can. One point of view came from the best influences in the young person's life, the people who loved and cared for him and looked out for his best interests. The other from local punks and sluts whom he knew would do him in for a nickel. He made his choice, alright—between the best and the worst that his society had to offer, between decency and profligacy, moral health and moral decay, self-discipline and self-centered lust.

But that was not the kind of choice the liberals want. It was not a fair choice. The cards were stacked in favor of the social values of the past, of Christianity. (Which, at the risk of annoying you by saying it

210

again, is the way it should be when a society tries to preserve itself as a civilization).

The sex-educator now, under SIECUS' direction, is to bring the immoral into the class and raise it to the level of an acceptable choice, an alternative lifestyle. But isn't that just an equal and fair intellectual proposition. Yes—like "shall I sell my sister to the highest bidding pimp?" Yes or no, class? And remember there are many experts who say there is much sense to both sides of the argument. Trash.

In a way it is a shame that the debate between parents and liberal educators can be raised to the proper level of intensity only over the issue of sex. There are many other liberal assaults against us that are just as dangerous. But that is O.K. Sex education can be a symbol of the others. It can point out by inference how much else of modern schooling is socially disruptive. People who cannot quite see the danger of promoting divisive thinking about the continuation of our national sovereignty, or our determination to remain confidently anti-Communist, can see this attack on their way of life in big bold letters. And then they can intuit how little the schools defend, protect, preserve and extend the rest of our cultural values, and how the schools, by self-definition, work to question the things dearest to us.

The place and propriety of sex in our lives simply are too important for us to proceed with the liberal assumption that there is no true position in relation to them. We have a right to treat the issue as another of those closed questions which we have decided upon, another of our self evident truths.

But are they really self-evident, in a rigid philosophical sense? Are we as certain of, say, monogamy as we are that 2+2=4? Certainly Christians—most noticeably traditionalist and fundamentalist groups—would say yes, without qualification. The truths we hold in our Faith are not mere propositions to them. Other Christians will admit that there are changes in attitude that develop in time over things like sexual propriety and standards of decency. Skirts above the ankles were considered indecent at one time (which does not mean that girls should have been encouraged to kick up their heels at that time in history if that did lead young men into temptation). Social changes in attitude do take place, but that is a far cry from legitimizing the sex-teachers claim that they are to take the leading directive role in promoting them. Teachers just do not have a right to pick out the new attitudes which they think best for society and promote them in sex-education classes. And the permissive, value-free, choose-your-life-style attitude promoted in "objective" sex-

211

education classes is a *specific attitude,* and one which is unacceptable to most parents. Educators are not missionaries. Not in public schools anyway. They are not the arbiters of America's destiny. They are paid representatives of the parents and the community, not of an elite organizing to convert that community.

CHRISTIAN LOVE

It would truly be a shame if the Christian community surrendered its own unique and revered contribution to man's knowledge about the proper relationship between a man and a woman. It is more than likely that the sad and pitiful discontent with being a woman evident in so much of the women's liberation movement is a result of American men not living as Christian men in their relationship with women—by not living up to the Christian code of knighthood, chivalry. The pagan notion of woman as slave and mistress was driven from the earth by the Christian vision of woman as an earthly image of the Blessed Virgin Mary. In the Christian scheme, the woman was the backbone of civilization, the one entrusted by God with bringing new life, new souls, into this world and raising that life to Christian consciousness on the way to salvation. The woman's task was the most important in the world. Man's role as defender of and provider for the family paled in comparison. The man was sworn to give his life if necessary to protect God's vessel of life, the woman. The man was to be courageous, strong, and true, in order to be worthy of the woman and children entrusted to his sword and shield. The women's liberation demand to be made an equal of man —to be able to work on an assembly line or sell insurance—to be freed from the chores and burdens of raising children is a reversal of priorities so grotesque that, if you did not know better, you would think it was a put-on. It is a distortion of reality so damnable as to question the vitality and very right to survive of the society which spawns it. Only a truly decadent people would bring to the surface as a legitimate and widespread social demand on the part of women the idea that day-care centers be set up so that women can leave their children somewhere to get out and do "meaningful" and "rewarding" work. Imagine—a woman not wanting to be with her children so that she can teach ceramics at the local junior high! And not to make money—that would be understandable. The demand is to escape the burden of being a "mere" mother!

Without the Christian understanding of life, the modern American woman is doomed to see herself as nothing more than a producer and pleasure-seeker competing unsuccessfully with men who have achieved a near monopoly over these things in our society. Instead of living in awe and solemn appreciation of God's gift of motherhood, the American women's-libber sees children as a stumbling block in the way of full material pleasure and business success. And godless, anti-Christian men can do no more than compound her misery by trying to explain to her in cost-analysis terms why she doesn't "have it so bad," that her hours and working conditions could be worse— "after all the kids leave home after twenty years or so anyway." And that she can eat out and go to shows more often if she gets a part-time job to pay for the babysitters. It is true, as someone has said, that when men are not men, it is difficult for a woman to be a proud woman.

When one thinks of the vast, ennobling literature of chivalry and its theme of self-sacrificing, spiritual love, and of how it has been ignored by modern man in favor of the cheap, spineless literature of sex-driven men who use women (and now of sex-driven women who achieve "liberation" by using men), it is no wonder that we are a civilization on the brink of suicidal madness, with a birth rate going down beyond the replacement level. A country which does not love life enough to replace itself, and to sacrifice to raise new and loving members of its social and spiritual order, has lost the will to survive. A society which sees conception as an unhappy "accident" and birth as a sloppy, bloody nuisance which does no one any good, and ruins a woman's shape, and children as a drain on a man's and a woman's vacation and nightclub time and bank accounts is a society in trouble.

What we had was so noble. Life and love, duty and sacrifice, tied together through the mystery of birth, in service to God. In ripping away God from man in the name of independence and self-seeking pleasure, the liberal has committed the sin of Adam and has caused a rupture in normalcy as severe as that which eroded life in the Garden of Eden. The future will be bad for baby doctors, but great for psychiatrists.

The Christian view of sex was balanced, healthy, normal. As C. S. Lewis put it "Christianity is almost the only one of the great religions which thoroughly approves of the body—which believes that matter is good, that God Himself took on a human body, that some kind of body given to us in Heaven is going to be an essential part of our happiness, our beauty, and our energy. Christianity has glorified marriage more than any other religion, and nearly all the great love poetry in the

213

world has been produced by Christians." What we are developing for ourselves and our posterity, in contrast to the Christian society, is a liberal madhouse in which the sick, bug-eyed view of sex of the massage-parlor freak is placed on the same level as marriage. C. S. Lewis again: "There is nothing to be ashamed of in enjoying your food: there would be everything to be ashamed of if half the world made food the main interest of their lives and spent their time looking at pictures of food and dribbling and smacking their lips."

The very structure of our family lives is being threatened as the self-control and self-sacrifice of the Christian married couple is made to appear unnatural and inhibitive of self-growth, in a world where instant and irresponsible sex-gratification is demanded as a human right. The constant drumbeat of pornography makes it a constant challenge for Christians to keep their balance about sex, and to live their lives with the self-denial demanded of them. Young couples today set out on a marriage voyage as competitors for maximum pleasure, demanding from each other their "sexual rights", the ones their teachers and Playboy and Cosmopolitan told them about, and seeking a divorce when the constant "thrill" of the "complete" sexual life they hear about from the porn merchants, in and out of school, is not provided. They come to see their marriage partners as tools for pleasure and judge and weigh each other on the basis of the latest best-selling pseudo-scientific sex manual. Pregnancy and childbirth become undesirable since they threaten the swinging lifestyle of the man and woman about town.

The shared sacrifices, responsibilities, and hardships which alone can bring man and woman together in the kind of full union described by Christ when he spoke of becoming one flesh, are tossed aside in favor of mere sensual encounters. And when the thrill is gone the marriage is over. One out of every three modern marriages in America ends in divorce. Maybe if SIECUS has its way they can get it up to two out of three. Or maybe abolish it altogether in favor of one of those "alternative lifestyles" they want America's children to learn to appreciate. Trash.

15

Is There an Answer?

There is an answer. It is the abolition of the American public school monopoly over education—and nothing short of that. The premise under which the public school system was founded no longer exists. The public school system is an idea whose time has gone.

For one thing the cost is becoming unbearable. Local school systems and tax-supported public universities are pushing the average citizen's tax load to the breaking point. That in itself would be reason enough to consider closing them down. You can't have what you can't afford. But the fact that the schools no longer serve the interests or wants of the American people makes the tax burden especially intolerable.

When America was a nation with a general consensus about its identity, when almost all Americans could agree on what they expected for themselves in life, and after death, it was no great trick to set up a school system which would reflect that consensus. The old caricature of the prim, grey-haired "schoolmarm" was an exaggeration, but an exaggeration of a type of schoolteacher which did predominate in the schools of yesterday. Teachers were like that. If anything, the old "schoolmarms" were too representative of Americans ideals. They taught the approach to life the parents wanted taught—with a vengeance. It was usually the parent's job to tone down the idealism of the schools, to let his children know that you could be a good man or woman without being quite as noble, truthful and patriotic as Miss Crabtree and James Russell Lowell, Longfellow and Francis Scott Key insisted you must be.

But where the Miss Crabtrees of old were too "goodie-goodie" and too "corny" about their patriotism, the modern bearded, booted, long-haired, blue-jeaned Mr. Liberal Fruitloop is the representative of a permissive and immoral lifestyle from the parental perspective— the counterculture. He does not defend and explain the parents' beliefs too rigorously. He challenges them, and demands an ever-increasing salary to do the job more effectively. And that is as ridiculous as it sounds, and cannot go on.

Students of the American scene—conservative and liberal alike— have pointed out the fragmentation of American life; what we could call the *tribalization*. Black parents want black studies, black teachers; young urban couples with "liberated" views want experimental, open, permissive schools for their children; traditional Christians want prayers and Bible-studies in the classroom; Jews want to preserve the competitive approach through which they have been able to rise to the top in American educational and professional circles; Hispanic-Americans want bilingual classes; and nobody, except the judges who issue the orders and a few millionaire politicians whose children are trained by private tutors or in elite private schools, wants busing to achieve an educational melting pot. Ethnic consciousness abounds. More people take to the street to protest the Turkish invasion of Cyprus or the Arab attacks on Israel than to commemorate Memorial Day. Young people's communes sprout up in the mountains, and old folks go to the desert to escape the frenzy, glitter and glare of the urban and suburban world which is so alien to their one-generation-old tastes.

Whether we will be able to survive the fragmentation of the nation is one question. And a big one. The answer just might be no. The search for "tribal" and ethnic identities came as a result of the shredding of the bonds of our national brotherhood. If we cannot feel proud and ennobled by being an "American," our social and community consciousness will seek to put down roots elsewhere—whether in our ancestors' old-world homeland or in one of the new American tribes—hippy, hardhat, Jesus freak, nostalgia nut, pothead, etc., etc. And it just has been a historic fact—whether we like it or not—that countries which become as divided as that collapse.

The primary task for Americans, then, should be the re-creation of the national consciousness, along with a proper and appropriately firm isolation of those who would deny us that process. But in the meanwhile, it is suicidal to go on allowing liberal academics, who represent just one of the many tribes (and the most socially disruptive at that) the right to set the educational atmosphere and moral tone for the children of the rest of us. There are permissive, free-thinking parents who want the kind of atmosphere the modern public school affords. Fine, let them have it. But let the rest of us have the kind of schools we want as well. Return to parents the God-given right to educate their children as they see fit.

How? Well there are a variety of methods that have been suggested. But they all center around one basic theme: return to parents the power to purchase the kind of schooling they want—break the public-school-tax-dollar monopoly.

The method of financing public schools and colleges in America varies little from state to state. Tax dollars. Everyone, young or old, single or married, ten children or none, who works and receives a salary has a portion of his pay taken for use by federal and state educational bodies. Property taxes on homes —all homes, whether children live there or not—make up the balance. Not a bad system— indeed, a very good one when all Americans could agree that there was a shared responsibility and a shared advantage in educating young Americans into their adult roles as responsible and productive citizens, and could agree that the public schools would do that job for us. But that was before our tribalization into opposed "lifestyles" and racial, religious and ethnic blocs. As a unified people the public schools fit the bill. Now we are being asked to pay more for more of what we do not want. We are being asked to support the missionary effort of one tribe against the rest of us.

The answer, then, lies in giving the tax dollars spent on education to the parents to spend on the school of their choice, instead of directing it to any one school system. If the parents want to use the money to pay the tuition costs in the local public school they can continue to do so. A public school or college which serves its clients' interests will go on as usual. Those which are unacceptable to the community will find themselves without students and without funds, and will have to either sell out their facilities to whatever local private school has

217

managed to attract all of their ex-students, or redesign their programs to attract back their students. With the tuition money in their hands parents will be able to select schools run by religious groups, military schools, schools with strict discipline, schools with no discipline—whatever school they and their children want. The school systems which will result will be ones which satisfy the community's wants and needs. Parents will have choice in education—schools with many sports activities, some with no sports but with expensively prepared music and art programs, some designed for future scientists, some for poets, some for tradesmen, some for the clergy, some for students who need extra help, some for students who need a great amount of free time. Freedom will return to American education.

Would teachers' salaries be decreased substantially? Certainly in some cases. Those teachers who have nothing to offer the community will be as out of work as accountants who cannot add. Those who have a skill and a presentation of material that satisfies community needs just might receive appreciably higher pay. Teacher unions could continue to organize, of course, and be as militant as they feel proper. But the nation will be spared the nightmare of a nationwide strike against the entire public school system—a nightmare which is becoming increasingly possible as teacher unions consolidate under the unified leadership of the New York-based American Federation of Teachers. A group of striking teachers would no longer be able to tell parents or children that their right to an education has come to a halt while salary negotiations are worked out. A school with a strike just might find its entire student body enrolling in some other school down the road. (Which—for those teacher-union advocates who are more interested in their own local school's welfare than in national union maneuvering—would force local school administrators to bargain in much greater fear of the consequences of a strike. And since the schools would be private schools in most cases strikes would not be against the law.)

Some schools would be able to operate efficiently. Those that could not would be forced to meet the standards of the more efficient school. The public school of today which spends some three thousand or so dollars per pupil would have to look again and again at how private schools run their operation at a fifth of that cost. Taxes to finance education would no longer climb year after year at the same rapid rate. Schools would have to explain why their costs are going up while another school with just as good an academic record is holding the line. The much-praised genius of American competition would be set to work.

Would the public schools become dumping grounds for students who would not be accepted in private schools? Perhaps. But if so—so? Additional funds could be channeled to these schools for problem students, and higher salaries could be—and should be—paid for those teachers willing to work under such conditions. But in all honesty, the only reason for a public school to become a dumping ground would be the fact that it offered a service judged to be undesirable by the community at large. And in that case it would deserve to be a dumping ground. If a public school offered a satisfactory program it would not have that many fewer of the better students—and no more of the troublesome kids than they have now, since they have almost all the troublesome kids now anyway.

The American people must take back the ultimate directive control over education from the band of cultural renegades who are trying to refashion our vision of how life is to be lived. The American people must end this academic imperialism, and reassert their determination to never surrender to a cabal of self-professed experts the final say over what kind of society we will be, and what kind of men and women our children will become. It is not a radical demand but a demand for the oldest and most basic of human rights.

Meanwhile, America's young people must issue their own interior, but determined, declaration of independence from their schools, and, as never before in our history, view their education as a process which goes on more outside the classroom than within. Parents, priests, pastors, rabbis, and other religious leaders must be consulted for reading lists and for a discussion of topics of concern. Church groups must take up the burden of working with their young people in a more organized and thorough way by organizing reading clubs and seminars on a regular basis.

The foundations of American life are worthy of our deepest respect. We do not have to hate ourselves. Schools which are not helping America's young to find their roots are denying them their heritage. Students must go beyond the modern school to the giants of intellect of our culture. Being proud of one's parents and their values will not make someone an "Archie Bunker patriot," for it can be said without reservation that those who stand on the shoulders of the giants, who base their judgements on the teachings of Moses and Christ, on the heritage of great books, and who trust the ennobling power of fine music and poetry rather than the "intellectual" fads of a season or two, are actually the party of the intellect at its best.

219

Index

Disney, Walt, 73
Dodd, Thomas, 164
Dos Passos, John, 29
Drake, Sir Francis, 16
Durham Case, 47

Einstein, Albert, 192
Elgin, Lord, 81
Eliot, T. S., 95
Ellington, Duke, 137
Enlightenment, 14f., 77 -
Euripedes, 37

Farrell, James T., 138
Federalist, 14
Federal Bureau of Investigation, 105
First Amendment, 80
Fleming, D. F., 148
Ford, John, 29
Founding Fathers, 18f., 82
Franco, Francisco, 127
Free School Movement, 101
"front group", 180
Frost, Robert, 29
Fuchs, Klaus, 177
Fulbright, William, 31

Galahad, Sir, 90
Galbraith, J. K., 68f.
Galileo, 15-16
Geiger, Theodore, 184
gnostics, 115
God, existence of, 190f.
Goldwater, Barry, 85
Gould, Elliot, 29
Gouzenko, Igor, 177
Greeley, Horace, 151
Gregory, Dick, 40
Guevara, Che, 128
Gulag Archipelago, 111, 118
Gupta, Yogi, 15

Hannibal, 38
Harvey, William, 17
Hawthorne, Nathaniel, 88, 92
Hazlitt, Henry, 57, 142
Hearst, Patricia, 168
Hebrews, 42
Hemingway, Ernest, 95
Henry VIII, 71
Herodotus, 141
Hiss, Alger, 123, 177
Hitler, Adolph, 23, 111, 128, 175, 189
Hoffman, Abby, 28
Hoffman, Dustin, 29
Ho Chi-minh, 116, 148, 181

Holmes, Sherlock, 167
Horowitz, David, 140
Hudson, Henry, 16
humanism, 16
Humphrey, Hubert, 39

imperialism, 151
in loco parentis, 112-113
Ives, Charles, 29

Jackson, Andrew, 88
Jacobins, 147
Jagger, Mick, 90
Jenner, Edward, 17
Jefferson, Thomas, 25, 75
Jews, 111, 125
Johnson, Lyndon, 31
Joplin, Janis, 94

Keats, John, 95
Kennedy, John, 121
Kendall, Willmoore, 13, 113
Kenyon, Dorothy, 184
Khrushchev, Nikita, 121
King, Mackenzie, 177
Kirk, Russell, 13, 88f., 91
Kirkland, Edward C., 109
Kissinger, Henry, 32
Kolko, Gabriel, 148
Kramer, Stanley, 94, 162
Krug, Allan S., 166
Ku Klux Klan, 110, 128, 132
Kunstler, William, 28

LaFeber, Walter, 153
laissez-faire, 53f., 58
Lattimore, Owen, 184
Lavoisier, Antoine, 17
League of Nations. 32
Lean, David, 94
Leary, Timothy, 15
"left", 147
Lenin, V.I., 33, 120
Leonidas, 37
Lennon, John, 84
Lewis, C. S., 198f.
liberalism, 11f., 70
Lincoln, Abraham, 65
Lindsay, John, 181
Locke, John, 18
Lomax, Louis, 135
London, Jack, 95
Louis XVI, 19
Luciano, Lucky, 136
Lukacs, John, 81, 96
Luther, Martin, 146
Lynd, Staughten, 148